Autopoietic Knowledge Systems in Project-Based Companies

Autopoietic Knowledge Systems in Project-Based Companies

Kaj U. Koskinen

First published 2010 by
PALGRAVE MACMILLAN

Palgrave Macmillan in the UK is an imprint of Macmillan Publishers Limited,
registered in England, company number 785998, of Houndmills, Basingstoke,
Hampshire RG21 6XS.

Palgrave Macmillan in the US is a division of St Martin's Press LLC,
175 Fifth Avenue, New York, NY 10010.

Palgrave Macmillan is the global academic imprint of the above companies
and has companies and representatives throughout the world.

Palgrave® and Macmillan® are registered trademarks in the United States,
the United Kingdom, Europe and other countries.

ISBN 978–0–230–27858–5   hardback

This book is printed on paper suitable for recycling and made from fully
managed and sustained forest sources. Logging, pulping and manufacturing
processes are expected to conform to the environmental regulations of the
country of origin.

A catalogue record for this book is available from the British Library.

Library of Congress Cataloging-in-Publication Data

Koskinen, Kaj U.
  Autopoietic knowledge systems in project-based companies/
Kaj U. Koskinen.
      p. cm.
    ISBN 978–0–230–27858–5 (hardback)
  1. Knowledge management.   2. Autopoiesis.   3. Project management.
I. Title.
  HD30.2.K6677 2010
  658.4'03801137—dc22   2010027528

10   9   8   7   6   5   4   3   2   1
19 18 17 16 15 14 13 12 11 10

Printed and bound in Great Britain by
CPI Antony Rowe, Chippenham and Eastbourne

I dedicate this book to my wife, Päivi

Contents

List of Figures and Tables

Figures

Tables

Foreword

I was most fortunate to be asked by Kaj U. Koskinen to write a short foreword for this book. I have listened to several of Kaj's IRNOP conference presentations and I have never failed to be stimulated by what he has to say. This book has provided me with a similar stimulating experience. I trust that readers will go away after reading this book seeing the project management (PM) world in a different way. I am sure that readers who have a traditional view of PM developed from twentieth-century literature will find this book an adventurous journey.

This is a clearly written text. It builds upon new ways of looking at projects which are important because any discipline stays alive by reflection and by re-framing ideas as they are challenged, argued, and clarified. Indeed, the word 'argument' derives from *agua* (water) and the notion is to clarify through argument issues until they are as clear as (pristine) water. Indeed, the role of language and culture in the exchange of information and knowledge, reflection, and understanding are recurring themes captured in this book that are critical to the theory of convergence of meaning between people.

One view that has been emerging from the knowledge management (KM) and organizational learning (OL) schools of thought is that projects are knowledge factories. They are places where knowledge is created, adapted, and re-framed as well as used to produce project outcomes. The very act of developing a project brief from an idea and then re-framing this through collaboration into a design and then further re-framing this knowledge by combining it with pragmatic operation knowledge from those that realize the project idea is an intensive KM process. Koskinen extends this idea and uses an autopoietic epistemology to illustrate how knowledge is perceived, created, transferred, and used in PM work. As he states at the close of Chapter 5 in this book, an autopoietic epistemology 'does not claim that the world is a pre-given, but instead that cognition is a creative function. Thus, knowledge is a result of autopoiesis, that is, of self-production processes'. He describes autopoiesis and how this way of understanding what is going on in project work can help us better manage the environment where knowledge is used in project work to deliver the benefits that a project should be established for.

This way of understanding project work builds upon a growing evolving literature of the role of knowledge in delivering projects and their intended and unintended outcomes. The 'rethinking PM' debates and investigations (Winter and Smith, 2006; Winter et al., 2006) and 'making projects critical' work (Hodgson and Cicmil, 2006a, b) as well as work on project business spearheaded by groups of researchers that have been centred around work undertaken by Karlos Arrto (Artto, 2001; Artto, Dietrich and Nurminen, 2004; Artto and Wikström 2005; Artto and Kujala, 2008; Artto et al., 2008) and Morris (2010, p. 145), also convincingly argues for appreciating the relevance of theoretically based and empirically grounded PM research that is focused upon project outcomes – and he acknowledges knowledge work as an important project process and outcome (Morris and Lock, 2004). He also highlights that knowledge management (KM) is a field of study within PM research that has only been focused upon recently, during the start of this twenty-first century (Morris, 2010, p. 145). All these researchers help redefine the concept of what it means to 'do project work'. The autopoietic epistemology to project knowledge work resonates with me as a progressive way of more clearly seeing the reality of PM and how the PM discipline is developing. This book is very strong on theory and cites many examples from empirical studies to support the argument and discussion that this book evokes.

I will be perhaps selfish and now outline what I personally got from reading this book and hope that this resonates with many readers. As an academic teaching PM, supervising doctorates, and undertaking research, I felt this to be an advanced PM text. It moves well beyond the introduction to KM and OL that I saw entering the PM literature over the first decade of twenty-first century (cf. Walker and Lloyd-Walker, 1999; Egbu, Botterill and Bates, 2001; Prencipe and Tell, 2001; Fernie et al., 2003; Jashapara, 2003; Sense, 2003; Dainty, Qin and Carrillo, 2005; Love, Fong and Irani, 2005; Love et al., 2005; Peansupap and Walker, 2005; Sense, 2005; Walker, Maqsood and Finegan, 2005; Maqsood, Walker and Finegan, 2007; Sense, 2008) to mention just a few salient examples of sources. Chapters 6 and 7 provide much useful discussion on more familiar aspects of KM and OL, and this is substantially extended in Chapter 8. Chapter 9 has a focus on knowledge flows in a PM context, building upon ideas proposed with more general management contexts by Bontis, Crossan and Hulland (2002), Crossan Lane and White (1999) and Lawrence, Mauws, Dyck and Kleysen (2005). Chapter 10 puts the project-based company as an autopoietic knowledge system into a PM context. This autopoietic project-based firm view of KM and OL had been largely unrepresented in the PM literature until this book.

The autopoietic epistemology also resonates with me because I recently supervised a doctorate where her research thesis theme shifted from a more traditional quality management and change management focus to one of understanding the way that culture underpins the construal of meaning, and how knowledge was shared in a highly challenging multi-cultural Middle Eastern context. This work of Koskinen, which is based upon many years of refinement in using an autopoietic epistemology with his colleagues (cited quite liberally throughout this book) and other work such as Small's (2009) thesis, is forging an exciting new way of understanding PM work and the nature of projects.

This book moves the agenda for seeing KM in project work solidly forward. Its clear way of explaining projects from a systems-thinking perspective is both interesting and valuable. The extensive references cited in the book also provide access to the ideas of many worthy books and papers that can be further explored by readers. I found myself chasing up many of these and will be using them in my preparation for research, teaching, and writing, so this book has proved invaluable to me.

Derek H. T. Walker is Professor of Project Management,
RMIT University, Melbourne, Australia,
and editor of the *International Journal of
Managing Projects in Business*.

About the Author

Dr (Tech.) Kaj U. Koskinen has worked for many years as a project manager in several international engineering companies, including Outokumpu and Honeywell. His main experience derives from process automation. Since 1997, he has been a senior lecturer (Docent) in Industrial Management and Engineering at Tampere University of Technology, Pori. Dr Koskinen's research interest is focused on knowledge and project management, and he has published several articles on these research areas, as well as the book *Knowledge Management in Project-Based Companies: An Organic Perspective* which was co-authored with Professor Emeritus Pekka Pihlanto.

Acknowledgements

I would like to extend my deepest thanks to Professor Emeritus Pekka Pihlanto who has acted as my tutor and paragon when we have co-produced our scientific texts.

1
Autopoietic Knowledge Systems: An Alternative View of Project-Based Companies

Traditional management wisdom focuses on the idea of conserving and maximizing capital. However, during the past 60 years, the world of business has shifted from being dominated by capital to being dominated by knowledge. This shift explains the interest in knowledge management and organizational learning that has emerged in the last 15 years. Managers recognize that, unless their companies can accelerate the rate at which they learn, their primary asset will stagnate, and their competitors will outpace them (e.g. de Geus, 1997). This emerging area of theory and practice has become identified as the 'knowledge-based view of the company', a feature of which is its ability to transcend the division between academic and management practice (Whitehill, 1997).

On the academic side, the knowledge-based view represents the confluence of a number of streams of research, the most promising being resource-based theory and epistemology. Contributing literatures include organizational learning, evolutionary economics, organizational capabilities and competencies, and innovation and new product development.

Among practitioners, companies are looking beyond information systems towards a broader conception of knowledge management. The first requirement is to identify the knowledge available within an organization. Knowledge audits seek to establish an inventory of proprietary technology and know-how in the same way that accounting systems identify and value a company's tangible assets. Formal systems for developing knowledge have focused on information technology and the role of networks and groupware in linking organizational members. Recognition that the major source of knowledge is the expertise and know-how of employees has directed attention to human resource planning and appraisal.

Extensive work on knowledge creation (i.e. learning) has been based on explaining a company's growth in terms of its resource capabilities (Penrose, 1959), and especially on the idea of a company's dynamic ability (Teece et al., 1997) to create, extend, and modify the way it operates. For example, in the context of project-based companies, Davies and Brady (2000) and Brady and Davies (2004) have developed valuable contributions based on perspective at the company level. Moreover, many scholars (e.g. Lindkvist et al., 1998; Koskinen and Pihlanto, 2008) assert that project success is contingent upon successful knowledge management.

Companies – including project-based companies – are essentially goal-seeking systems. As human systems, companies must provide something of value to their members in exchange for the resources and capabilities they provide to it. Thus, a company must pursue and, at least to an acceptable extent, achieve a goal or set of goals for creating value in ways that can be shared with, and will be appreciated by, providers of the resources and capabilities it needs. To sustain its goal-seeking activities, a company must behave like a system that not only uses the resources and capabilities of its own members, but also draws on resources and capabilities of people and entities external to the company. This means that a company's interaction with various external providers of resources – as well as its interaction with other organizations competing to attract the same resources – embeds it in large economic, social, technological, and legal systems.

System properties that affect a company's ability to sustain adaptive change and to gain competitive advantage have been studied by systems researchers as well as by strategists. For example, General Systems Theory as an area of academic research was founded by biologist Ludwig von Bertalanffy and others in the early 1950s. The aim was to create a genuinely trans-disciplinary field of research (von Bertalanffy, 1968; Skyttner, 1996). On the grounds that different academic disciplines often dealt with very similar theoretical problems, it was believed that there was scope for synergies to be exploited. The idea was to abstract the solutions found within a specific field of research to a general level in order to help other disciplines re-specify and apply them to their respective fields (Seidl, 2005).

The common ground on which those synergies were to rest was a specific approach to the objects of research: the systems approach. It was argued that the conventional approach of explaining the characteristics of an object of observation solely on the basis of an analysis of its parts leads to 'analytical reductionism': many objects of observation possessed properties that could not be explained on the basis of the properties of their parts. An understanding of these so-called emergent properties required a view of the object as a whole: as a system.

In contrast to an earlier phase of systems theory, which was based on the notion of closed systems and only analysed the internal relations between the parts and the whole, the General Systems tradition, as formulated by von Bertalanffy, assumed an open systems model. It replaced the conceptualisation of systems according to the difference between 'whole and parts' with that between 'system and environment' (Luhmann, 1995b). This was often explained in terms of thermodynamics: according to the second law of thermodynamics, the entropy of a closed system always increases, and, further, any closed system sooner or later dissolves. At the centre of the open systems model was the idea of systems transforming inputs from the environment into outputs into the environment. The system could be described as a particular input-output relation (Luhmann, 1995b).

In formulating his 'law of requisite variety', for example, Ashby (1956) observed that to survive in a complex environment while maintaining internal stability, a system must be able to generate a requisite variety of responses to a changing environment. Forrester's (1961, 1968) industrial dynamics modelling helped to clarify the important impacts on the dynamics of industries and the economies of information feedback loops, as well as on time delays in adjusting stocks of resources. Researchers in the systems dynamics field extended the industrial dynamics framework to the analysis of organization processes and dynamics (e.g. Morecroft, 1988, 2007; Sterman, 2000; Warren, 2007). Simon (1981) also identified a number of basic properties shared by systems of all types, whether purely physical systems, natural systems, or human systems.

A radical further step within the systems tradition was taken in the 1970s with the development of the concept of self-referential systems. In contrast to the open systems model, the concept of self-referential systems was not so much concerned with input-output relations as with the self-determination of the system through its own operations. One of the most important contributions to this new phase of systems theory was the theory of autopoiesis developed by two Chilean biologists, Humberto Maturana and Francisco Varela.

The traditional representation-based view (i.e. the open systems model) on management and organizations implies that business activities are contingent on external influences and respond to demands from the environment through internally representing a pre-given environment. In other words, in this view, *knowledge* is a representation of a pre-given reality: universal, objective, and transferable. On the contrary, the autopoietic perspective reflects the belief that cognitive activities in organizations are simultaneously open and closed. This means that (according to autopoietic epistemology which is based on the autopoiesis theory) knowledge is created and based on the observation of distinctions, it is dependent on history and sensitive to context, and is not directly transferable. As will be seen throughout this book the autopoietic perspective not only sheds light on existing issues but it also opens up the management and organizational study realms for new probes into the unknown.

The objective of this book is to give the reader an alternative observational scheme to better understand knowledge creation and learning in project-based companies. The suggested conceptual system is based on autopoiesis theory.

Keywords of the book

- Project-based companies
- Systems thinking
- Autopoietic systems
- Autopoietic epistemology
- Knowledge management.

Structure of the book

Chapter 1 highlights the emergence of a systems approach and of autopoiesis within knowledge management research. The chapter argues that the conventional way of solely explaining the characteristics of parts of an object leads to analytical reductionism, that is, many properties of an object cannot be explained on the basis of the properties of parts of an object. Instead, a systems approach – and particularly autopoiesis theory – is needed to explain the properties of an object.

Chapter 2 briefly describes the project business. The purpose of the chapter is to present a general discussion of the concepts of Project-based companies, Project teams, and Project team members.

Chapter 3 illustrates Systemic View and Systems Thinking. Then, the chapter briefly describes the basics of Systems Theory and Systems, and the concepts of Complexity in Systems, Open and Closed Systems, Boundaries of Systems, Cybernetics and Feedback Loops, System Dynamics and Causality, and the Company as a System.

Chapter 4 is about autopoiesis. The purpose of the chapter is to briefly explain autopoiesis theory and the essential features of an autopoietic system such as Structural Coupling and Self-Referential Systems, Autonomy, Simultaneously Open and Closed Systems, Observing, and Organizational Autopoiesis.

Chapter 5 deals with epistemological assumptions. The idea of the chapter is to describe some basic features of Cognitivist-, Connectionist-, and Autopoietic epistemologies and to give an explanation of why Autopoietic Epistemology is chosen to be an observational scheme for the understanding of knowledge creation and learning in project-based companies.

Chapter 6 looks at the concepts of knowledge, competence, and organizational memory. The chapter deals with the concepts of Meaning, Knowledge, Individual Knowledge, Organizational Knowledge, Project Knowledge, Resources, Capability and Competence, Emotional Intelligence and Emotional Competence, Organizational Memory, and Intellectual Capital.

Chapter 7 is about evolution and learning. The chapter deals with the concepts of Intuition, Interpreting and Mental Models, Learning, Learning Organizations, Organizational Learning, Expansive Learning Seen through Activity Theory, Organizational Ecology, and Socio-Cognitive Engineering.

Chapter 8 describes 12 components of project-based companies in terms of an autopoietic knowledge system. This chapter is broken down into the following sub-chapters: Identity, Perception of the Environment, Strategy and Strategic Management, Knowledge Management, Knowledge Sharing, Boundary Elements and Perturbations, Interactivity, Boundary Objects, Commitment and Motivation, Information and Communication Systems, Organizational Climate and Organizational/Project Culture, and Trust.

Chapter 9 is about two major knowledge flows within an autopoietic knowledge system. The chapter deals with the concepts of Sensing, Memory, and Recursivity.

Chapter 10 puts together the ideas of the preceding chapters and describes project-based companies as Autopoietic Knowledge Systems. This chapter is divided into the following sub-chapters: Evolution and learning in project-based company and Improving a project-based company's potential to be an autopoietic knowledge system.

Finally, the Epilogue sums up the conclusions of the book.

2
Project Business

During the second half of the twentieth century, there was a shift from functional organization to project-based organization (e.g. Prencipe and Tell, 2001). This shift was caused by the changing nature of work from mass production, with essentially stable customer requirements and slowly changing technology, to the current situation in which every product supplied may be made to a bespoke design, and in which technological changes are continuous and rapid (Turner and Keegan, 1999). In that sense, project-based business is part of a wave of 'new organizational forms' that has entered most industries during the past two decades (Kerfoot and Knights, 1998; Packendorff, 2002).

Project business thus denotes the activities of a company that carries out project deliveries to its customers. As a whole, project business includes the key business-related activities of project companies, such as project sales and marketing, financing, as well as operation support, maintenance, and other after-sale services (Artto and Wikström, 2005; Artto and Kujala, 2008). In essence, companies engaged in project business can be divided into four categories: manufacturing-oriented companies, designers, integrators, and companies contracting on project-management services (Artto et al., 1998). This scheme of categories can be used to depict the key segments of a company's activities and the core knowledge its operations are based upon. However, many companies have expertise in more than one sub-field of categorization. For example, suppliers of complex capital goods (e.g. telecom networks, paper machines, and ships) design, produce, and sell complex products and services as one-offs or in small tailored batches to meet the individual needs of business or institutional customers (Hobday, 1998).

Thus, increasingly, technology-based as well as service-providing companies that operate in dynamic environments, organize their operational and developmental activities in projects (DeFilippi and Arthur, 1998; Gann and Salter, 1998; Hobday, 2000; Prencipe and Tell, 2001; Grabher, 2002). Therefore, companies that strongly privilege the project dimension and carry out most of their activities in projects, are referred to as project-based companies.

Project-based companies

Project-based companies are organizations in which the majority of products are made to bespoke designs for customers. These types of organizations may be stand-alone, making products for external customers, or subsidiaries of larger firms, producing for internal or external customers. They may also be consortiums of organizations that collaborate in order to serve third parties (Turner and Keegan, 1999).

Project-based companies are usually involved in several projects simultaneously. A typical example might be a consulting company. The company as an organization with an identity is permanent, but its mode of production is dominated by projects. The governance of such companies is a challenging task. Their heavy reliance on projects implies that a high degree of discretion is granted to lower levels. These projects may be interrelated which calls for knowledge sharing efforts among projects: projects that seem to be separate and independent may compete for resources, attention, commitment, and legitimacy (Blomquist and Söderholm, 2002). Since projects enjoy autonomy, they easily become separated from each other, with the risk of turning the company into a series of disconnected projects. Therefore, project-based companies will tend to suffer from certain weaknesses – for example, failure to bring about company-wide development and learning (Hobday, 2000), and difficulties in linking projects to firm, level business processes (Gann and Salter, 2000). Furthermore, projects typically comprise a mix of individuals with highly specialized competences, belonging to functionally differentiated world views (Dougherty, 1992), making it difficult to establish shared understandings and a common knowledge base.

Indeed, project-based companies tend to be not only strongly decentralized but also quite loosely coupled (Orton and Weick, 1990). This also applies to the knowledge dimension. Relevant pieces of knowledge are distributed (Tsoukas, 1996) into a multitude of local settings and a great amount of knowledge resides in individual members. Governance in such a context must take into account the organization's fundamental dependence on its knowledgeable individuals, and its potential weaknesses in dealing with issues of company integration and development.

As noted earlier, a project-based company is often involved in several projects simultaneously. These projects are intended to meet an often vague, but unique need for something new. Within a project-based company an individual project is an organization of people dedicated to a specific purpose or objective. Projects often involve large, expensive, unique, and high risk undertakings that have to be completed by a certain date, for a certain amount of money, within some expected level of performance. At a minimum, all projects should have well-defined objectives and sufficient resources to carry out all the required tasks. However, unfortunately, this is not often the case (e.g. Steiner, 1969; Pinto and Kharbanda, 1995; Cicmil, 1997; Kerzner, 1997).

The temporary nature of projects means that starting and completion dates are specified for each assignment. Assembly line production (i.e. part of a functional organization) is an example of an activity without specified starting and completion dates. The key to understanding the nature of project work, as opposed to assembly line production, is that unlike assembly line production that can continue into the indefinite future, a project is a temporary enterprise (cf. Lundin, 2000; Lundin and Hartman, 2000). A project fulfils its goal within time and money limits – that is, within project constraints. The differences between an ordinary functional organization and a project organization can be described as depicted in Table 2.1.

However, the division between functional and project-based organizations is not at all clear-cut. According to Lundin (2000), functional organizations (i.e. permanent organizations) and project-based organizations (i.e. temporary organizations) are bonded more closely than present theory indicates (cf. Anell and Wilson, 2002; Thiry and Deguire, 2007). That is, functional organizations appear to be growing more project-based, while project-based organizations are becoming more 'routinized' – that is, they are taking on the characteristics of functional organizations.

Table 2.1 Functional vs project-based organization

Functional organization	Project-based organization
Continuous operations	Temporary arrangement
Emphasis on working processes	Emphasis on goals
Stable	Dynamic
Inflexible, hierarchic	Flexible, non-hierarchic
Centralized decision-making	Decentralized decision-making
Bureaucratic	Adhocratic

Source: Koskinen and Pihlanto (2008).

In any case, the time and money limits of individual projects may cause problems when it comes to knowledge sharing. These limits can lead individual team members to act in an extreme hurry and in an untrustworthy manner, in order to avoid caring, and to refuse to offer their feedback during the learning process. In other words, the limits of time and money may make a project reactive rather than proactive, and could create an unpleasant working environment (cf. von Krogh et al., 2000). A related problem is that during the implementation of a project, there is hardly any time for reflection (Raelin, 2001) and learning between projects due to over-optimistic time schedules and a constant shortage of resources (Packendorff, 2002).

Project team

A *project team* is a group of people working together for a common goal. It shares responsibility and resources to achieve its collective mission: problem solving and decision making are natural activities of a project team. While projects have quite specific goals or expectations, it is up to the team to find out how the problems should be solved. Project teams thus typically enjoy a considerable amount of autonomy within the limits set (cf. Lundin and Söderholm, 1995; Lindkvist and Söderlund, 2002).

Briner et al. (1990) divide project team membership into 'visible' team members who are part of the organization but not permanently in the project and 'invisible' team members who are stakeholders in the project but not members of the organization. Examples of the latter would be subcontractors and suppliers. The heart of the visible team is the core team that is permanent but not necessarily full-time. Other visible team members are temporary in the project. According to this definition, project team membership does not necessarily involve mutual social awareness, commitment to a common goal, the same performance norms, or accountability for outcomes (Mäkilouko, 2001).

In a well-functioning project team, open and informal communication is prolific. Project team members motivate, respect, and support each other. According to Smith and Berg (1987, p. 140) 'It is clear that a group can function only if the members are able to depend on each other. It is ultimately the mutual dependency that makes the group a team. To deny this dependency or to try to make it into something other than what it is retards the group's capacity to come together a whole'. This means that organizing a project at the very beginning of the project life cycle forms a base for the building of a successful project team. In other words, at the beginning of a project, the tuning of a group to work as a team is the most intensive task of the project management.

A number of scholars have studied teams, looking for the characteristics that make a team successful. Larson and LaFasto (1989) studied high-performance groups as diverse as a championship football team and a heart transplant team, and detected eight characteristics that are always present:

- A clear, elevating goal
- A results-driven structure
- Competent team members
- Unified commitment
- A collaborative climate
- Standards of excellence
- External support and recognition
- Principled leadership.

In other words, a project team must know how to work together in order to be productive and successful. If a team can work together, it will be able to raise and resolve issues that are standing in the way of accomplishing a goal (e.g. LaFasto and Larson, 2001). Working together may not be easy at first, but with proper training the team will be able to adapt quickly. If people are working together effectively rather than working by themselves, a lot more work will be accomplished.

According to Kerzner (1997), in exemplary companies teamwork has the following characteristics:

- Employees and management share ideas with each other and establish high levels of innovation and creativity in group work
- Employees and managers trust each other and are loyal to each other and to the company
- Employees and managers are committed to the work they do and the promises they make
- Employees and managers share knowledge freely
- Employees and managers are consistently open and honest with each other.

Constructive co-operation is critical both within and outside the project team. Relationships between team members and with customers, suppliers, and the other teams are important. All the members, especially the team leader, must set an example. Project team members can develop the

behaviours necessary to work as a team through observation and imitation. Informal communication is essential in most team activities: the
strength of the team lies in the individuality and experience of each of
its members.

Project team members

Drucker (1993) makes the important point that, in many companies,
the true source of competitive advantage is not so much technology or
even knowledge itself, but people, the knowledge workers – *project team
members* – whose skills and expertise are the foundation of all progress.
He continues by arguing that, on one hand, knowledge workers need
the organization (e.g. project team and/or project-based company) in
order to put their knowledge to work and, on the other hand, they own
the chief means of production, and can take their knowledge through
the door at a moment's notice. 'The more an organization becomes an
organization of knowledge workers, the easier it is to leave it and move
elsewhere' (Drucker, 1993, p. 11). As a result, every organization is
always in competition for its most essential resource: qualified, knowledgeable people. The only way to attract and keep the best people is to
provide them with an environment that allows learning and innovation
to flourish. 'Loyalty can no longer be obtained by the paycheque. The
organization must earn loyalty by providing to its knowledge employees exceptional opportunities for putting their knowledge to work'
(Drucker, 1993, p. 13). Grant's writings (1996, 1997) on the 'Knowledge
Based Theory of Firm' also chime with Drucker's thinking.

However, projects are short-lived and therefore the people working
on them have to engage in swift socialization and quickly find a way
to carry out complex tasks within the limits set. As many people have
experienced, the project goals are very 'strong' and there appears to be
little incentive or even perceived time available for engaging in private
strategizing. The quite limited overlap between specialist competencies
also means that people can help others without risking their ability to
capitalize extensively on people's advice (cf. Lindkvist, 2004).

One way to observe individual differences in a project work context
is to look for differences in individual style and personality (Flannes
and Levin, 2001). 'Style' covers areas such as how people direct their
energy, how outgoing or quiet they are, what their approach is when
addressing a particular situation, how they make decisions, and how
they attempt to order their world. Because of these differences it is often
difficult to form a project team that has the 'right mix' of personal styles

and personalities. However, the right mix is the glue that holds the team together during a project's rough times. It is also the right balance of styles that allows each team member to find an appropriate niche among the project member functions.

As project work typically involves public interaction, those who do not contribute actively and share their knowledge with others run the risk of developing a bad reputation and low demand for their services. Getting a reputation for non-co-operative behaviour would be devastating in many organizations, since this would mean that nobody would ask individuals to participate in projects or ask for their advice. In a limited labour market no one can escape his or her history (cf. Lindkvist, 2004).

Summary

Project business denotes the activities that deliver projects for customers. This business is no longer purely about delivering required projects on time: it is now about systematically creating a disciplined way of prioritizing effort and resolving trade-offs, working concurrently on all aspects of the project in multifunctional teams, and much more. This chapter has described three basic concepts of the project business, namely: project-based companies, project teams, and project team members. Some of the key factors are the following:

A project-based company is an organization in which the majority of products are made according to bespoke designs for customers – that is, the company's mode of production is dominated by projects. Production of the project-based companies takes place through project teams.

A project team is a group of people working together for a common goal – that is, for project delivery. Knowledge sharing, problem solving, and decision making are some of the main activities of a project team. Project teams typically enjoy a considerable amount of autonomy within the limits set.

An individual becomes a project team member by interacting with other people. In this book the concept of 'project team member' primarily means a knowledge worker, whose skills and expertise are the foundation of successful project implementation.

3
Systemic View and Systems Thinking

A *systemic view* of organizations is trans-disciplinary and integrative. This view transcends the perspectives of individual disciplines, integrating them on the basis of a common 'code', that is, on the basis of the formal apparatus provided by systems theory (e.g. Bell and Morse, 1999). The systemic view gives primacy to the interrelationships, rather than to the elements of a system. It is from these dynamic interrelationships that new properties of the system emerge.

Systems thinking comes from a rigorous scientific discipline called General Systems Theory, which developed from the study of biology in the 1920s. The theory centred on the natural world, the living systems therein, and the common laws governing those systems (Haines, 1998). Its major premise was that such laws, once known, could serve as a conceptual framework for understanding the relationships within any system, and for handling any problems or changes encompassed by that system.

Systems thinking is, therefore, a basis for clear thought and communication, a way of seeing more and further (e.g. O'Connor and McDermot, 1997; Mingers, 2006). This means that obvious explanations and majority views are not always right. With a wider and different perspective, an individual can see exactly what is happening and can then take actions that are best in the long run. Systems thinking looks at the whole, the parts, and the connections between the parts, studying the whole in order to understand the parts. It is the opposite of reductionism: the idea that something is simply the sum of its parts. A collection of parts that do not connect is not a system, it is a heap.

Systems thinking is any process that estimates or infers how actions or changes influence the state of neighbouring systems. It is an approach to problem solving that views problems as parts of an overall system, rather than one that reacts to present outcomes or events, potentially contributing to the further development of undesired issues or problems. In other words, systems thinking is a framework that is based on the belief that the components of a system can best be understood in the context of relationships with each other and with other systems, rather than in isolation. The only way to fully understand why a problem or element occurs and persists is to understand the part in relation to the whole. This means that systems thinking is a way to view and mentally frame what we see in the world; a world view and way of thinking whereby we see the entity or unit first as a whole, with its placement within and relationship to its environment as primary concerns.

The reason that habitual thinking is insufficient to deal with systems is because it tends to see simple sequences of cause and effect that are limited in time and space, rather than as a combination of factors that mutually influence each other. In a system, cause and effect may be far apart in time and space. The effect may not be apparent until days, weeks, or even years later. At the same time, people have to act without delay (O'Connor and McDermott, 1997).

In recent years, systems thinking has developed to provide techniques for studying systems in holistic ways to supplement traditional reductionist methods. In this more recent tradition, systems theory in organizational studies is considered by some as a humanistic extension of the natural sciences.

Another concept from social science is the notion of systemic view – the view that all social systems are composed of interrelated sub-systems. A whole is not just the sum of its parts, but the system itself can be explained only as a totality. The systemic view is, then, the opposite of elementarism, which views the total as the sum of its individual parts. The systemic view is thus the basis of the systems approach. In traditional organization theory, as well as in many of the sciences, sub-systems have been studied separately, with a view to putting the parts together into a whole at some later point. The systemic view emphasizes that this is not possible and that the starting point has to be the total system.

In sum, the systemic view and systems thinking attempt to illustrate that events are separated by distance and time, and that small catalytic events can cause large changes in systems. Acknowledging that an improvement in one area of a system can adversely affect another area of the system promotes organizational communication at all levels in order to avoid the silo effect.

Systems theory and systems

Systems theory is an interdisciplinary field of both science and of the study of systems in nature, society, and science. It is a framework by which one can analyse and/or describe any group of objects that work in concert to produce some result. This could be, for example, an organization or company, or informational artefact. Systems theory, then, serves as a bridge for interdisciplinary dialogue between autonomous areas of study (e.g. Capra, 1996).

Thus, the scientific research field which is engaged in the study of systems is based on the properties of systems theory, systems science, and is systemic. It investigates the abstract properties of matter and organization, examining concepts and principles independent of the specific domain, substance, type, or temporal scales of existence

A *system* is a set of interacting or interdependent entities, real or abstract, forming an integrated whole. The concept of an 'integrated whole' can also be stated in terms of a system embodying a set of relationships which are differentiated from relationships of the set to other elements, and from relationships between an element of the set and elements not a part of the relational regime. Thus, the term 'system' has the following meanings (e.g. Capra, 1996):

- A collection of organized things, analogous to a solar system
- A way of organizing or planning
- A whole composed of relationships between the members

Further, using Flood's definition (1990), a system is an abstract organizing structure that has many different paradigmatic interpretations, some of which attach systems to processes in the world, while others attach systems to processes of consciousness. The main ideas are of a whole characterized by richly interactive parts, and this is then expanded and/or interpreted according to various paradigms. Hence, when an individual uses the term 'system', it has two very distinct elements:

- The actual system
- The part of the system people are aware of.

Most systems share the same common characteristics. These common characteristics include the following:

- Systems have structures that are defined by their parts and processes

- Systems are generalizations of reality
- Systems tend to function in the same way – they are concerned with the input and output of material that is processed, causing it to change in some way.
- The various parts of a system have functional as well as structural relationships with each other. The characteristics of systems have been studied in General Systems Theory

(von Bertalanffy, 1968)

A system from this frame of reference is composed of regularly interacting or interrelating groups of activities (e.g. Kim, 1999). For example, in organizations which are complex social systems, reducing the parts from the whole reduces the overall effectiveness of the organization (Schein, 1980). This is different from conventional models that centre on individuals, structures, departments, and units, separate from the whole, instead of recognizing the interdependence of groups of individuals, structures, and processes that enable an organization to function. Laszlo (1972, pp. 14–15) explains that the new systemic view of organized complexity went 'one step beyond the Newtonian view of organized simplicity' in reducing the parts from the whole, or in understanding the whole without relation to the parts. The relationship between organizations and their environments became recognized as the foremost source of complexity and interdependence. In most cases the whole has properties that cannot be known from an analysis of the constituent elements in isolation.

Similar ideas are found in theories of learning that developed from the same fundamental concepts, emphasizing that understanding results from knowing concepts both in part and as a whole. That is, interdisciplinary perspectives are critical in breaking away from industrial-age models and thinking.

There are some startling implications to the simple definition of a system. Systems function as a whole, and as a result have properties above and beyond the properties of the parts that comprise them. These are known as *emergent properties* – they 'emerge' from the system when it is working (e.g. Batterman, 2001). For example, the movement of a car is an emergent property. A car needs a carburettor and the fuel tank in order to move. But when an individual puts the carburettor or the fuel tank on the road, he or she sees how far they go on their own. Properties can emerge like the beauty of a rainbow when rain, atmosphere, and the angle of sunlight fit together perfectly. Because people live with emergent properties, they take them for granted, and yet they are often unpredictable and surprising.

The interaction between systems and their environments are categorized in terms of absolutely closed, relatively closed, and open systems (see more extensive descriptions of these terms later in this chapter). The case of an absolutely closed system is a rare, special case. Important distinctions have also been made between hard and soft systems (Checkland and Scholes, 1990; Checkland, 1999; Flood, 1999). Hard systems are associated with areas such as systems engineering, operations research, and quantitative systems analysis. Soft systems are commonly associated with concepts developed by Checkland (1999) through Soft Systems Methodology (SSM), involving methods such as action research and emphasizing participatory designs. Where hard systems might be identified as more 'scientific' than soft systems, the distinction between them is actually often hard to define.

Banathy (2000) developed a methodology that is applicable to the design of complex social systems. This technique integrates critical systems inquiry with soft systems methodologies. Consequently, systems can be grouped into three categories based on the techniques used to tackle a system:

- Hard systems – involving simulations, often using computers and the techniques of operations research. Useful for problems that can justifiably be quantified. However, this category cannot easily take into account unquantifiable variables (opinions, culture, politics, etc.), and may treat people as being passive, rather than having complex motivations.
- Soft systems – for systems that cannot easily be quantified, especially those involving people holding multiple and conflicting frames of reference. Useful for understanding motivations, viewpoints, and interactions, and addressing qualitative as well as the quantitative dimensions of problem situations.
- Evolutionary systems – evolutionary systems, similar to dynamic systems are understood as open, complex systems, but with the capacity to evolve over time. Banathy (2000) uniquely integrated the interdisciplinary perspectives of systems research (including chaos, complexity, cybernetics), cultural anthropology, evolutionary theory, and others.

Evidently, there are many types of systems that can be analysed both quantitatively and qualitatively. According to Gaines (1979, p. 1), 'A system is what is distinguished as a system'. This means that the observer has a choice in how to define the system that he or she intends to analyse.

Taken together, systems theory is the interdisciplinary study of systems in science and society. It offers frameworks to describe and analyse groups of objects that work together to produce a result.

A system is a set of interacting or interdependent entities forming an integrated whole. There is a wide variety of system types such as physical systems, chemical systems, biological systems, social systems, and so on. This means that a conceptual framework is required for an observer to be able to characterize the system. This framework will determine the types of systems that can be described and should lead to some specific criteria as to how systems can be categorized. However, Klir (1985) maintains that no classification is complete and perfect for all purposes, and defines systems in terms of abstract, real, and conceptual physical systems, bounded and unbounded systems, discrete to continuous systems, pulse to hybrid systems, and so on.

Complexity in systems

Theories of *complexity* can be characterized and classified in several ways. According to Sanchez (1997), two theoretical perspectives, systems theory and complexity theory, provide convergent insights into the composition, interrelationships, and dynamics of complex systems.

First, systems theory focuses on understanding how entities linked by interdependencies and feedback mechanisms compose systems that even in their simplest forms may have the capability to generate complex behaviour and to maintain 'quasi-stable' internal conditions while adapting to changing environmental conditions. Examples of such robust (adaptable) systems include cells, organs, human beings, groups of people (e.g. project teams), organizations (e.g. project-based companies), and societies. System theorists build system models based on deterministic variables that are nevertheless capable of exhibiting complex patterns of behaviour that range from chaotic to adaptive. Growing interest in organizational learning as adaptive behaviour has revived interest in systems thinking, for example, in strategic management studies.

Second, complexity theory, in contrast, starts with complex phenomena that exhibit 'chaotic' behaviour and explores ways in which system elements have interactions that can generate chaotic patterns of behaviour. In the midst of chaotic phenomena, 'quasi-stable' patterns of behaviour may emerge. Complexity theorists tend to use advanced mathematical techniques to analyse complex phenomena and to infer underlying relationships between system elements that are capable of exhibiting 'quasi-stable' behaviour.

According to Mitleton-Kelly (2003), theories of complexity provide a conceptual framework, a way of thinking, and a way of seeing the world, but there is no single unified theory of complexity. Instead, there are several versions of complexity that arise from various natural sciences such as biology, chemistry, and physics. Mitleton-Kelly advocates that 'complex social (human) systems' should be studied in their own right because natural and social domains may have fundamental differences, including the capability of humans to reflect and to make deliberate choices and decisions. A theory of complex social systems is needed to explain phenomena of self-organization (the capability to create order), emergence, and adaptation in human systems. Thus, the concept of complexity can be defined and measured in several ways, depending on the field of research.

Complex evolving systems are characterized by ten generic principles: connectivity, interdependence, feedback emergence, co-evolution, far-from-equilibrium, historicity and time, space of possibilities, path dependence, and self-organization (Mitleton-Kelly, 2003). In general, these aspects of complexity enable the creation of new order:

- *Connectivity* refers to interrelatedness and resulting interdependence among system elements. Complex evolving systems may create new order by changing the rules that govern interactions between system elements.
- *Co-evolution* means that the evolution of one domain or entity depends at least in part on the evolution of other domains or entities (Kauffman, 1993). There is thus a difference between adaptation to an environment and co-evolution with the environment. The first expression emphasizes the dichotomy between the system and its environment and reflects the contingency theory basis for much of the management theory, whereas the latter expression reflects an assumption of interaction between a system and its environment and the idea that co-evolution takes place within an ecosystem.
- A *far-from-equilibrium* state – also called the 'edge of chaos' state – is one in which established patterns have been disrupted and new forms of organization may emerge.
- *Historicity* and *path dependence* reflect the importance of investigating an organization's space of possibilities in exploration, decision-making, and flexibility. Mitleton-Kelly (2003) comments that there seems to be a balance between an organization's rate of discovery and what the ecosystem can effectively sustain. Excessive rates of discovery and change may be dysfunctional for an organization.

- *Feedback mechanisms* (or in the social context, *feedback processes*) are in complex systems and far-from-equilibrium conditions subtler than in conventional systems theory. In human systems, such as companies, positive and negative feedback loops are intertwined and interact on several levels (micro and macro), and their outcomes may be difficult to predict.
- *Self-organization* refers to a phase transition, to the emergence of a spontaneous order that is internally coherent. Emergence is a process that creates irreversible (dissipative) structures or reversible (conservative) new order together with self-organization. Self-organization may occur as a result of being pushed into a state of far-from-equilibrium, but the self-organization to produce new order does not necessarily happen: a system may also simply run down. In an organizational context, the concept of self-organization may take the form of self-organizing teams but may also include management in which empowered individuals make decisions. Self-organization can include increasing connectivity, sharing knowledge, and the creation of new ideas and structures. In theories of self-organizing systems, it is especially important to remember the dynamic and temporal nature of the otherwise spatial terms 'closure' and 'boundary': both refer primarily to a set of operations and only secondarily to whatever physical structures accompany them.

(Livingston, 2006)

According to Senge (1990), there are two kinds of complexity. *Detail complexity* refers to the large number of variables that must be managed so that they do not overwhelm an organization and render it dysfunctional. *Dynamic complexity* refers to the way the essential elements of an organization and its environment evolve. Conventional forecasting, planning, and analysis methods that are often oriented toward detail complexity are not well equipped to analyse dynamic complexity. In addition, increasing the level of detail complexity in models of organizational structures and processes does not help people to understand the processes of learning and renewal that are essential in managing dynamic complexity.

The 'structural complexity' of an organization as a system (e.g. Scott, 1987) arises in the first instance from the number of elements that make up the organization as a system and from number, nature, and intensity of the interactions between the elements. To this internally generated structural complexity we must add the additional structural complexity that arises from system elements that interact with entities outside an organization, and from the number, nature, and intensity of those interactions. The structural complexity of a system increases with the number of interacting elements inside and outside the system, and with the number and variety of significant interactions between them. Structural complexity increases faster than the rate of increase in the number of interesting system elements.

Most organizations have significant structural complexity, with perhaps tens of interacting system elements generating hundreds of important interactions and interdependencies. The hierarchy of complexity based on Boulding (1956) is depicted in Table 3.1.

Indeed, how stable a system is depends on many factors, including the size, number, and variety of the sub-systems within it, and the type and degree of connectivity between the sub-systems. A complex system is not necessarily an unstable one. Many complex systems are remarkably stable and therefore resistant to change. For example, businesses can still function even when there are policy disagreements between different departments.

In sum, a complex system is a system composed of interconnected parts that as a whole exhibit one or more properties (behaviour being one of the possible properties) not obvious from the properties of the individual parts.

A system's complexity can be defined and measured in many ways. For example, it may be divided into two forms: detail complexity and dynamic complexity. In essence, detail complexity refers to a very large number of parts, and dynamic complexity addresses the way the elements of an organization and its environment evolve. Examples of complex systems include human economies, human beings, as well as modern telecommunication infrastructures. Many systems of interest to humans are complex systems.

Open and closed systems

Systems are generally classified as *open systems* or *closed systems* and they can take the form of mechanical, biological, or social systems. Open systems (e.g. Katz and Kahn, 1966) refer to systems that interact with other systems or the outside environment, whereas closed systems refer to systems having relatively little interaction with other systems or the outside environment. Living organisms are considered open systems because they take in substances from their environment such as food and air and return other substances to their environment. For example, some organizations consume raw materials in the production of products and emit finished goods and pollution as a result. In contrast, a watch is an example of a

Table 3.1 The hierarchy of complexity

Level	Description	Characteristics	Type of relations	Example
1	Structures and frameworks	Static, spatial patterns	Topology (where)	Bridge, mountain table
2	Single mechanistic systems	Dynamic-predetermined changes, processes	Order (when)	Clock, tune, computers
3	Control mechanisms, cybernetic systems	Error-controlled feedback, information	Specification (what)	Thermostat, body temperature
4	Living systems	Continuous self-production	Autopoietic Relations (first-order autopoiesis)	Cell, amoeba, single-celled bacteria
5	Multicellular system	Functional differentiation	Structural coupling between cells (second-order autopoiesis)	Plants, fungi, moulds, algae
6	Organisms with nervous systems	Interaction with relations	Symbolic, abstract relations	Most animals
7	Observing systems	Language, self-consciousness	Recursive, self-referential-relations	Human beings
8	Social systems	Rules, meanings, norms, power	Structural coupling between organisms (third-order autopoiesis)	Families, organizations
9	Transcendental systems			

Source: Mingers, (1997, based on Boulding, 1956).

closed system in that it is a relatively self-contained, self-maintaining unit that has little interaction or exchange with its environment.

Open-systems theory originated in the natural sciences and subsequently spread to fields as diverse as computer science, ecology, engineering, management, and psychotherapy. As discussed earlier, in contrast to closed-systems, the open-system perspective views an organization as an entity that takes inputs from the environment, transforms them, and releases them as outputs in tandem with reciprocal effects on the organization itself along with the environment in which the organization operates. This means that the organization is part and parcel of the environment in which it is situated. Open systems of organizations accept that organizations are contingent on their environments and these environments are also contingent on organizations.

As an open-systems approach spread among organizational theorists, managers began incorporating these views into practice. Two early pioneers in this effort, Daniel Katz and Robert Kahn, began viewing organizations as open social systems with specialized and interdependent sub-systems and processes of communication, feedback, and management linking the sub-systems. Katz and Kahn argued that the closed-system approach fails to take into account how organizations are reciprocally dependent on external environments. For example, environmental forces such as customers and competitors exert considerable influence on corporations, highlighting the essential relationship between an organization and its environment as well as the importance of maintaining external inputs to achieve a stable organization.

The open-systems approach serves as a model of business activity; that is, business as a process of transforming inputs to outputs while realizing that inputs are taken from the external environment and outputs are placed into this same environment. Companies use inputs such as labour, funds, equipment, and materials to produce goods or to provide services, and they design their sub-systems to attain these goals. These sub-systems are thus analogous to cells in the body, while the organization itself is analogous to the body, and external market and regulatory conditions are analogous to environmental factors such as the quality of housing, drinking water, air, and the availability of nourishment. Furthermore, open systems are subject to linear and non-linear feedback mechanisms. In an organization wishing to improve quality, linear effects would be observed when implementing more quality checks to reduce the number of defects reaching the customer. Non-linear effects would occur when deciding on a training programme to educate staff in total quality management (Teale et al., 2003).

To summarize, any system falls into one of two basic categories: open or closed. An open system accepts inputs from its environment, acts on the inputs to create outputs, and releases the outputs to its environment. In contrast, a closed system is isolated and hermetic; an experimental, sterile chemistry lab would be an example. Virtually every system within which people operate is an open system, although some are more open than others.

Boundaries of systems

All systems have *boundaries*, a fact that is immediately apparent in mechanical systems such as the watch, but much less apparent in social systems such as organizations.

The concept of boundaries helps us to understand the distinction between open and closed systems. A closed system has rigid, impenetrable boundaries, whereas an open system has permeable boundaries between itself and a broader system (Kast and Rosenzweig, 1981). Boundaries set the domain of the system's activities. In a physical, mechanical, or biological system, boundaries can be identified. In a social organization – as in a project-based company – boundaries are not easily definable and are determined primarily by the functions and activities of the organization. Such an organization is characterized by rather vaguely formed, highly permeable boundaries.

Indeed, the boundaries of open systems, because they interact with other systems or environments, are more flexible than those of closed systems, which are rigid and largely impenetrable. Instead, a closed-system perspective views systems as relatively independent of environmental influences. For example, the closed-system approach conceives of the company as a system of management, technology, personnel, equipment, and materials, but tends to exclude competitors, suppliers, distributors, and governmental regulators. This approach allows managers and organizational theorists to analyse problems by examining the internal structure of a business with little consideration of the external environment.

According to Morecroft et al. (2007), the entire social and business world may be viewed as one large system. However, individuals are usually interested in understanding some more limited part of the world, such as a given organization (e.g. a project-based company), or unit (e.g. a project) within an organization. To focus on a sub-system of the business world, individuals commonly place boundaries around a collection of people and things of interest (e.g. project teams), and then refer to that bounded collection as a system. If correctly placed, the boundaries of a system demarcate the elements that have relatively intense and frequent interactions (those that are inside the boundary of the system) from elements that have relatively less intense or frequent interactions (those elements that are then regarded as being outside the system). Although people may place boundaries around a system for the purpose of analysis or management, all systems nevertheless remain open systems in the sense that there will always be some form and level of interaction between the elements 'inside' a system with elements 'outside' the system. Thus, to some extent, the boundaries of a system are inevitably artificial and somewhat arbitrary in their placement, and are always porous to some degree.

Evidently the concept of boundaries furthers our understanding of the distinction between open and closed systems. Relatively closed systems have rigid, impenetrable boundaries, whereas open systems have permeable boundaries between themselves and the broader system.

All systems have boundaries which separate them from their environments. For example, boundaries set the domain of a project-based company's activities. However, in this case the boundaries are rather vaguely formed, that is, they are highly permeable boundaries.

Cybernetics and feedback loops

Cybernetics is the study of feedback and it is derived from concepts such as communication and control in living organisms, machines, and organizations. Its focus is on how an object (digital, mechanical, or biological) processes data, reacts to data, and changes or can be changed to better accomplish the first two tasks.

The terms 'systems theory' and 'cybernetics' have been widely used as synonyms. Some authors use the term cybernetic systems to denote a proper subset of the class of general systems, namely those systems that include *feedback loops*. Cybernetics, catastrophe theory (e.g. Gilmore, 1981), chaos theory (e.g. Levy, 1994), and complexity theory have a common goal which is to explain complex systems that consist of a large number of mutually interacting and interrelated parts in terms of those interactions.

Systems theory recognizes that the interaction between elements may be of two basic types, each of which has a very different impact on the internal dynamics of a system. When an increase or decrease in a system element leads to a corresponding increase or decrease in another system element, the first element is said to have a 'positive' influence on the second element. When a change in one system element leads to an opposite change in another system element, the first is said to have a 'negative' influence on the second (O'Connor and McDermott, 1997; Morecroft et al., 2007).

Feedback and regulation are self-related. Negative feedback helps to maintain stability in a system in spite of external changes. It is related to homeostasis. Positive feedback amplifies the possibilities for divergences (evolution, change of goals); it is the condition to change, evolution, growth; it gives the system the ability to access new points of equilibrium.

Thus, the types of feedback are:

- *Positive feedback* which seeks to increase the event that caused it. This is also known as a *self-reinforcing* loop. Such loops tend to be open-ended leading to runaway growth.
- *Negative feedback* which seeks to cancel the event that caused it. This is also known as a self-correcting or *balancing* loop. Such loops tend to be goal-seeking (Figure 3.1).

The terms 'negative and positive feedback' can be used less formally to describe or imply criticism and praise, respectively. This may lead to confusion with the terms positive and negative reinforcement, which both refer to something that increases the likelihood of the behaviour. Further, there are some subtle points relating to feedback loops. Balancing loops are sometimes prone to hunting, which is an oscillation caused by excessive or delayed goal-seeking, resulting in over-correction. Self-reinforcing loops are often a part of a larger balancing loop, especially in biological systems such as regulatory circuits.

To summarize, the principle of feedback seems to be so simple, so ubiquitous, that people take it for granted. Feedback allows machines to work without direct human control. Machines built with feedback circuits are more powerful, more controllable, and do not need constant human supervision. The steam engine, for example, revolutionized existing technology, gave impetus to the industrial revolution, and changed our lives and the way we work. Now electronic feedback

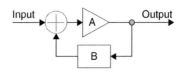

Figure 3.1   Ideal feedback model.

circuits power the information revolution; they form the driving force of computers and all devices that rely on microchip technology, from washing machines to missiles.

System dynamics and causality

To understand and improve an organization's effectiveness in building a powerful and co-ordinated portfolio of resources, a rigorous, comprehensive set of tools for operationalizing the accumulation and depletion of strategic 'asset-stocks' (Dierickx and Cool, 1989) is required. *System dynamics* provides ideal tools for this purpose, including a rigorous means of formulating the mathematical integration underlying these accumulation and depletion processes. System dynamics frameworks can capture the dynamic interdependencies between resources, leading to powerful models of a company's performance as a 'dynamic resource-system' (Warren, 2007). This is because system dynamics deals with feedback loops and time delays that affect the behaviour of the entire system. What makes using system dynamics different from other approaches to studying complex systems is the use of feedback loops, as well as stocks and flows. These elements help describe how even seemingly simple systems display baffling nonlinearity.

The basis of system dynamics is the recognition that the structure of a system – the many circular, interlocking, sometimes time-delayed relationships among its components – is often just as important in determining its behaviour as the individual components themselves. Examples are chaos theory and social dynamics. It is also claimed that, because there are often properties of the whole which cannot be found among the properties of the elements, in some cases the behaviour of the whole cannot be explained in terms of the behaviour of the parts. An example is the properties of those words which when considered together can give rise to a meaning which does not exist in the words by themselves. This further explains the integration of tools, like language, as a more parsimonious process in the human application of easiest path adaptability through interconnected systems.

Causality denotes a necessary relationship between one event (called cause) and another event (called effect) which is the direct consequence (result) of the first. Though cause and effect are typically related to events, other candidates include processes, properties, variables, facts, and states of affairs. Which of these comprise the correct causal relations, and how best to characterize the nature of the relationship between them, has no universally accepted answer, and it remains under discussion.

According to Sowa (2006), up until the twentieth century, three assumptions described by Max Born in 1949 were dominant in the definition of causality:

- Causality postulates that there are laws by which the occurrence of an entity B of a certain class depends on the occurrence of an entity A of another class, where the word entity means any physical object, phenomenon, situation, or event. A is called the cause, B the effect
- Antecedence postulates that the cause must be prior to, or at least simultaneous with, the effect
- Contiguity postulates that cause and effect must be in spatial contact or connected by a chain of intermediate things in contact.

Thus, changes in the independent variable are assumed to cause changes in the dependent variable. However, it is possible to make an incorrect assumption about causality when relationships are found. For example, early behavioural scientists found that there was a relationship between employee satisfaction and productivity. They concluded that a happy worker was a productive worker. Follow-up research has supported the relationship, but disconfirmed the direction: the evidence more correctly suggests that high productivity leads to satisfaction rather that the other way around (Robbins and Judge, 2009).

Senge (1990, p. 23) argues, with reference to organizations, that 'We learn best from our experience, but we never directly experience the consequences of many of our most important decisions'. This means that people tend to think that cause and effect will be relatively close to one another. That is, when faced with a problem, it is the contiguous 'solutions' individuals focus upon. Traditionally, people have looked at actions that produce improvements in a relatively short time span. However, when viewed in systems terms, short-term improvements often involve very significant long-term costs. For example, cutting back on research and design can bring very quick cost savings, but can severely damage the long-term viability of an organization.

Part of the problem involves the nature of the feedback we receive. Some of the feedback will be reinforcing, with an accumulation of small changes generating further changes. 'Whatever movement occurs is amplified, producing more movement in the same direction. A small action snowballs, with more and more and still more of the same, resembling compound interest' (Senge, 1990, p. 81). An appreciation of systems will lead to recognition of the use of, and problems with, such reinforcing feedback, and also an understanding of the place of balancing feedback. A further key aspect of systems is the extent to which they inevitably involve delays, 'interruptions in the flow of influence which make the consequences of an action occur gradually' (Senge, 1990, p. 90). Senge (1990, p. 92) concludes: 'The systems viewpoint is generally oriented toward the long-term view. That's why delays and feedback loops are so important. In the short term, you can often ignore them; they're inconsequential. They only come back to haunt you in the long term'.

Further, Senge (1990) advocates the use of 'system maps' – diagrams that show the key elements of systems and how they connect. However, people often have a problem 'seeing' systems, and it takes work to acquire the basic building blocks of systems theory, and to apply them to one's organization. On the other hand, failure to understand system dynamics can lead people into 'cycles of blaming and self-defence: the enemy is always there, and problems are always caused by someone else' (Bolman and Deal, 1997).

To summarize, system dynamics is an approach to understanding the behaviour of complex systems over time. It deals with internal feedback loops and time delays that affect the behaviour of an entire system. What makes using system dynamics different from other approaches to studying complex systems is the use of causal loops. These loops help describe how even seemingly simple systems display baffling nonlinearity. System dynamics has found application in a wide range of areas, for example ecological and economic systems, which usually interact strongly with each other. Besides this, system dynamics has been used to investigate resource dependencies, and the resulting problems in product development projects (cf. Repenning, 1999, 2001).

Company as a system

According to Mitleton-Kelly (2003), organizations like companies are, by their very nature, complex evolving systems and need to be considered as such for two reasons. First, the characteristics of complexity cannot be mapped directly from other scientific domains into the social domain because humans have volition that generates behaviours that differ from the predictable behaviours of other objects of scientific research. Second, using the principles of complexity from the physical sciences only as metaphors or analogies in studying human systems would be too limiting.

Visualizing a company as a system is useful because it helps individuals to see its basic elements quite clearly. The basic elements of a company are its inputs, processes, outputs, and feedback. Inputs to a company include materials, ideas, and employees. Processes are what the company itself does to the inputs in order to transform them into outputs; outputs are primarily a company's products; feedback includes any sort of information that describes the outputs, such as how information about the outputs has been perceived by customers, competitors, or regulators (e.g. André, 2008).

For example, a manufacturing company collects inputs in the form of raw materials and processes them into an output called a product. Its customers buy the product and comment on its utility and quality, and thus give the company's managers important feedback about how to improve the product. In a similar way, innovative companies take in information and raw materials, transform them via creative processes, and produce new technologies. Universities, for example, take in students and turn out educated citizens.

Indeed, complex adaptive systems like project-based companies have the capacity to create order from chaos and to generate new emergent properties in an accumulative manner (Kauffman, 1993; Holland, 1998). Such capabilities are described as self-organizing and self-structuring decentralized processes (Doz and Prahalad, 1993), self-renewal (Chakravarthy and Doz, 1992; Nonaka, 1988), and emergent internal closure (Spender, 1996a). Achieving self-organization and emergence in complex human adaptive systems, however, requires reduced levels of centralized control. Although certain basic approaches have been identified as facilitating self-organization (Holland, 1995) they do not fully address the interconnectedness that impacts on an organization's capability to evolve and to create and utilize knowledge.

Equifinality is an important characteristic of social systems. In physical systems there is a direct cause-and-effect relationship between the initial conditions and the final state. However, biological and social systems operate differently. The concept of equifinality says that final results may be achieved with different initial conditions and in different ways. This view suggests that the project-based company can accomplish its objectives with varying inputs and with varying internal activities. Consequently, the social system is not restrained by the simple cause-and-effect relationship of the closed systems.

Thus, the equifinality of social systems is of major importance for the management of complex organizations like project-based companies. A closed-system cause-and-effect view adopted from the physical sciences would suggest that there is a preferred way to achieve a given objective. The concept of equifinality suggests that a manager can utilize a varying bundle of inputs into an organization, transform them in a variety of ways, and can achieve satisfactory output. Extending this view further suggests that the management function is not necessarily one of seeing a precise, optimal solution but rather one of having a variety of satisfactory alternatives available.

To summarize, the system approach to the study of companies combines the often contrasting positions and considerations of the classical and human relations schools, and embraces both the technical and social aspects of a company. It also recognizes the presence of contingent environmental factors which, even though they may lie outside the organizational boundaries, nevertheless influence organizational activity. Attention is focused on the whole company, the relationships between its technical, mechanical, or structural parameters and its behavioural, social, or human elements, as well as its relationship with the business environment. Furthermore, 'learning organizations', and 'management by walking around' are concepts that most managers would be familiar with. What these concepts are pointing to is the idea of the organization as a system or a living organism, rather than just a set of boxes on an organizational chart or flowchart.

Summary

One of the biggest breakthroughs in how individuals understand and guide change in organizations is systems theory. Therefore, this chapter has described the basic concepts of systemic view and systems thinking. Some of the key factors are the following:

A systemic view of organization often requires a change in the mindset of an observer from reductionist to holistic paradigms.

Systems thinking is a way of seeing and talking about reality that helps people better understand and work with systems to influence the quality of their lives. In this sense, systems thinking can be seen as a systemic view.

Systems theory is the interdisciplinary study of the abstract organization of phenomena, independent of their substance, type, or spatial or temporal scale of existence. It investigates both the principles common to all complex entities, and the models which can be used to describe them.

In the most basic sense, a system is any group of interacting, interrelated, or interdependent parts that form a complex and unified whole that has a specific purpose. The key thing to remember is that all the parts are interrelated and interdependent in some way. Without such interdependencies, we have just a collection of parts, not a system.

Thus, a system is a complex whole, a set of connected things or parts, an organized body of material or immaterial things.

Emergent properties arise out of more fundamental entities and yet are novel or irreducible with respect to them. For example, it is sometimes said that consciousness is an emergent property of the brain.

The concept of complexity refers to the basic components of a system as it exists in the real world – such as elements, relationships, and interconnectedness – but is more specifically associated with the attributes of these, or the kinds of behaviour which arise because of the types of relationship. That is, a complex system is a system composed of interconnected parts that as a whole exhibit one or more properties (behaviour being one of the possible properties) not obvious from the properties of the individual parts. Theories of complex evolving systems may lead to ideas about 'enabling environments' and 'enabling infrastructures' – socio-cultural and technical conditions that facilitate learning and the sharing of knowledge that supports self-organization.

Open systems adapt quickly to the environments in which they exist by possessing permeable boundaries through which new data and ideas are readily absorbed. By incorporating viable, new ideas, an open system ultimately sustains growth. Open systems possess a stronger probability for survival due to this adaptability. Conversely, a closed system that resists the incorporation of new ideas can be deemed unnecessary to its parent environment, and risks atrophy. By not adopting or implementing viable ideas, a closed system ceases to properly serve the environment it lives in.

All systems have boundaries which separate them from their environments. These boundaries help people to understand the distinction between open and closed systems. A closed system has rigid, impenetrable boundaries, whereas an open system has permeable boundaries between itself and a broader system.

There are two types of feedback. Positive feedback is when changes in the system come back and amplify a change, leading to more change in the same direction. The system moves away ever faster from its initial point. Positive feedback can lead to runaway exponential growth. Negative feedback is when changes in the whole system feed back to oppose the original change and so dampen the effect. It leads to less of the action that is creating it. Negative feedback keeps the system stable and resists attempts to change it.

System dynamics is an approach to understanding the behaviour of complex systems over time. It deals with internal feedback loops and time delays that affect the behaviour of the entire system.

Characteristics of complex systems are regulated by causal principles and causal couplings that are not describable by a linear chain of causes and effects.

A system approach to studying companies combines the often contrasting positions and considerations of the classical and human relations schools, and embraces both the technical and social aspects of companies. A system approach also recognizes the presence of contingent environmental factors which, even though they may lie outside the organizational boundaries, nevertheless influence organizational activity.

The equifinality of social systems has major importance for the management of complex organizations like project-based companies. This concept suggests that a manager can utilize a varying bundle of inputs into a company, transform them in a variety of ways, and can achieve satisfactory output.

All systems have a goal – even if that goal is only survival. The goal is its desired state where the system is at rest or balanced. Negative feedback acts to reduce the distance between where a system is and where it 'should' be. It drives the system towards a goal.

4
Autopoiesis

The concept of *autopoiesis* reached the international scientific community through an article published by Varela, Maturana, and Uribe in
1974 (Varela et al., 1974), sponsored by von Foerster (Varela, 1996). Its
roots lie in cybernetics and in the neurophysiology of cognition. The
autopoietic approach was subsequently refined and developed over a
period of five years (Maturana, 1975, 1978; Varela, 1979; Maturana and
Varela, 1980a). Two readings edited by Zeleny (1980, 1981) established
in quite a definite manner the essence of the autopoiesis paradigm, and
also outlined the differences between Maturana and Varela regarding
the possibility of its application to the social sciences.

The term autopoiesis literally means 'auto (self)-creation' (from the
Greek: *auto* for self, and *poiesis* for creation or production), and expresses
a fundamental dialectic between structure and function (Maturana and
Varela, 1980a). Thus:

- an autopoietic machine is a machine organized (defined as a unity)
  as a network of processes of production (transformation and destruction) of components which
- through their interactions and transformations continuously regen-
  erate and realize the network of processes (relations) that produced
  them, and
- constitute it (the machine) as a concrete unity in space in which they
  (the components) exist by specifying the topological domain of its
  realization as such a network.

Maturana and Varela wanted to gain a better understanding of the nature
of living systems. The most fundamental question they addressed was:
'What is common to all living systems that allows us to qualify them

34

as living?' The answer, they discovered, lay in self-production, which they labelled autopoiesis. The term autopoiesis was originally conceived as an attempt to characterize the nature of living systems, and most famously adapted by German sociologist Luhmann, who describes the same concept in social systems.

Since its introduction, autopoiesis theory has gradually evolved into a general systems theory (Varela, 1979; Luhmann, 1987; van Twist and Schaap, 1991). It has even been claimed that autopoiesis is a theoretical paradigm rather than a unified theory. The development of autopoiesis in understanding social systems has become intertwined with the main thrust of systems theory thinking (e.g. Buckley, 1967) over the last three decades, that is, towards seeing systems as adapting to their environment and, thus, being ever more open.

Autopoiesis theory has been combined with configuration theory to better understand societal steering. In the debate on ecological consciousness and company responsiveness to environmental issues, autopoiesis theory has helped increase the awareness of communication problems and advanced possible ways to overcome these problems (Luhmann, 1992). Autopoiesis theory has also increased our understanding of how computers and their functioning are related to the evolution of human language, thought, and action (Winograd and Flores, 1987). In the field of management, the concept of autopoiesis has been used to understand the company as a living system (Becker, 1991; Maturana, 1991; Maula, 2006) and to address the development of organizational knowledge (von Krogh and Vicari, 1993; von Krogh et al., 1996a). It has also formed a reference point for understanding evolutionary change in organizations (Smith, 1982; Weathly, 1992; Morgan, 1996).

Autopoietic systems

An *autopoietic system* (e.g. Mingers, 1995; Capra, 1996; Morgan, 1996) is a distinguishable complex of component-producing processes and their resulting components, bounded as an autonomous unity within its environment, and characterized by particular kinds of relations among its components and component-producing processes. The components, through their interaction, recursively generate, maintain, and recover the same complex of processes which produced them.

A canonical example of an autopoietic system is the biological cell. The eukaryotic cell, for example, is made of various biochemical components such as nucleic acids and proteins, and is organized into bounded structures such as the cell nucleus, various organelles, a cell membrane, and cytoskeleton. These structures, based on an external flow of molecules and energy, produce the components which, in turn, continue to maintain the organized bounded structure that gives rise to these components.

More generally, the term autopoiesis resembles the dynamics of a non-equilibrium system. This refers to organized states (sometimes also called dissipative structures) that remain stable for long periods of time despite matter and energy continually flowing through them. Additionally, from a very general point of view, the notion of autopoiesis is often associated with that of self-organization. However, an autopoietic system is autonomous and operationally closed in the sense that every process within it directly helps maintain the whole. Further, a system must be self-organized before it can be autopoietic. Moreover, autopoietic systems are structurally coupled with their environment in a dialect dynamic of changes that can be recalled as sensory-motor coupling. This continuous dynamic is considered as knowledge and can be observed in different life forms.

The relations among the components include the processes of interaction, production, transformation, and destruction. A particular complex of such processes, assembling the components into identifiable unity, is referred to as its *organization*. The organization of a system, as a complex of processes, manifests itself in a given environment of components so that it forms a particular spatio-temporal arrangement of components which realize the system as a concrete entity. This is referred to as the *structure* of the system. Consequently, *an autopoietic system is the unity of its organization and structure*.

Biggiero (2001) gives an example: suppose we can define a chair as a network of relations between components (i.e. horizontal plane supported by at least one strut). That is the organization of the seat class. Since both plane and strut can be made of various materials (i.e. wood, iron, plastic, etc.), each member of the seat class may have a different structure. A specific member of the seat class, together with its defined structure, is a system. Von Krogh and Roos (1995a) give another example: the organization of a bicycle requires two wheels connected by a frame. But the structure of a bicycle may be modified by replacing wooden tyres with rubber tyres, and a stainless steel frame with an aluminium frame. Then, in order to understand autopoietic systems, we need to understand both the interrelations that define them and how the interrelations that constitute them are brought forth in the system.

Thus, the organization of a system identifies it only as a distinguishable unity (e.g. a project-based company) – independent of the concrete attributes of its components (e.g. projects). Its structure then refers to the actual components and their station-temporal relations which must be satisfied if they are to participate in constituting a given system. Obviously, the same organization (e.g. the project-based company) can be realized or can manifest itself in many different structures (e.g. different types of project-based companies or different projects). Less obvious, but still disturbingly conceivable, is the fact that different organizations could give rise to identical (or relatively indistinguishable) structures.

However, reproducing either the organization or the structure of a given system is insufficient for achieving its full explanation. Both aspects, organization and structure, must be reproduced and their relationship specified if an explanation is intended. In order to define a system as a unity (i.e. the class of unities to which it belongs; e.g. the project-based company is a specific type of company) it is necessary and sufficient to reproduce (or to describe) its organization. And, in order to define a system as a particular concrete unity, it is also necessary to describe its structure. Describing the structure alone, by identifying its components and their relationships in a concrete space, is insufficient for explaining a system's properties as a unity. However, it is true that through acquired experience we may recognize a known system by simply identifying its components and describing its structure. But an unknown system and its functioning as a unity cannot be defined or explained by simply reproducing its structure.

An autopoietic system can be contrasted with an *allopoietic system*, such as a car factory, which uses raw materials (components) to generate a car (an organized structure) which is something *other* than itself (the factory). In other words, the product of an autopoietic system is the system itself, it maintains its own identity under a continuing turnover of its concrete components. A system, which only produces something other than itself, is an allopoietic system. In other words, an allopoietic system produces components which do not participate in its constitution as an autonomous unity. Even if a system is capable of producing an exact replica of itself, a clone, it has produced something other than itself and has thus remained allopoietic.

The above comments should not be interpreted as implying that an autopoietic system cannot produce anything other than itself: reproduction of autopoietic systems refers to their ability to produce autopoietic unities that are distinct from themselves. They are of course also capable of producing allopoietic unities. However, it is the self-renewal of their own unity which is primary, while their reproductive capabilities are only secondary as they do not participate in the constitution of the original unity.

To determine whether a system is or is not autopoietic in its organization, Varela et al. (1974, pp. 192–3) have developed six key points or criteria that should be applied to the system. Their criteria are stated as follows:

1. Determine, through interactions, if the unity has identifiable boundaries. If the boundaries can be determined, proceed to 2. If not, the entity is indescribable and we can say nothing.
2. Determine if there are constitutive elements of the unity, that is, components of the unity. If these components can be described, proceed to 3. If not, the unity is an un-analyzable whole and therefore not an autopoietic system.
3. Determine if the unity is a mechanistic system, that is, if the component properties are capable of satisfying certain relations that determine the unity, the interactions, and transformations of these components. If this is the case, proceed to 4. If not, the unity is not an autopoietic system.
4. Determine if the components that constitute the boundaries of the unity constitute these boundaries through preferential neighbourhood relations and interactions between themselves, as determined by their properties in the space of their interactions. If this is not the case, you do not have an autopoietic unity because you are determining its boundaries, not the unity itself. If 4 is the case, however, proceed to 5.
5. Determine if the components of the boundaries of the unity are produced by the interactions of the components of the unity, either by transformation of previously produced components, or by transformations and/or coupling of non-component elements that enter the unity through its boundaries. If not, you do not have an autopoietic unity; if yes, proceed to 6.
6. If all the other components of the unity are also produced by the interactions of its components as in 5, and if those which are not produced by the interactions of other components participate as necessary permanent constitutive components in the production of other components, *you have an autopoietic unity in the space in which its components exist.* If this is not the case and there are components in the unity not produced by components of the unity as in 5, or if there are components of the unity which do not participate in the production of other components, you do not have an autopoietic unity.

Thus, the successful application of the six-point key to a system will determine whether the system is autopoietically organized or not.

Autopoietic systems can be classified into three types according to the kind of autopoiesis they incorporate. The idea of first-, second-, and third-order autopoiesis is based on the emergence of increasingly complex and abstract structures such as societies and social organizations (Mingers, 1997). *First-order autopoiesis* explains the principles of a self-producing, living system (a cell, for example). *Second-order autopoiesis* explains structural coupling between living systems. It describes a multicellular system, characterized by functional differentiation (plants, for example). *Third-order autopoiesis* explains structural coupling between organisms. This level includes social systems, such as human societies that involve multiple organisms.

In sum, autopoiesis theory conceives living systems as being continually self-reproducing in terms of the processes that made them, not in terms of their relationship with their environment, nor in terms of their components, per se. Therefore, the autopoietic system's production of components does not depend on an input-output relation with the system's environment. Everything the system needs for self-production (i.e. its autopoiesis) is already in the system. In other words, in contrast to allopoietic systems, the elements of an autopoietic system are not produced by something outside the system. Thus, an autopoietic system is a unity of its organization and structure.

Structural coupling and self-referential systems

Teubner (1991, p. 133) suggests that *structural coupling* at the level of social systems can be defined in the following way: 'A system is structurally coupled to its environment when it uses events in the environment as perturbations in order to build up its own structure'.

Structural coupling is a reformulation of the idea of adaption, but with the important proviso that *the environment does not specify the adaptive changes that will occur*. They will either occur, and thus maintain autopoiesis, or they will not occur and the system will disintegrate. Moreover, it is important to understand that, for example, the project-based company must become structurally coupled not only to its environment but also to other systems (Koskinen, 2009a). The behaviour of one system becomes a trigger for the behaviours of the other systems through the selections of their individual structures.

As outlined above, an autopoietic system is realized through a particular structure, and the changes that it can undergo are determined by that structure so long as autopoiesis is maintained. These changes may preserve the structure as it is, or they may radically alter it. Where this is possible, the structure is said to be plastic (Mingers, 1995). Plastic structure exists within an environment that perturbs it and can trigger changes. However, the environment does not determine the changes, but it can be said to select states from among those made possible at any instant by the system's structure. In an environment characterized by recurring states, continued autopoiesis will lead to selection in the system of a structure suitable for that environment. The system becomes structurally coupled to its environment and, indeed, to other systems within that environment.

Consequently, the system is never idle; by observation it distinguishes events in the environment, and it uses energy to discuss these events within the rules of its language. The system uses such events to discover new themes, issues, opportunities, threats, strengths, and weaknesses. Gradually, new arguments are made that construct a description of the environment.

Indeed, systems exist in a network of continuous structural coupling, and change together congruently in a process that spontaneously lasts as long as the autopoietic system is conserved. In these circumstances, an autopoietic system lives only as long as its internally generated structural changes occur with the conservation of autopoiesis, and its encounters in the environment do not trigger a disintegration in it. Disintegration does not happen as long as there is an operational dynamic congruence between the environment and the system through which the system is conserved. That is, all systems as well as the environment with which they interact recursively are systems that change together congruently forming a network of multidimensional structural coupling. In other words, the systems become structurally coupled not only to their environment but also to other systems. These interlocked triggering behaviours may have direct importance as such or they may be purely symbolic and essentially arbitrary, such as a particular form of greeting in a particular language. In the latter case, it does not matter what the actual behaviour is, but only that it has been implicitly agreed through structural coupling.

The concept of *self-reference* is an abstraction that allows people to distinguish a particular class of systems by its functioning. Self-reference means that the knowledge accumulated by the system about itself affects the structure and operation of that system. Autopoietic systems are, therefore, self-referential (Goguen and Varela, 1979; Varela, 1979). In contrast, non-autopoietic systems, for example a computer, refer to something given from the outside, like software, and consequently have a different relating operation.

An autopoietic system may be self-referential with respect to a specific space-time combination, but also self-referential with respect to its own evolution (Jantsch, 1980). Once this circularity arises, the processes attain coherence through their own operation, not through interventions from the environment. Further, implications emerge for how human beings attain knowledge: we gain knowledge through reference to our previous knowledge. Thus, self-referentiality is a way of abstracting that what we know is influenced by what we knew, and what we will know depends on what we know (von Krogh and Roos, 1995a).

Thus, the structure of a system changes both as a result of its structural coupling and as a result of its self-reference. The structural changes triggered in the interactions of a system arise moment after moment determined by its structure. As a consequence, in this process the structure of the system and the structure of the environment change together congruently as a matter of course, and the general result is that the history of interactions between two or more systems becomes a history of spontaneous recursive coherent structural changes in which all the participant systems change together congruently until they separate or disintegrate.

Autonomy

Autonomy means self-control, that is, maintaining identity. This means that a system is autonomous if it can specify its own laws for its own functioning (e.g. Morin, 1982). Autopoietic systems are autonomous units: they subordinate all changes to the maintenance of their own organization. 'Autonomy is the distinctive phenomenology resulting from an autopoietic organization: the realization of the autopoietic organization is the product of its operation' (Varela et al., 1974, p. 188). Because an autopoietic system reproduces its own components and recreates its own organization and identity, it acquires its autonomy. The rules for its functioning are found in the system's organization and the way it reproduces itself. Autonomy is, therefore, a property of living systems in general: 'autonomy appears so obviously an essential feature of living systems that whenever something is observed that seems to have it, the naive approach is to deem it alive' (Varela, 1979, p. 3).

The autonomy of an autopoietic system refers to its capability of being determined by its own internal rules, instead of inputs received from the environment. The enactors are the circular causality of the system and its environment. In such a context, the coupling between the system and its surroundings is not given by any 'input-output' scheme, but by a 'perturbation-dissipation' effect, which is the direct consequence of the self-maintenance of the autopoietic system. In other words, to be cognitive means to be able to maintain a physical autonomous stability, despite the environment's constant perturbations (cf. von Krogh and Roos, 1995a).

Autonomous systems are distinct from systems whose coupling with the environment are specified or designed through input-output relations, like a computer: allopoietic systems. In other words, an open organization of components and component-producing processes (linear, treelike, or other noncyclical concatenations) leads to allopoiesis; that is, the organization is not recursively generated through the interactions of its own products. In this sense, as mentioned earlier, the system is not self-producing; it produces something other than 'itself'. This particular (allopoietic) concatenation of processes is capable only of production, not self-production. Allopoietic organizations are still invariant and can be spontaneously concatenated (under favourable conditions).

A particular concatenation of production processes can be assembled by humans through a purposeful design. We then speak of *heteropoiesis*. Man-made machines and contrivances, and their own productions as well, are heteropoietic – they are produced by another system. A machine, for example, is characterized by an organization of components produced by other processes (a person or another machine), and of processes of production whose products do not constitute the machine itself. So far, all heteropoietic systems are allopoietic (i.e. non-living).

It should be noted that the property of autonomy makes autopoietic systems distinct from self-organizing systems (Jantsch, 1980; Andrew, 1989). They differ with respect to the criteria of autonomy they imply: systems first have to be self-organized before they can become autopoietic (cf. sub-chapter autopoietic system in this chapter). In other words, autopoiesis is not synonymous with self-organization, as suggested by some authors (e.g. Zimmerman and Hurst, 1993).

To summarize, an autopoietic system can select its elements (i.e. structure) autonomously. This means that, for example, a project-based company can decide, with respect to every communication, whether to conceive an input as an element of its structure or not.

Simultaneously open and closed systems

Operational closure is a fundamental concept, which should be analysed using the notions of operations and closure. The former refers to component actions which are determined by the component's role and nature, and by their reciprocal interconnections. Operations are all self-contained, which explains autonomy and self-reference. Only energy, matter, and information can be exchanged with the environment, provided that the latter is not in the form of components. Closure refers to the relationship between system and environment. Any environmental change is selected (perceived, enacted) by the system, in order to maintain its organization (i.e. its autonomy, identity). A system can give rise to structural changes as needed to adapt to environmental changes, always maintaining (preserving) the existing organization (i.e. identity). If it fails to do so, then that systemic identity perishes and the autopoietic system may transform itself (Biggiero, 2001)

- into another autopoietic system, with a new organization
- into an allopoietic system, owing to the loss of its autonomy
- it can disintegrate and disappear.

However, boundaries cannot be understood only as the discrete limits of an autopoietic system in space and time, just as closure and openness cannot be fully understood in terms of the semi-permeable membranes that separate the inside from the outside. That is, in several different but related ways, autopoietic systems are both open and closed. First, and in the most limited sense, autopoietic systems seem to work out a simple compromise between closure and openness in the form of some kind of semi-permeable membrane. Boundaries do more than produce closure by keeping certain things out and others in; they also allow traffic that they channel and manage. But they do more than just allow traffic: they create traffic by producing differentials between sides of boundaries, thus also producing more openness. This means that one has to acknowledge that boundaries and the autopoietic systems built around them more than simply create traffic, they are traffic (Livingston, 2006).

An autopoietic system filters, enacts, and reacts to the environment in order to maintain its autopoiesis, that is, its self-production. This property is what was initially called organizational closure and subsequently operational closure. A system exchanges – is open to exchange – matter, energy, and information with the environment, but it neither receives inputs nor gives outputs. That is, the lack of conventional inputs and outputs does not imply that the system is isolated from its environment. The system does not direct energy to the perturbation, as is the case in allopoietic systems. Perturbations can only stimulate processes in the system itself, which act always follows the self-defined rules of the system. Because the environment cannot ever determine, direct, or control these changes, the autopoietic system perceives its environment by perceiving itself (e.g. Dupeuy, 1988). Similarly, although the system, per se, may be the cause of structural changes in the environment, the final result can never be determined by the autopoietic system. Thus, the perturbations are reciprocal. From this it follows that autopoietic systems are *simultaneously open and closed*. And therefore it is possible to conclude that knowledge is not picked up or transferred from the environment, but it is formed within the autopoietic system (see chapter 5: Autopoietic epistemology later in this book).

It is important to note that the unity-characterizing complex of processes is assumed to be invariant; it is being continually recovered as the same complex of processes. Furthermore, the components, as the end products of component-producing processes, are indispensable prerequisites for the activation of the component-producing processes themselves. These processes, in order to occur at all, require specific co-operation of their own end products. It is only in this sense that a complex of such processes can be called closed.

Thus, it is important to understand that openness is not the same as open system, and closure is not the same as closed system. Moreover, it is also important to note that openness and closure are neutral and analytical system concepts that explain certain characteristics of a system's behaviour and should not be associated with any value judgments (Maula, 2006).

Openness and closure can be described by two dimensions, boundary and feedback. In a very simplistic interpretation they could have the following values:

- Boundary of the system is closed (closure) or open (openness)
- Feedback exists (closed feedback) or is missing (the system is open).

It can also be assumed that boundary and feedback may represent degrees of openness and closure. Openness does not only mean receiving input but also proactive interaction and co-evolution with the environment. Furthermore, it can be assumed that feedback exists always in one way or another, in a shorter or longer period, directly of indirectly even if it may be difficult to identify. Therefore, the characterization above will be redefined by Maula (2006) as follows:

- *Boundary:* The boundary is closed (closure; no input or interaction) or open (interactive openness through open interaction and co-evolution with the environment).
- *Feedback:* The system is characterized by self-referentiality and internal closure (internal closure) or by feedback loops via the external environment ('open feedback' through external closure).

The combinations of the two variables and their values result in four theoretical alternatives:

1. *A connected system* (open boundary; internal closure) co-evolves with its environment through reciprocal interaction with it. It is simultaneously characterized by an open boundary through input or interaction (interactive openness, co-evolution) and internal closure (e.g. self-referentiality). This kind of organization is capable of acquiring new knowledge and it has access to its earlier accumulated knowledge.

2. *A double-open system* (open boundary; 'open feedback' via environment) is connected to its environment via an open boundary (interactive openness, co-evolution) and has an 'open feedback-loop' from the external environment. This kind of organization is very open to external input, but learning does not accumulate or the organization does not have access to its earlier accumulated knowledge through self-referentiality and internal closure.

3. *An isolated, double-closed system* (closed boundary, internal closure) is not connected to its environment but is instead based on internal closure. This kind of organization does not react to signals from its environment and does not interact and co-evolve with it. However, it has access to its earlier accumulated knowledge. Because of the lack of new input, there is a danger that existing knowledge becomes outdated and irrelevant.

4. *A passive, closed and open system* (closed boundary, 'open feedback' via environment) does not react to signals from its environment and does not interact with its environment. Moreover, learning does not accumulate or the system does not have access to its earlier accumulated knowledge. This kind of passive organization is not connected to the environment and has access neither to new knowledge nor to its own earlier knowledge.

Indeed, the analysis of openness and closure provides a more diversified characterization of systems than the mere division between an 'open system' and a 'closed system'. The analysis shows that openness and closure are not mutually exclusive features. Rather, a system can be simultaneously open and closed according to the variables of boundary and feedback.

Furthermore, openness and closure are neutral and analytical system concepts that explain certain characteristics of a system's behaviour and should not be associated with any value judgments. Indeed, as noted earlier, openness is not the same as an open system, and closure is not the same as a closed system.

In sum, an autopoietic organization is characterized by an organizational closure of its constitutive processes. At least some of the products become necessary ingredients or conditions for their own production. In this sense, autopoietic systems are organizationally closed. However, they remain of course open with respect to the environmental perturbations of their structure. In other words, they have contact with their environment. This contact with the environment is regulated by the autopoietic system, that is, the system determines when, what, and through what channels energy or matter is exchanged with the environment. This simultaneous open and closed condition of the autopoietic system becomes particularly important when considering cognitive processes. For Maturana and Varela (1973, 1980b, p. 13), the concept of living is directly linked to the concept of cognition: 'Living systems are cognitive systems, and living as a process is a process of cognition'.

Observing

'If there is anything like a central intellectual fascination in this century it is probably the discovery of the observer' (Baecker, 1996, p. 17).

Spencer Brown (1979) suggests treating *observation* as the most basic concept for any analysis (Seidl, 2005). As a concept it is supposed to be even more basic than, for example, that of thing, event, thought, action, or communication (Luhmann, 2000). This means, of course, that the term 'observation' is not used in its usual sense as referring merely to optical perception. Instead, 'observation' is used as an abstract concept referring to any operation from communication to thought and even to the operation of a machine; even the observer is treated as an observation (Spencer Brown, 1979).

The concept of observation (Spencer Brown, 1979; Latour, 1986) does not focus on the object of observation but on the observation itself as a selection of what to observe. In this sense, the underlying question is not: *what* does an observer observe, but *how* does an observer observe; *how* is it that an observer is observing what he or she is observing, and not observing something else (Seidl, 2005).

Every observation is construed from two components: a distinction and an indication. An observer chooses a distinction with which he or she demarcates a space into two spaces (states or contents). Of these two states, he or she has to choose one which he or she indicates. That is to say, the observer has to focus on one state, while neglecting the other. It is not possible to focus on both simultaneously. In this sense, the relation between the two states is asymmetrical (e.g. Cooper, 1986; Chia, 1994).

However, the role of the observer is usually ignored in systems writing (Weinberg, 2001). The most popular way of ignoring the observer is to move right into a mathematical representation of a system – a so-called mathematical system – without saying anything about how that particular representation was chosen. For example, Hall and Fagen (1968, p. 81) give this definition: 'A system is a set of objects together with relationships between the objects and between their attributes'. These authors rightly emphasize 'relationships' as an essential part of the system concept, but fail to give the slightest hint that the system itself is relative to the viewpoint of some observer.

The real world gives the subset of what is; the product space represents the uncertainty of the observer. The product space may therefore change if the observer changes, and two observers may legitimately use different product spaces within which to record the same subset of actual events in some actual thing. The constraint is thus a relation between observer and thing; the properties of any particular constraint will depend on both the real thing and on the observer. From this it follows that a substantial part of the theory of organization will be concerned with properties that are not intrinsic to the thing itself but are relational between observer and thing (Ashby, 1968).

Thus, because the autopoietic process is not directly accessible to anything or anybody except the system, it is only open to observation, and any characterization of an autopoietic system can only be given from the standpoint of an observer (von Foerster, 1972). An observer, or observer-community, is 'one or more persons who embody the cognitive point of view that created the system in question, and from whose perspective it is subsequently described' (Varela, 1979, p. 85).

The observer can choose to either focus his or her attention on the internal structure of the system, or on its environment. In the former case, the observer sees the environment as background, and the properties of the system emerge from the interaction between its components. In the latter case, he or she treats the system as a simple entity with a particular interaction with the environment. That is, a system is a way of looking at the world.

Knowledge, therefore, depends very much on the point of observation of an individual. In autopoiesis theory 'knowledge' and 'observation' are closely related, since observing systems are autopoietic systems (cf. Piaget, 1936). To be more precise, in autopoiesis theory distinctions and norms are two central categories (Varela, 1979; Luhmaan, 1986,

1988). Knowledge is what makes individuals able to make distinctions in their observations and, based on their norms, determine what they see. The distinctions reveal the knowledge of the distinguisher.

Organizational autopoiesis

The question of whether human social systems (e.g. companies and/ or organizations) can be described as autopoietic has been discussed quite extensively, and different scholars have proposed various answers (e.g. Luhmann, 1986; Fleischaker, 1992; Mingers, 1995; Biggiero, 2001; Pamkowska, 2008). The central problem is that autopoiesis has been defined precisely only for systems in physical spaces and for computer simulations in mathematical spaces. Because of the 'inner world' of concepts, ideas, and symbols that arises with human thought, consciousness, and language, human social systems exist not only in the physical domain but also in a symbolic social domain.

However, although the definition of autopoiesis refers to the production of components that constitute the entity and a boundary that separates the entity from its environment, 'the definition does not specify that these must be physical components. Then, if they are not, what precisely is their domain of existence?' (Mingers, 1995, pp. 120, 124).

Mingers (1995) differentiates several alternative ways to apply autopoiesis theory to organizations. The approaches contain assumptions about the autopoietic nature of an organization:

- Autopoiesis theory can be applied naively to the social domain. This means that basic characteristics such as boundaries and the production of components remain unexplained.
- Social systems have characteristics of autopoiesis but they are not autopoietic as such. These autonomous systems are characterized by organizational (internal) closure, autonomy, and structure dependence. They are without the specification of physical processes of component production.
- Social systems are not themselves autopoietic, but they constitute a medium where other autopoietic systems (such as human beings) exist and interact within the consensual domain (Maturana and Varela, 1980a).
- Autopoiesis theory can be modified or enlarged to cover non-physical production. This means that it is possible to conceive of non-physical systems such as games or computer-based models as autopoietic (Varela, 1979; Mingers, 1995, 1997).

• Autopoiesis acts as a metaphor, without the ontological commitment that social systems are autopoietic (Tsoukas, 1993; Morgan, 1996).

While behaviour in the physical domain is governed by cause and effect – the so-called laws of nature – behaviour in the social domain is governed by rules generated by the social system and often codified in law. The crucial difference is that social rules can be broken while natural laws cannot. Human beings can choose whether and how to obey a social rule whereas molecules cannot choose whether or not they should interact (cf. Fleischaker, 1992; Mingers, 1995).

Maturana (1988) does not see human social systems as being autopoietic, but rather as the medium in which human beings realize their biological autopoiesis through 'languaging' (Maturana, 1988). However, Varela (1981) argues that the concept of a network of production processes, which is at the very core of the definition of autopoiesis, may not be applicable beyond the physical domain, but that a broader concept of 'organizational' closure can be defined for social systems. This broader concept is similar to that of autopoiesis but does not specify processes of production (Varela, 1981). According to him, autopoiesis can be seen as a special case of organizational closure.

Other authors have asserted that an autopoietic social network can be defined if the description of human social systems remains entirely within the social domain. For example, Luhmann's (1990a) central point is to identify the social processes of the autopoietic network as processes of communication. A product development team, for instance, can be defined as a network of conversations exhibiting inherent circularities. The results of conversations give rise to further conversations, so that self-amplifying feedback loops are formed. The closure of the networks results in a shared system of explanations and understanding – a context of meaning – that is continually sustained by further conversations.

According to Luhmann (1990a), the communicative acts of the network of conversations include the 'self-production' of the roles by which the various team members are defined and of the team's boundary. Since all these processes take place in the symbolic social domain, the boundary cannot be a physical boundary. It is a boundary of expectations, confidentiality, loyalty, and so on. Both the individual roles and boundaries are continually maintained and renegotiated by the autopoietic network of conversations.

Indeed, there seem to be several ways in which autopoiesis theory may be applied to the social domain. The mode of application is important because claiming that an organization is truly autopoietic, and not just metaphorically so, raises significant ontological issues (Mingers, 1995). In metaphorical applications, basic characteristics of autopoietic systems such as boundaries, the production of components, organizational closure, autonomy, and structure dependence may be asserted, but do not specify the processes of component production.

Moreover, in order to exist, organizations must be able to reproduce their specific organizational dynamics and at the same time to evolve and shape themselves in a vital structural coupling with the ever changing dynamics of their environments. Therefore, the crucial survival process of the interlocked adjustment of internal chaotic dynamics to the chaotic dynamics of the environment is here referred to as *organizational autopoiesis*.

In sum, organizations are open systems that are subject to diverse external and internal forces, the combination of which gives birth to organizational dynamics. If people working in organizations are unable to cope with these dynamics, organizations are inevitably thrown into either a fixed order and rigidness, or into uncontrollable chaos and collapse.

Summary

Autopoiesis is the process whereby a system produces itself. This chapter has described autopoiesis theory, concepts of autopoietic system, and organizational autopoiesis. Some of the key factors are the following:

An autopoietic system is an autonomous and self-producing unity which contains component-producing processes. The components, through their interaction, generate recursively the same network of processes which produced them.

An autopoietic system is organizationally identified and structurally defined. A system's structure determines its organization and the effects of perturbations on the organization.

The concept of organization refers to the interrelations between the components of the system, which – independently of the components themselves – define the system as a distinct system in a given space-time continuum. In this sense, the organization of the living system is autopoiesis. In order to speak of the same system, the organization of the system has to remain the same.

In contrast to the organization, the structure is not constitutive of the system. Structures can change, and yet one can still speak of the same system. Hence, the theory of autopoietic systems distinguishes strictly between the continuation of autopoiesis and the stabilization of particular structures. That is, an autopoietic system is structurally coupled to its environment: the structure reacts to its environment through compensation.

Organizational closure does not imply independence from the environment or from other systems. However, all activity must maintain autopoiesis or else the system will disintegrate. All processes are processes of self-production; the system's activity closes in on itself.

Boundaries are necessary for autonomy and organizational closure, that is, they separate the system from its environment and other systems. Further, boundaries must be products of self-production, that is, boundaries are generated and maintained by the system.

Boundaries of autopoietic systems are 'fuzzy'; that is, boundaries function as regulatory mechanisms in structurally coupled interactions. From this it is possible to conclude that autopoiesis theory is a relational theory and it emphasizes the dependence of the observer and the focus and level of observation. In other words, when one focuses on learning processes, an organization is autonomous and controlled by its internal structure. When one focuses on production (transformation) processes, the control approach can be used where the environment determines the system's functioning.

Boundaries in particular cannot be understood only as the discrete limits of an autopoietic system in space and time, just as closure and openness cannot be fully understood in terms of the semi-permeable membranes that separate the inside from the outside of living things.

A system is structurally coupled to its environment when it uses events in the environment as perturbations in order to build up its own structure.

Self-referentiality means that new knowledge refers not only to past knowledge but also to potential future knowledge. People use already established knowledge to determine what they see, and they use what they already know to choose what to look for in their environment. Knowledge is therefore highly dynamic, as people make new observations, talk, use their fantasies to envision possible futures, and formulate problems.

Autopoietic systems are autonomous units; they subordinate all changes to the maintenance of their own organization, that is, the autonomy of an autopoietic system lies in its capability of being determined by its own internal rules, instead of inputs received from the environment.

In several different but related ways, autopoietic systems are simultaneously both open and closed. This simultaneous openness and closure of the autopoietic system becomes particularly important when considering cognitive processes.

Openness and closure can be described by two variables, boundary and feedback, and it is possible that a system is simultaneously open and closed:

- *Boundary.* The boundary is closed (closure; no input or interaction) or open (interactive openness through open interaction and co-evolution with the environment)
- *Feedback.* The system is characterized by self-referentiality and internal closure (internal closure) or by feedback loops via the external environment ('open feedback' through external closure).

The concept of observation does not focus on the object of observation but on the observation itself as a selection of what to observe. In this sense, the underlying question is not: what does an observer observe, but how does an observer observe; how is it that an observer is observing what he or she is observing, and not observing something else.

There are several ways in which autopoiesis theory may be applied to the social domain. Here autopoiesis is seen as a special case of organizational closure, and therefore applicable to social systems like project-based companies.

Thus, through its biological roots, autopoiesis theory focuses on processes and relations between processes realized through components, rather than on properties of the components of the systems, per se. All metacellulars, like human beings, reproduce themselves through the coupled cells that they are composed of. Because all metacellulars are autopoietic systems, we are all autopoietic systems (von Krogh and Roos, 1995a).

Furthermore, the main argument of autopoiesis theory is that living systems are created and recreated in an *autonomous, simultaneously open and closed, self-referencing,* and *observing* manner. The basic characteristics of autopoietic systems are depicted in Table 4.1.

The interpretation and model presented in this book goes beyond metaphor to propose that a project-based company can be a self-producing, autopoietic system in the sense of autopoiesis. That is, this book will build on the assumption that autopoiesis theory explains organizational non-physical, autopoietic production.

Table 4.1 Basic characteristics of an autopoietic system

Characteristic	Definition
Autopoiesis (self-production)	An organization produces its own components and boundaries, and renews itself in a way that allows the continuous maintenance of its integrity
Identity	Being composed of components and their relationships. Being distinguishable from other organizations
Components	Non-physical parts of the system that are continually produced by the organization
Boundaries	Non-physical parts of the system that connect the system to its environment through reciprocal interaction. Here: boundary elements
Triggers	Signals that are treated as perturbations, not as an input to the organization
Structural coupling	Reciprocal interaction (mutual relationship or correspondence) with the environment. History of recurrent interactions leading to structural congruence
Interactive openness	The organization interacts with the environment and compensates for the perturbations by improving knowledge (distinctions) and changing its 'structure'
Organizational closure ('Operational closure')	The product of the transformation is the very organization itself. Any change in the organization becomes a structural change
Self-referentiality	Accumulated knowledge affects the structure and operation of the organization. The organization affects the (creation of) new knowledge
Social coupling	Reciprocal interaction (communication) by using language

Source: Based on Maturana and Varela (1980a, 1987); Mingers (1995, 1997); von Krogh and Roos (1995a); von Krogh et al. (1996a); Maula (2006).

5
Epistemological Assumptions

The literature of organizational knowledge reveals that companies can be regarded as knowledge-intensive systems (e.g. Newell et al., 2002). However, the *epistemological assumptions* have not been well clarified in this literature. Therefore, an attempt to improve the knowledge-based theory of a company is necessary here (Spender, 1996a).

Epistemology is a branch of the grand divisions of philosophy and it deals with approaches to interpreting knowledge, that is, with ways of knowing. With an epistemology, it is possible to construct a theory of how and why individuals and organizations, like project teams and project-based companies, attain knowledge. Epistemology deals with the following questions: what is knowledge, how does it develop, and what are the conditions necessary for knowledge to develop (cf. von Krogh and Roos, 1995a).

Differences in epistemology are manifested in different ways of categorizing knowledge. This means, for example, that by uncovering the epistemological roots of a company one can better understand the characteristics of knowledge creation needed in that company. 'In order to manage knowledge assets, we need not merely to identify them but to understand them – in depth – in all their complexity: where they exist, how they grow, how managers' actions affect their viability' (Leonard-Barton, 1995, p. xii). According to Venzin et al. (1998), to be familiar with different possible epistemologies means having a larger knowledge management repertoire, and a better understanding of the limitations of each approach. The following three sub-sections provide short illustrations of *cognitivist, connectionist,* and *autopoietic* epistemologies (cf. Varela et al., 1991; von Krogh and Roos, 1995a).

Cognitivist epistemology

Traditional cognitivist epistemology is based on the idea that the human mind has the ability to exactly represent reality in the way that corresponds to the outer world, be it objects, events, or states. This is also frequently referred to as the 'intentionality of the mind' (cf. Goldman, 1986). Broadening this idea, organizations like project-based companies are considered to be systems that develop knowledge by formulating increasingly accurate representations of their pre-defined worlds. Because knowledge is seen as a representation of these worlds, knowledge accumulation and dissemination are the major knowledge development activities in an organization: the more knowledge an organization can gather, the closer the presentation is to reality.

Learning in the cognitivist epistemology means to improve representations of the world through assimilating new experiences (von Krogh et al., 1996a; Varela, 1979). According to Bruner and Anglin (1973, p. 397), an individual actively constructs knowledge by relating incoming information to a previously acquired frame of reference. In other words, when gathering information from the external environment an individual stores facts, relates them to existing experiences, and creates a picture of the world. The world is considered to be a pre-given object, event, or state, which can be perceived in an objective way. What varies from individual to individual is the ability to represent reality. The truth of knowledge is understood as the degree to which an individual's inner representations correspond to the world outside. As new things are learned, this truth will constantly be improved.

Connectionist epistemology

Representationism, as it has been described in cognitivist epistemology, is still prevalent in connectionist epistemology (von Krogh and Roos, 1995a). In connectionism, however, the rules of how to process information are not universal, but vary locally. Organizations are seen as self-organized networks composed of relationships, and driven by communication (Varela et al., 1991; Mingers, 1995). The main method in connectionist epistemology is to look at relationships and not to focus on the individual or the entire system. The connectionist's models are built upon a large number of integrating units that are able to influence one another by sending activation signals down interconnecting pathways. Organizations are seen as networks. Like the cognitivists, the connectionists consider information processing to be the basic activity of the system. The connectionists see the process of shaping an organization as dependent not only on the stimuli entering the system but also on the system itself. Relationships and communication are the most important issues of cognition.

Cognitivist and connectionist epistemologies share two assumptions. First, an individual or an organization is directed to resolve a task. This means that an individual or an organization must identify and represent that task as inner creation of the cognitive system. Second, information processing is the basic activity of an individual or an organization. For an individual, information is taken in from the environment through the senses and will activate various components in the network of components that compose the individual (von Krogh and Roos, 1995a).

However, cognitivist and connectionist epistemologies also differ. While cognitive theories assume that information processing depends only on stimuli from the environment, connectionists claim that it may also arise from within the system itself. The two epistemologies also assume that organizations acquire representations in different ways. Cognitive theories regard learning as a process of creating increasingly accurate representations of the external world, while connectionist theories understand representation as resulting from global states in a history-dependent system (von Krogh and Roos, 1995a). The network as a whole learns from perceived patterns in its environment (Mingers, 1995; cf. Maula, 2006).

Autopoietic epistemology

Compared to cognitivist and/or connectionist epistemology, autopoietic epistemology provides a fundamentally different understanding of the input coming from outside a system (e.g. Hall, 2005). Input is regarded not as knowledge but as data, that is, knowledge is data put into a certain context. This means that knowledge cannot be directly transferred from an individual to another individual, because data have to be interpreted by the receiving individual before it can become knowledge. According to autopoietic epistemology, information does not equal knowledge, but is a process that enables knowledge production and sharing to take place. Von Foerster (1984, p. 193) states that 'information is the process by which knowledge is acquired'. In other words, books (this book, for example), manuals, memos, computer programmes, and so on, are data, not information.

As outlined earlier, an autopoietic system is self-referential, rather than an input-output relationship with the environment. This means that its knowledge structure is made up of closed components of interactions that make reference only to them, that is, in this sense an autopoietic system is autonomous. However, although the autopoietic system is autonomous, it will be perturbed by changes in its environment. For example, when an individual interacts in a recurrent manner, data produced elsewhere reach him or her as perturbations. These perturbations trigger information processes in that individual (i.e. in the receiving system). This means that the perturbations trigger learning but do not specify it. An individual's own knowledge structure (i.e. his or her cognitive map) determines which perturbations are allowed to enter the system, and what changes in the existing knowledge structure are available at a given point in time.

For example, if a teacher delivers a speech to two students, each student will gain different knowledge from it. The transmission by the teacher is the same for both students, but the knowledge created is different: knowledge therefore cannot be transmitted but only created or produced with the help of existing knowledge (Vicari and Troilo, 1999). That is, the only way to acquire new knowledge (i.e. to learn) is to utilize existing knowledge.

Summary

The field of management and organization studies has not paid enough attention to the fundamental issues of epistemology. Knowledge has mostly been taken for granted, often as a fuzzy and substitutable concept. This chapter has, therefore, described three different epistemologies, namely: cognitivist, connectionist, and autopoietic epistemologies. Some of the key factors are the following:

Traditional cognitivist epistemology is based on the idea that the human mind has the ability to exactly represent reality in the way that corresponds to the outer world.

Connectionist epistemology is based upon a large number of integrating units that are able to influence one another by sending activation signals down interconnecting pathways. Therefore, organizations are seen as networks. Like the cognitivists, the connectionists consider information processing to be the basic activity of the system.

Unlike cognitivist or connectionist epistemology, autopoietic epistemology does not claim that the world is a pre-given, but instead that cognition is a creative function. Thus, knowledge is a result of autopoiesis, that is, of self-production processes.

The characteristics of the cognitivist, connectionist, and autopoietic views of knowledge are depicted in the Table 5.1.

Table 5.1 Three approaches to knowledge

Cognitivist view	Connectionist view	Autopoietic view
Knowledge represents the pre-given world	Knowledge represents the pre-given world	Knowledge is created
Knowledge is universal and objective	Knowledge is emergent and history-dependent	Knowledge is emergent, history-dependent, self-referential and context-sensitive
Knowledge is created through information processing by using categories	Knowledge emerges by using simple rules and a few representations	Knowledge is based on distinction-making through observation and experience
Knowledge resides in the individual and in organizational memories	Knowledge resides in the individuals and in the connections between them	Knowledge is embodied in individuals as well as in the internal structures and distinctions of the organization
Knowledge can be transferred	Knowledge can be transferred	Knowledge can be communicated through structural and social couplings

Source: Based on Varela et al. (1991); von Krogh and Roos (1995a); Maula (2006).

In this book, autopoietic epistemology is the basis for an understanding of knowledge, learning, and knowledge transfer. The choice is based on the idea of presenting a fresh and alternative observational scheme for the understanding of knowledge creation in projects and project-based companies.

6
Knowledge Dividend

The central insight of the knowledge in organizations is that *knowledge inputs are necessarily embedded in a context* – cognitive and behavioural, individual and social – which powerfully constrains their discovery, their transfer from one set of actors to another, and their usefulness in different situations (Postrel, 1999). This insight, implicitly or explicitly, drives discussions of path dependence in capabilities (Penrose, 1959) (according to autopoietic epistemology, what you already know biases what you are likely to learn next), imitation of others' technologies (Cohen and Levinthal, 1990) (absorbing new ideas requires a basis of prior knowledge), and transfer of best practices from one site to another (Nelson and Winter, 1982; Kogut and Zander, 1992; Zander and Kogut, 1995) (routines often rely on a context of tacit cues from other people or from machines, which must be articulated in an understandable way in order to be replicated).

This contextual understanding separates the knowledge perspective from research programmes that bear a superficial similarity. For example, the data processing approach (Burton and Obel, 1995) treats the organization as a communication net, linking a group of individuals who are treated as a set of boundedly powerful sensors and processors. As Kogut and Zander (1996, pp. 506, 509) point out, this approach ignores the real difficulties of communication between people, which has to do with such things as conflicting conceptual categories and semantic ambiguities.

Contingency theory (e.g. Smith, 1984) has always had an appreciation for the existence of limits on understanding across individuals, but the different causes of these limits, such as motivational issues and restrictions on attention and knowledge, tend to get blurred (Postrel, 1999). Knowledge is not a central construct in this tradition, although its properties may be implicitly included in discussions of other issues. The properties of the knowledge that organizations use to get work done end up buried in assessments of the simplicity or complexity of the environment, where they are relatively inaccessible to analysis.

Kogut and Zander (1996, pp. 505–6) identify this problem of knowledge division and co-ordination across individuals as being central to the performance of companies. They point out that the extensive specialization found in modern economic life results in a situation where each individual is largely ignorant of the activities of his or her fellows, and stress that bridging these knowledge gaps in some way is essential to the co-ordination of economic activity. They argue that this gap is bridged by social identification processes, behavioural routines, and evolved modes of discourse which allow different individuals to coordinate their activities over time at the cost of some inflexibility and suboptimality of behaviour. This statement of the problem of the division of labour makes one wonder how different patterns of the division of labour and knowledge affect output.

Yet another way of addressing knowledge relies on an organic metaphor. From this perspective, knowledge is viewed as a creative phenomenon that requires the right environment. In other words, it is a complex, self-organizing system. In the organic view of knowledge, the culture of the organization plays a major role. The organizational environment is the 'garden' in which knowledge grows. This viewpoint emphasizes culture, leadership, behaviours, and norms, as well as secondary enablers, such as supporting technologies and communication flows. This perspective draws on concepts from systems theory and uses terms such as 'ecology of knowledge' (Allee, 1997).

Meaning

As originally developed by Husserl (1948, 1950), the concept of *meaning* denotes the surplus of references to the other possibilities of an experience or action. The meaning of 'knife', for example, is its reference to actions and experiences like cutting, stabbing, eating, operating, cooking, and so on. Thus, the knife is not only 'knife' as such but 'knife' with regard to something beyond the knife (Seidl, 2005). In this context, Luhmann (1995b, p. 60) writes: 'Something stands in the focal point, at the center of intention, and all else is indicated marginally as the horizon of an "and so forth" of experience and action'.

According to Seidl (2005), meaning is the difference between the real and the possible, or between actuality and potentiality. A momentarily actual experience or action refers to other momentarily, not actual but possible, experiences. The significance of this distinction becomes clear if one looks at it from a dynamic perspective. While one side of the distinction indicates what is momentarily actual, the other side indicates what could consequently become actual (Luhmann, 1995b, p. 74).

Thus, meaning is an event that disappears as soon as it appears. It marks a merely temporal point after which something else has to follow. The combination of this instability with the co-presentation of possible ensuing events results in the particular dynamic of meaning. Every meaning event disappears as soon as it takes place, but it produces further meaning events to succeed it. For Luhmann this 'auto-agility' of meaning events is 'autopoiesis par excellence'.

According to Pihlanto (2005), all the knowledge an individual has acquired is accumulated into his or her world view in the form of meanings. Meanings can be classified in different categories, and, therefore, knowledge can also be categorized accordingly. Knowledge can be defined in both a narrow and a wide sense. The former contains scientific research results and other more or less factual types of knowledge. In a wide sense, tacit knowledge can also be considered as knowledge.

For instance, intuition is a type of meaning and therefore knowledge in a wide sense. Further, such mental conditions as feeling, belief, and will are meanings, and therefore relevant to the understanding of phenomena by an individual. In a wide sense, all types of meanings are knowledge because an individual understands what the world is like on the basis of these types of meanings.

In addition to the complicated intermingling of different types of meanings, meanings are not always clear and unambiguous: they may be in many cases unclear, ill-structured, distorted, or even erroneous, but they are nevertheless meanings, on the basis of which a decision maker understands the issue at hand in one way or another. Meanings are not only concrete in content but may also be abstract, or ideal (e.g. mathematical relationships), which means that the meaning has not emerged from any real object, but instead from an abstract object. Moreover, in the mind, a continuous process of restructuring of meanings occurs, in which meanings are also often forgotten, fading into unconsciousness, possibly to be later retrieved.

Thus, meaning is a relationship between ontology and truth.

Knowledge

The concept of *knowledge* has different definitions, depending on the discipline where it is used. Here the concept of knowledge means 'human understanding of a specialized field of interest that has been acquired through study and experience'. Knowledge is based on learning, thinking, and familiarity with the problem area. According to autopoietic epistemology, knowledge is not information, and information is not data. Davenport and Prusak (1998) define knowledge as 'a fluid mix of framed experience, values, contextual information, and expert insight that provides a framework for evaluating and incorporating new experience and information'. This means that to be able to manage knowledge, people need a clear understanding of the nature and characteristics of knowledge. Knowledge is a multifaceted construct and is difficult to come to grips with (cf. Ahmed et al., 2002).

There are many ways to categorize knowledge into different types. A traditional method is to make distinctions between data, information, and knowledge. Data is seen as unprocessed raw facts. It is the symbolic representation of numbers, letters, facts, or magnitudes, and is the means through which knowledge is stored and transferred. Information, in turn, is the grouping of these outputs and the placing of them in a context that makes a valuable output. In other words, information is an aggregation of meaningful data. Knowledge, in turn, is considered to be the sum of an individual's perception, skills, and experience. Knowledge involves the individual combining his or her experience, skills, intuition, ideas, judgements, context, motivations, and interpretation. It involves integrating elements of both thinking and feeling. Thus, knowledge, information, and data are, according to cognitivist epistemology, distinct entities. Moreover, data contained in computer systems is not a rich vessel of human interpretation, which is necessary for potential action. Knowledge is in the user's subjective context of action, which is based on data that he or she has interpreted.

Another way to categorize knowledge is to ascertain whether it is tacit or explicit (Polanyi, 1966; Ancori et al., 2000; Cowan et al., 2000; Baumard, 2001). Tacit knowledge represents knowledge – and meanings – based on the experience of individuals. It is expressed in human actions in the form of evaluations, attitudes, points of view, commitments, motivation, and so on (e.g. Myers and Davids, 1992; Nass, 1994; Nonaka, 1994; Blackler, 1995; Nonaka and Takeuchi, 1995; Lam, 2000). It is usually difficult to express tacit knowledge directly in words, and often the only ways of presenting it are through metaphors (e.g. Tsoukas, 1991), drawings, and methods of expression that do not require the formal use of language.

On a practical level, many experts are often unable to express clearly all the things they know and are able to do, and how they make their decisions and come to conclusions (Lyles and Schwenk, 1992; Starbuck, 1992; Koskinen et al., 2003). Tacit knowledge is context dependent and situation sensitive (Varela et al., 1991). '[K]nowledge depends very much on the point of observation. Where you stand or what you know determines what you see or what you choose to be relevant' (von Krogh et al., 1996a, p. 164). This means that tacit knowledge is not abstract but is embodied in the individual's world view. Rosenberg's (1982, p. 43) description of traditional technological knowledge, accumulated in crude empirical ways with no reliance upon science, provides a good definition of tacit knowledge in technology companies as 'the knowledge of techniques, methods and designs that work in certain ways and with certain consequences, even when one cannot explain exactly why'.

According to Haldin-Herrgard (2000), the main problem in sharing tacit knowledge is related to perception and language. It is not so much that people have difficulty expressing and articulating what they know, but that they may not be conscious of what it is that they know, or the interconnection between their tacit and explicit knowledge. Another problem deals with the time it takes for the internalization of tacit knowledge. In many work practices, time is a scarce resource that is rarely set aside for the sharing of tacit knowledge.

According to Leonard-Barton and Sensiper (1998), there are three main ways in which tacit knowledge can be potentially exercised to the benefit of the organization:

- *Problem solving:* The most common application of tacit knowledge is for problem solving. The reason experts on a given subject can solve a problem more readily than novices is that the experts have in mind a pattern born of experience, which they can overlay on a particular problem and use to quickly detect a solution. The expert recognizes not only the situation in which he or she finds himself or herself, but also what action might be appropriate for dealing with that situation. Writers on the topic note that 'intuition may be most usefully viewed as a form of unconscious pattern-matching cognition'.
- *Problem finding:* A second application of tacit knowledge is to the framing of problems. Some researchers distinguish between problem finding and problem solving. Problem solving is linked to a relatively clearly formulated problem within an accepted paradigm. Problem finding, on the other hand, tends to confront the person with a general sense of intellectual unease leading to a search for better ways of defining or framing the problem. Creative problem framing allows the rejection of the obvious or usual answers to a problem in favour

of asking a wholly different question. Intuitive discovery is often not simply an answer to the specific problem but is an insight into the real nature of the dilemma.

- *Prediction and anticipation:* The deep study of a subject seems to provide an understanding, only partially conscious, of how something works, allowing an individual to anticipate and predict occurrences that are subsequently explored very consciously. Histories of important scientific discoveries highlight that these kinds of anticipations, and a reliance on inexplicable mental processes, can be very important in invention. Authors writing about the stages of creative thought often refer to the preparation and incubation that precede flashes of insight.

Explicit knowledge, unlike tacit knowledge, can be embodied in a code, or a language, and as a consequence can be communicated easily (Lyles, 1988; Blackler, 1995; Lam, 2000; Zollo and Winter, 2002). In other words, the meanings representing explicit knowledge in the world view are rather clear and conscious, and therefore an individual can easily retrieve them from his or her world view. However, they represent knowledge only in a narrow sense. That is, the code may be words, numbers, or symbols like grammatical statements, mathematical expressions, specifications, manuals, and so forth (Nonaka and Takeuchi, 1995). For example, explicit knowledge implies factual statements about such matters as material properties, technical information, and tool characteristics.

However, there is no dichotomy between tacit and explicit knowledge: tacit and explicit knowledge are mutually constituted (Tsoukas, 1996). In other words, they should not be viewed as two separate types of knowledge, but these kinds of meanings are intermingled in the world view. This means that for any explicit knowledge, there is some tacit knowledge. That is, explicit knowledge is an extension of tacit knowledge to a new level (Mooradian, 2005). Hence, if there is value in identifying tacit knowledge, it is in relation to making explicit knowledge understandable. Tacit knowledge is an enabling condition of explicit knowledge and of the sharing of knowledge. This means that tacit knowledge is knowledge that is active in the world view (mind) but not consciously accessed in the moment of knowing. Therefore it grounds, enables, causes, or somehow brings about the explicit knowing connected with individuals. In addition to explicit and tacit knowledge, other kinds of meanings – such as feelings and beliefs – are also present in the world view and mingled with the above mentioned in a very complicated way.

As noted earlier, there are many ways to categorize and characterize knowledge. Day and Wendler (1998) characterize all types of knowledge as follows:

- *Knowledge is 'sticky':* some knowledge can be codified, but because tacit knowledge is embedded in people's minds or worldviews, it is often 'sticky' as it tends to stay in people's 'heads' (cf. von Hippel, 1994). Even with modern tools, which can quickly and easily transfer data from one place to another, it is often very difficult and time consuming to transfer knowledge from person to person, since those who have knowledge may not be conscious of what they know or how significant it is. As knowledge is 'sticky', it often cannot be owned and controlled in the way that plants and equipment can.

- *Extraordinary leverage and increasing returns:* network effects can emerge as more and more people use knowledge. These users can simultaneously benefit from knowledge and increase its value by adding, adapting, and enriching the knowledge base. Knowledge assets can grow in value as they become a standard upon which others can build. This is unlike traditional company assets that decline in value as more people use them.

- *Fragmentation, leakage and the need for refreshment:* as knowledge grows, it tends to branch and fragment. Today's specialist skill becomes tomorrow's common standard, as fields of knowledge grow deeper and more complex. While knowledge assets become more and more valuable, others, like expiring patents or former trade secrets, can become less valuable as they are widely shared.

- *Knowledge is constantly changing:* new knowledge is created every day. Knowledge decays and gets old and obsolete. Thus, it is hard to find and pinpoint knowledge.

- *Uncertain value:* the value of an investment in knowledge is often difficult to estimate. Results may not come up to expectations. Conversely they may lead to extraordinary knowledge development. Even when knowledge investments create considerable value, it is hard to predict who will capture the lion's share of it.

- *Most new knowledge is context specific:* knowledge is usually created in practice for a particular use, and as such is context specific. Therefore the question is, what aspect of it can be transferred? This would suggest that concepts such as 'best practice' are of limited use.

- *Knowledge is subjective:* due to its subjective nature, not all employees might agree what specific knowledge is usable, or on best practice.

According to Hall and Andriani (1999, 2002) knowledge, which is new to a project, has to be either invented internally in the project or acquired from external sources. This new knowledge may add to or be a substitute for the project's existing knowledge base. Thereby Hall and Andriani categorize this new knowledge as either additive or substitutive knowledge (e.g. Nooteboom, 1996).

Consequently, it would appear that no one is really in charge. At its core, knowledge is a social process. Only people together make knowledge happen. No one individual makes knowledge happen. What this means is that no one person can take responsibility for collective knowledge. Knowledge managers cannot really manage knowledge itself. However, they can and do help devise and support processes for acquiring, creating, sharing, and applying knowledge. A knowledge manager can also attend to strategies for removing barriers and creating a knowledge-sharing culture (Allee, 1997).

Individual knowledge

Human beings rely on their experiences and creativity in defining the problem and the possible solutions to the problem. A theory of knowledge rooted in autopoiesis theory suggests that knowledge is not abstract but embodied: everything known is known by somebody (Maturana and Varela, 1987). As human beings confront new situations, experiences are gained through thinking, sensing, and moving (von Krogh and Roos, 1995a). Knowledge is formed through actions, perception, and sensory processes (Merleau-Ponty, 1963; Schutz, 1970; Varela et al., 1991). Autopoiesis theory also recognizes that human beings use past experiences to orient themselves in new situations. Thus, previous experience will affect new experiences gained.

A person's knowledge is embodied, self-referential, and allows for distinction-making in observations, and is brought forth in an organizational setting (von Krogh and Roos, 1995a). This view of embodied knowledge leads to a startling view of the relationship between the world and a person's knowledge. A key claim is that situations, or the world, and knowledge are structurally coupled, and hence co-evolve. Knowledge enables people to perceive, act, and move in a world, and as they act, perceive, and move, the world comes forth as a result of their actions and observations. In the words of Maturana and Varela (1987): knowledge is what brings forth a world. In the words of Schutz (1970), the world refers to subjective experience and comprehension. It is somebody's world, namely the concretely experiencing individual.

The view of embodied knowledge also maintains the concern with autonomy that is so critical for autopoiesis theory. Knowledge develops in an autonomous manner for the human being, and thus cannot be transferred directly to other humans. In other words, a human being's history is unique, and is structurally coupled with the world. As humans, we each have our own history of movement and observation, our own pattern of structurally coupled interaction with the world. As a result, evolving knowledge, because it is formed in structural coupling, is also unique (von Krogh and Roos, 1995a). That is to say, an individual's knowledge is a result of directly experiencing tasks through a history of structural coupling.

The concept of self-reference has strong implications for the way human knowledge is viewed. Knowledge is intimately connected to creativity, action, observation, hearing, smelling, and so on. The broad repertoire of human activity contributes to knowledge. Cognitive processes refer to themselves. All knowledge will always be self-knowledge: when an individual knows (brings forth a world) this will reveal something about himself or herself (Morgan, 1996). Even when individuals are acting spontaneously (Schutz, 1970), in hindsight their actions reveal something about themselves to themselves.

Thus, in the case of an individual 'knowledge is the individual ability to draw distinctions within a collective domain of action, based on an appreciation of context or theory, or both' (Tsoukas and Vladimirou, 2001, p. 979). This means that an individual's capacity to exercise judgement is based on an appreciation of context in the ethno-methodological sense, that a social being is knowledgeable in accomplishing a routine and taken-for-granted task within a particular context as a result of having been through processes of socialization.

Organizational knowledge

Scholars of organizational behaviour and strategic management have attempted to bridge individual cognition with social cognition of the organization (e.g. Ginsberg, 1990; Lyles and Schwenk, 1992; Spender, 1996b). Many of these scholars have concluded that individuals have private knowledge that can be a basis for organizational knowledge when conveyed through speaking, gesturing, writing, and so on (von Krogh et al., 1996a). This means that knowledge of the organization is shared knowledge among organizational members. Organizational knowledge allows for shared distinction-making in observations made by organizational members of events, situations, and objects that are internal and external to the organization. These distinctions are created and maintained in conversations between organizational members and hence allow for new knowledge to develop in a self-referential manner.

A prerequisite for organizational knowledge to develop is the cardinal distinction between the organization and its environment, for example, 'What do we know about our environment?' Social norms are necessary to coordinate the opinions of organizational members with regard to what they observe. They also highlight conflict regarding observations, and provide guidelines when organizational members need to negotiate the content of observations (e.g. Daft and Weick, 1984).

As outlined above, knowledge is a process brought forth by individuals, groups, departments, organizations, and so on. According to von Krogh and Roos (1995a), knowledge development takes place at various organizational scales depending on people's observational schemes, that is, autopoiesis at various scales. A theory of scaling helps people understand the relations between individual and organizational knowledge development, and the dynamics of individual and social systems. Scaling concerns the design of nature, its multi-level, even hierarchical structure (Bonner, 1969).

Scaling is a fundamental aspect of nature and, therefore, possibility of autopoiesis on different organizational levels. A growing tree and the weather are dynamic and nonlinear phenomena and processes, whose states change over time and space, that is, across scale. Because size has vast consequences for human beings and the behaviour of things, spatial scaling is perhaps the most discussed type of scaling. For example, the enlargement of a photograph is a scaled version of the original in proportion to it. Its corresponding angles are the same and the corresponding line segments, oblique or not, have the same scaling-factor. Indeed, scaling is a profound property of nature, and everything in nature and all dimensions can be scaled (cf. von Krogh and Roos, 1995a).

For any given system, change from one state of equilibrium to another yields a set of predictable and unpredictable outcomes, and the boundary between these states is not binary, it is 'fractal'. This term describes systems with fractional dimensionality (Mandelbrot, 1967). Formally, a fractal has infinite detail, infinite length, and no slope or derivative. A property of fractals is 'self-similarity', which means invariance with respect to scaling. That is, self-similarity is about patterns, not at one scale or another, but across scales it is a way to collapse complexity (Horgan, 1994). Lorenz (1993, pp. 170–1) explains self-similarity of fractals: 'in many fractal systems, several suitably chosen pieces, when suitably magnified, will each become identical to the whole system. This implies, of course, that several sub-pieces of each piece, when magnified, become equivalent to that piece, and hence to the whole system. Other fractals are only statistically self-similar; small pieces, when magnified, will not superpose on the entire system, but they will have the same general type of appearance'.

What is essential for the fractal structure is that it does not become simpler when one goes from a higher to a lower level. The whole of the organizational structure consists of 'wholes' of sub-organizational structures. The complexity of an individual employee is at least as large as the complexity of the whole organization. The fractal structure is vital for the realization of the reproductive mechanism embedded in the process of autopoiesis.

Organizational ecology is an example of a self-similar theory within the realm of management studies. Organizational ecology is a macro-sociological theory of organizations that builds on general ecological and evolutionary theories of change in populations (Hannan and Freeman, 1989, p. 7): 'an ecology of organizations seeks to understand how social conditions affect the rates at which new organizations and new organizational forms arise, the rates at which organizations change forms, and the rates at which organizations and forms die out'. Concepts frequently used in the organizational ecology discourse include demography, populations, boundaries of forms, niche, selection, and mortality. All these concepts have been imported from biological theories, that is, from theories pertaining to life cycles on a different scale, that of biological life (von Krogh and Roos, 1995a). Indeed, the autopoietic knowledge development process is not only scaled in general, but similar across scale.

So, organizational knowledge depends largely on the experiences of individual people, and it is formed through actions and perceptions (von Krogh and Roos, 1995a). Exposure and sensitivity to the environment, boundary elements, and work processes influence the availability of new experiences for individuals (Maula, 2006). Knowledge flows commonly extend beyond temporal, hierarchical, functional, and organizational boundaries. Several studies emphasize language and conversations between organizational members (von Krogh and Roos, 1995a; Vicari et al., 1996). Interpretation has an increasing role in organizations (Mingers and Stowell, 1997), and language can be used to manage knowledge (von Krogh et al., 1996a). As to information systems, self-referentiality, communication, and action have an increasingly important role (Hirschheim et al., 1995).

The behaviour of organizations has long been captured in the form and formats of organizational routines. For example, according to Cyert March (1963) and Lant and Mezias (1990), organizations function as their routines prescribe. These routines have been based on successful behaviour of organizational members or what is imagined to be necessary behaviour for successful task performance. Alternatively, organizations function not in accordance with their written routines, but rather by their unwritten or tacit routines (Argyris and Schön, 1978). Over time, organizational members repeat their behaviour and knowledge as they become socialized into the values and norms of the organization, giving rise to more informal routines (Nelson and Winter, 1982; Hatchuel and Weil, 1995). A necessary implication of this view of human cognition and task performance is that the organization at various moments may appear as highly fragmented where each individual holds his or her own view of what the organization is (e.g. Østerberg, 1988; Frost et al., 1990). Thus, for management of organizations, a critical task becomes the coordination and integration of these highly fragmented views (Deal and Kennedy, 1982; Peters and Waterman, 1982; Schein, 1985). By coordination one achieves the necessary stability for routinized behaviour.

Organizational knowledge has, therefore, been evident in Penrose's (1959) work on the theory of the firm. According to her, firms have discretion over how they use their resources and, therefore, over the services derived from them. According to this view, organizational knowledge is the set collective understanding embedded in an organization – in a project team and/or project-based company – which enables it to put its resources to particular uses.

Project knowledge

According to Reich (2007), there are four knowledge categories vital to the success of projects:

- Process knowledge
- Domain knowledge
- Institutional knowledge
- Cultural knowledge.

Instead, Reich and Wee (2006) suggest only two types of knowledge which are important in the context of project work – process and domain knowledge.

Process knowledge is knowledge that the project team members and sponsors have about the project structure, methodology, tasks, and time frames (Chan and Rosemann, 2001; Meehan and Richardson, 2002; Bresnen et al., 2004). This knowledge allows a project team member to understand his or her part in the overall project and to understand what kind of project delivery is expected to be achieved and when it is to be delivered. This kind of knowledge also allows a project team or sub-team to self-organize, since the team knows the outputs required, and the time frames, and can, if authorized, decide how the work can best be accomplished.

Domain knowledge is knowledge of the industry, firm, current situation, problem, opportunity, and potential solutions (including technology and process). Chan and Rosemann (2001) specify three sub-categories of knowledge that make up domain knowledge: business, technical, and production knowledge. This knowledge is widened within and outside the project team. The project sponsor may be the most well-informed about the industry and the problem or opportunity being tackled. Technical experts inside and outside the company have knowledge about the technologies that could be utilized in project. Project team members will have profound knowledge about the company and its business processes.

Institutional knowledge is a blend of an organization's history, power structures, and values. This knowledge is transferred by means of stories or anecdotes told by insiders and observers of an organization. It is not as much about facts as it is about how the facts can be interpreted in order to understand 'what is really going on'. This knowledge is particularly important for an external project manager or a vendor in order to get difficult problems dealt with and key decisions made in the course of a project.

Cultural knowledge means, for example, that a project manager is required to understand how to manage people who are thought to have fairly unique cultural norms. However, in a broader context, with project teams being comprised of many disciplinary groups (e.g. organizational expansion experts, IT engineers) and people from many cultural backgrounds, the idea that cultural knowledge, both discipline-based and national, might be important, is a very useful idea.

To summarize, there are many types of knowledge needed within a sole project. The more complex and innovative the organization, problem or opportunity, or the technology within the project, the more significant it will be to organize, share, and make use of these different types of knowledge.

Resource, capability, and competence

The terms 'resource', 'capability', and 'competence' have been the subject of much semantic debate. For example, according to Amit and Schoemaker (1993, p. 35), resources are 'stocks of available factors that are owned or controlled by the firm ... converted into final products or services by using a wide range of other firm assets and bonding mechanisms', and capability is 'a firm's capacity to deploy resources, usually in combination, using organizational processes ... that are firm-specific and are developed over time'. However, Warren (2007, p. 48) is not satisfied with this definition and redefines it more accurately as 'the rate at which the firm is able to build a strategic resource, for any given availability of the other resources needed for that task'.

In the opinion of Long and Vickers-Koch (1995), the people who create strategy plans use the terms competence and capability more or less interchangeably. Therefore, they have defined the relationship between these two concepts (Figure 6.1): competencies relate to the skills, knowledge, and technological know-how that give a special advantage at specific points in the value chain, which, in combination with the strategic processes that link the chain together, form core capabilities.

Strategists in the competence perspective have proposed a model of organizations as goal-seeking open systems composed of various tangible and intangible resources (Sanchez et al., 1996; Heene and Sanchez, 1997; Sanchez and Heene, 1997). This model explicitly recognizes

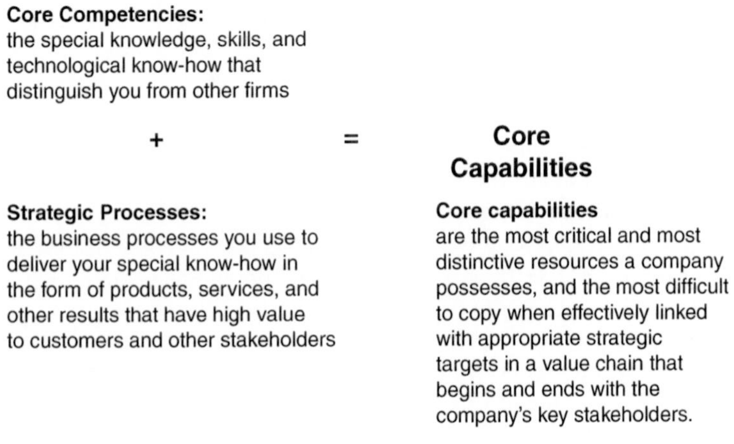

Core Competencies:
the special knowledge, skills, and technological know-how that distinguish you from other firms

+　　　　　**=**　　　　　**Core Capabilities**

Strategic Processes:
the business processes you use to deliver your special know-how in the form of products, services, and other results that have high value to customers and other stakeholders

Core capabilities
are the most critical and most distinctive resources a company possesses, and the most difficult to copy when effectively linked with appropriate strategic targets in a value chain that begins and ends with the company's key stakeholders.

Figure 6.1 Core capabilities.

that an organization's ability to strategically re-configure its resources depends on:

- The *cognitive processes* through which managers try to determine what kinds of resource stocks and flows an organization should try to develop and what uses an organization's available resources may best be applied to
- Managers' ability to *coordinate* both intra-organizational and inter-organizational flows of resources and capabilities in processes of organizational change
- Managers' ability to maintain processes of *organizational learning* that continuously renew an organization's base of knowledge as a critical strategic resource.

(Sanchez, 2001)

Furthermore, Spencer and Spencer (1993, p. 9) have defined competence as 'an underlying characteristic of an individual that is causally related to criterion-referenced effective and/or superior performance in a job or situation'. Hofer and Schendell (1978, p. 25) describe competence under the heading of resource deployment. Specifically, they define competence as 'patterns of ... resource and skill deployments that will help the firm achieve its goals and objectives'.

Indeed, competence seems to be a term that is widely used but which has come to mean different things to different people. Nevertheless, it is generally accepted to encompass knowledge, skills, attitudes, and behaviours that are causally related to superior job performance (e.g. Boyatzis, 1982; Hamel and Prahalad, 1994; Boisot et al., 1996). So, strictly speaking, an individual's competence is simply the particular knowledge and skills that an individual possesses, and the superior way he or she uses them. As Figure 6.2 suggests, an individual's personal competence can be divided into *knowledge-based competencies* and *socially-based competencies*.

Knowledge-based competencies are seen to consist of an individual's tacit and explicit knowledge (e.g. Nonaka and Takeuchi, 1995). As described above, tacit knowledge is knowledge which an individual has collected and stored in his or her world view while he or she has performed different tasks and duties in different contexts and situations of his or her life. This means that tacit knowledge is acquired by an individual as a result of active work (e.g. Polanyi, 1966). However, tacit knowledge can also refer to distorted knowledge that is culturally assimilated, and thus passively given to an individual (e.g. Popper, 1977). Unlike tacit knowledge, explicit knowledge can be embodied in a code, or a language, and,

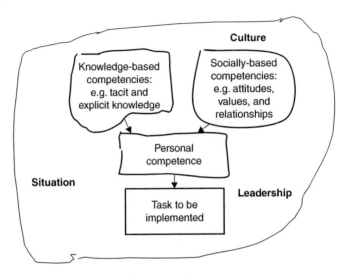

Figure 6.2   Individual's personal competence.

therefore, it is in the form of clear meanings in the world view. Thus, it can be communicated easily.

Social based competencies are seen as abilities to integrate thinking, feeling, and behaviour to achieve social tasks and outcomes valued in the context and culture of a company. Recent evidence suggests that socially adept personnel contribute strongly to a companies' success (e.g. Baron and Markman, 2000). Specifically, organizations made up of people who are especially good at perceiving others' emotions accurately and at expressing their own emotions clearly earned significantly higher income from their businesses than organizations with staff who possessed fewer of these skills.

For example, an individual's personal competence in a technology company context as a whole includes the mastery of a body of job-related knowledge and skills (which can be technical, professional, or managerial), and also the motivation to expand, use, and distribute work-related knowledge to others (cf. Spencer and Spencer, 1993, p. 73). Acquisition and sharing of competencies depend on motivation as much as on the technical knowledge involved. According to Spencer and Spencer (1993), these two aspects of an individual's competence are crucial in transforming knowledge and skills into effective work results.

However, it is crucially important to understand that the usefulness of an individual's competence always depends on the context and his or her personal situation (in Figure 6.2, situation, leadership style, culture) in which that competence is utilized (e.g. Koskinen, 2003; Koskinen et al., 2003). Furthermore, it must also be noted that 'knowledge is about specific insights regarding a particular topic, competence is about the skill to carry out work' (von Krogh and Roos, 1996a, p. 424). From this it follows that the competencies of an individual are not fixed properties. Rather, they are created continuously in his or her situated practices. When an individual's performance is seen as his or her dynamic engagement with a task, personal competence is understood as emerging from situated practice. The focus then is on understanding the conditions (e.g. human and infrastructural) under which the performance of an individual is more or less likely to be enacted.

It is also important to understand that the performance of individuals varies over time. This means that people's competencies evolve in the course of their lives as they cumulate new meanings into their world views, which are shaping their performances, too. Figure 6.3 illustrates, in principle, how the competence of an engineer has changed in the course of his or her working life. The explicit technological knowledge that an engineer gains in his or her formal education has transformed into diverse tacit knowledge, like work related know-how, relationships between people, business skills, and so on.

The competencies of senior-level people are often socially based and they include a lot of tacit knowledge. This is because seniors have had many opportunities to work in different contexts and situations, and therefore they have also been able to collect experiences that have become their tacit knowledge. This means, as discussed earlier, that the explicit knowledge an engineer gains as a junior in a university transforms in the course of his or her lifetime into diverse tacit skills. This type of reasoning is also supported by the significant evidence of Wagner and Sternberg (1985), and Sternberg et al. (1995), according to which old timers and more experienced people tend to utilize more tacit knowledge than juniors and less experienced people. Thus, a senior-level person's competencies often equal practical know-how.

An important sub-concept within the main concept of competence is core competence (Hamel and Prahalad, 1989; Prahalad and Hamel, 1990; Lampel, 2001; Orlikowski, 2002). The premise is that a company's strategy is based on learning, and that learning depends on competencies. Core competencies arise from collective learning in organizations, especially from the co-ordination of skills and the integration of technologies.

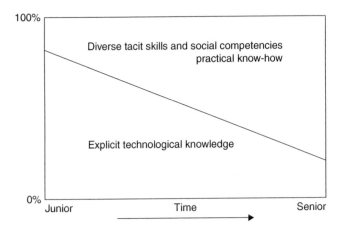

Figure 6.3 Competence transformation of an engineer in the course of working life.

By their nature, core competencies do not diminish in value but need to be nurtured as knowledge and skills are lost over time.

Core competencies that are complex can generate ambiguity (Reed and DeFilippi, 1990). Complexity and, thus, ambiguity arise from large numbers of technologies, organization routines, and individual- or team-based experience. Complexity within and between a company's competencies guarantees that few individuals, if any, have sufficient breadth and depth of knowledge to grasp the overall performance package (Nelson and Winter, 1982).

According to Mollona (2008), at a higher level of abstraction, companies are characterized as architecture(s) of organizational competencies (Rumelt, 1995) or hierarchies of organizational capabilities (Nelson and Winter, 1982). In this hierarchical mode of analysis, a company's competence can be seen as the 'ability to sustain the coordinated deployment of assets and capabilities in ways that promise to help a firm to achieve some desired results (goal) through specific actions' (Sanchez et al., 1996, p. 8). The existence of a capability in marketing, for example, relies on a prior higher-order capability in hiring, training, and coordinating marketing people. Following from this, a company's competence is realized through its ability to integrate and connect resources and capabilities.

In sum, although the terms 'resource', 'capability', and 'competence' have been the subject of much semantic debate, they form the basis of a company's competitive advantage – the project-based company in our case.

Emotional intelligence and emotional competence

Emotional intelligence refers to the emotional side of life, such as the ability to recognize and manage an individual's own and others' emotions, to motivate oneself and restrain impulses, and to handle interpersonal relationships effectively (Goleman, 1995).

Emotional competence, in turn, refers to a learned capability based on emotional intelligence that results in outstanding performance at work. Individuals' emotional intelligence determines their potential for learning practical skills based on the following five elements:

- Self-awareness
- Motivation
- Self-regulation
- Empathy
- Adeptness in relationships.

Individuals' emotional competencies show how much of that potential they have translated into on-the-job competencies (Goleman, 1995). This means that emotional competence refers to an individual's competence in expressing or releasing his or her emotions. It implies an ease around emotions which results in emotionally competent people being relaxed about other people being emotional. The concept of emotional competence is rooted in the understanding of emotions as being normal contents of a world view, and as useful aspects of being human. Anger is a reaction to aggression and gives an individual the strength to repel aggression. Grief is a reaction to the abandonment of feeling loved, and it has the effect of eliciting sympathetic responses from others. Fear is a response to danger and has a clear physiological effect: it heightens individuals' senses and speeds up reactions. From this it follows that the suppression of emotion is not useful and that teaching people to suppress their emotions is part of trying to control them. Emotionally competent people will express emotions appropriate to the situation and their needs, and they will not seek to suppress emotions in others.

According to Druskat and Wolff (2001), interpersonal understanding and perspective-taking are two ways that groups can become more aware of their members' perspectives and feelings. But just as important as awareness is the ability to regulate those emotions – to have a positive impact on how they are expressed and even on how individual team members feel. Further, it is fairly widely believed that if appropriate emotions are not expressed, some sort of memory of them becomes stored in a person's world view. Later events may trigger off the old emotions resulting in inappropriate emotional responses. Releasing old emotions is a key feature of co-counselling.

Humanistic approaches to assertiveness (Dickson, 1982, 2000) emphasize the importance of working with emotions. In particular, they recognize the need to address manipulative or passive (an individual does not say what he or she wants) aggressive (an individual tries to force another person to do what he or she wants) behaviour in which the manipulator exploits the feelings of the other in trying to get what he or she wants. Building up emotional competence is a way of learning to handle such behaviour.

Thus, emotional competence can lead to improved health through avoiding stress that would otherwise result from suppressing emotions. Emotional competence can, therefore, also lead to improved relationships, since inappropriate emotions are less likely to be expressed and appropriate behaviour is not avoided through fear of triggering some emotion.

Organizational memory

Organizational memory relates the dialectics of planning, communicating, decision-making, and knowledge management in organizations. For example, Argyris and Schön (1978, p. 11) claim 'for organizational learning to occur, learning agents' discoveries, inventions, and evaluations must be imbedded in organizational memory'. Weick (1979) argues that organizations must accept and live with their memories because memory is an important co-producer of the personality of a company. Furthermore, Schatz (1991) generalizes these observations by suggesting that organizational memory provides knowledge that enables an organization to function effectively. This means that in order to carry out their work, project team members frequently need to learn things already known in other projects (i.e. they need to acquire and assimilate organizational memory). And this means, in turn, that project team members draw on both the company's memory and contribute to it. The more effectively they carry out these actions, the more effective they are, and the more effective their projects and companies will be (e.g. Cohen and Bacdyan, 1994; Lundin and Midler, 1998; Huber, 1999; Love et al., 2005).

According to Weick and Roberts (1993), collective mind is conceptualized as 'a pattern of heedful interrelations of actions in a social system'. Organizational memory is then seen as the ability to both store and retrieve knowledge in organizations, analogous to the brain. So, the self-similar theories discussed within the realm of organization studies have been applied across machinery, computers, organizations, people, and brains.

Literature (e.g. Walsh and Ungson, 1991; Cross and Baird, 2000; Paoli and Prencipe, 2003) mentions numerous different types of repositories (e.g. minds or world views of people and company databases) which form an organizational memory, and where organizational knowledge is maintained and into which newly acquired knowledge is deposited for later use by other people and teams of companies. The minds of project team members, particularly those in an organic project work environment (Koskinen, 2004, 2009b), may play an important role in solving different problems. One form of organizational memory is the different routines and machinery individuals find when they move to new projects.

The knowledge connected with implementing projects and running a business is partly explicit, and transferring it with the help of documents and computers is fairly easy. On the other hand, the transfer of tacit knowledge requires personal contacts and interaction. According to Davenport and Prusak (1998), it is generally felt that the more tacit knowledge there is in a company the more technology should be used in distributing that knowledge. However, only explicit knowledge can be stored in databases. In large companies the efficient transfer of explicit knowledge is not possible without information technology. In any case, it is the values, norms, and behaviours of individuals that finally determine the efficient transfer of knowledge needed to solve problems.

Nevertheless, in many organizations, distributed technology is at the heart of organizational memory (e.g. Burt, 1987; Szulanski, 1996). Most initiatives have concentrated on identifying relevant data in various places of an organization in order to build a technical infrastructure to support the capture and dissemination of knowledge. Knowledge repositories often contain reports, memos, and other work documents (Keegan and Turner, 2001; Newell et al., 2006). Ideally, these technologies allow an organization to apply its collective intellect to any problem, regardless of time or geographic location. However, according to Cross and Baird (2000), databases only complement the personal networks of those seeking answers to problems. No matter how robust the search is functionally, a person's network of human relationships often determines what knowledge he or she can access. People usually take advantage of databases only when colleagues direct them to a specific point in the database. Rather than engage in an extensive search through an organization's repository of knowledge, employees turn to friends and peers to learn where to find relevant knowledge.

In practice, it is rare for a single person to know enough to solve the complex problems in projects. In many projects, knowing how to find and apply relevant knowledge efficiently is more practical than trying to master a large amount of knowledge. However, it is often assumed in projects that people turn to databases and procedure manuals to obtain data. In practice people often rely upon a network of relationships for knowledge and advice (cf. Rogers, 1995). Rather than turning to databases they seek knowledge from trusted and capable colleagues. In the opinion of Handy (1994), people are about five times more likely to turn to friends or colleagues for answers than to other sources of knowledge. In short, *whom* you know significantly affects *what* you eventually know (Cross and Baird, 2000).

It should be understood that organizational memory is often more than the sum of individual knowledge. Part of what an individual knows is shared by other members of a project team and company. Like holograms, individuals maintain the values, norms, and images of the organization (Stein, 1995). Mead (1962) likens these networks of minds to a 'social mind', and Smith (1982) refers to culture as a means to retain organizational memories through icons, symbols, and stories, which are manifestations of a collective mind. However, it should also be understood that social systems are notoriously resistant to adopting new ideas and practices. Organizational memory is thus essential to organizational learning, while learning is a necessary condition for organizational memory.

In fact, the concept of archiving and using learning histories is already an old one in project-based companies. For example, in many companies it is considered good practice to create documents of what has been learned in a project. However, according to Conklin (2001), even in those companies in which this practice is a normal routine, it is very difficult to find instances of the resulting document actually being referenced in the next project. In addition to this, some project teams have attempted to capture their learning by videotaping their meetings. However, these teams often end up with a staggering amount of information on tape. The important pieces of data they may require later on are in there somewhere, but no one has time to watch it all to find them.

These two examples of capturing organizational memory seem to give an impression that project-based companies cannot create a useful memory store just by capturing lots of data, but must somehow organize it in ways that create a coherent whole. These examples also give the idea that the creation and use of organizational memory cannot be a by-product, an extra bit of work hanging on the side, of the organization's main production process (Conklin, 2001). Further, the people working for project-based companies do not necessarily have time to reflect, being bombarded by urgent problems and pressing deadlines (Jashapara, 2004). Therefore, project-based companies should find ways of preserving the asset of knowledge they have to look within the practices of everyday teamwork.

In any case, in project-based companies the knowledge management systems need to be designed to collect, share, and utilize knowledge produced in projects. For project-created knowledge, Conroy and Soltan (1998) have defined three knowledge bases to include knowledge that is created and used in project implementation:

- The organization knowledge base, which includes knowledge specific to organizations and environments in which projects are implemented
- The project management knowledge base, which includes knowledge of the theory and application of project management
- The project-specific knowledge base, which includes project-specific knowledge acquired within project implementation.

The knowledge produced within the implementation of a project is especially project-specific knowledge. However, according to Conroy and Soltan (1998), the bases of organization and project management knowledge are also developed during project implementation. That is, new knowledge of all three knowledge bases is initially held only by project team members. Therefore, it is necessary to identify, capture, and make this knowledge available to the organizational memory of the company.

Conroy and Soltan (1998) divide project-created knowledge into three general categories:

- *Technical:* relating to techniques, technologies, work-processes, costs, etc., involved in the production of discipline-specific issues of the project; new knowledge needs to be fed back to the company's organizational memory.

- *Project management:* relating to the methods and procedures for managing the implementation of projects; this knowledge should be available to all project managers working in the company.
- *Project related:* knowledge of customer and other things that are of value for the future business of the company.

In sum, organizational memory is the body of data, information, and knowledge relevant to an individual organization's existence. Falling under the wider disciplinary umbrella of knowledge management, it has two repositories – an organization's archives, including its electronic databases, and individuals' memories.

Intellectual capital

The market value of a company (e.g. a project-based company) consists of its financial capital and 'everything else' (Wiig, 1997). Financial capital represents the company's book value and consists of the value of its financial and physical assets. 'Everything else', defined as the *intellectual capital*, consists of assets created through intellectual activities ranging from acquiring new knowledge (learning) and inventions to creating valuable relationships.

Intellectual capital management focuses on renewing and maximizing the value of the company's intellectual assets. Skandia's well-known definition of intellectual capital consists of several entities as follows (Edvinsson and Malone, 1997):

- *Human Capital* – consists of the competence and capabilities of the employees. When a company educates its employees, it increases its human capital. A company cannot own, only rent, its human capital.
- *Structural Capital* – consists of the results of intellectual activities in data and knowledge bases, documents, etc. In accordance with that, 'structural capital is what is left after the employees have gone for the night'.
- *Customer Capital* – consists of the value of the company's relationships with its customers.
- *Organizational Capital* – consists of embedded knowledge assets in the process and innovation areas.
- *Process Capital* – consists of the company's value-creating processes such as its organizational structure, management practices, systems and procedures, infrastructure, computer systems, and the like.

- *Innovation Capital* – consists of both explicit knowledge and hard-to-identify intellectual assets such as a positive culture.
- *Intellectual Property* – consists of documented and captured knowledge such as innovations, operational practices, patents, technology, educational programs, company knowledge bases, and designs and specifications of products and services.
- *Intangible Assets* – consists of the value of positive culture, community image, etc.

All companies that pursue intellectual capital management should understand that intellectual capital defines the future capabilities of the company. They should also indicate that its value – both real and potential – is typically greater than that of the financial capital (Teece, 1998). However, the emphasis and attention given to it by management is usually far less. The value placed on intellectual capital is often obtained by market valuations based on perceived and qualitative impressions by investors and financial analysis instead of that established by diligent study.

In sum, the intangibleness refers to the fact that intellectual capital is not easily translatable in financial terms. All other assets of a company, such as a piece of real estate or a credit note, can be monetized: that is, there exist standard criteria for expressing their value in currency. Intellectual capital, instead, is mainly made of elements (such as the quality of employees or the reputation of a brand among consumers) for which there is no consensual model for monetary expression.

Summary

Knowledge and competence in different forms, contexts, and situations are concepts that are extremely meaningful, promising, and hard to pin down. This chapter has explored these concepts and organizational memory. Some of the key claims and suggestions include the following:

The central insight of the knowledge in organizations is that knowledge inputs are necessarily embedded in a context – cognitive and behavioural, individual and social – which powerfully constrains their discovery, their transfer from one set of actors to another, and their usefulness in different situations.

All types of meanings are knowledge because an individual understands what the world is like on the basis of these types of meanings. For example, intuition, feeling, belief, and will are meanings through which an individual understands phenomena.

Knowledge is an individual's perception, skills, and experience, which are all dependent on what experiences the individual's world view contains in the form of meanings. This means that knowledge involves the individual combining his or her experience, skills, intuition, ideas, judgements, context, motivations, and interpretation.

Traditionally, knowledge has been categorized by distinguishing between data, information, and knowledge. However, here these terms are understood by stressing the human dimension, that is, that data is raw knowledge, information is interpretation process, and knowledge is located in the world view of an individual. Furthermore, we put the emphasis on the categorization according to which knowledge is divided into tacit and explicit knowledge. In many cases, within project work, tacit knowledge is seen as the most important knowledge that is typically transferred between team members through face-to-face interaction.

The knowledge of an individual is embodied, self-referential, and allows for distinction-making in observations, and is brought forth in an organizational setting.

Organizational knowledge allows for shared distinction-making in observations made by organizational members of events, situations, and objects that are internal and external to the organization. These distinctions are created and maintained in conversations between organizational members and hence allow for new knowledge to develop in a self-referential manner.

There are many types of knowledge needed within a sole project. The more complex and innovative the organization, the problem, or opportunity, or the technology within the project, the more significant it will be to organize, share, and make use of these different types of knowledge.

The value of knowledge relates to the effectiveness with which the managed knowledge enables project-based companies (and project teams within them) to deal with their current activities and effectively envision and create their future.

An individual team member's competence is not only his or her knowledge but it also includes social aspects, which arise from the situation of an individual. Furthermore, an individual team member's knowledge is about his or her insight of a task at hand, and competence is about his or her skill in carrying out the task-related work. An individual's competence evolves in the course of his or her life and is accumulated into the individual's world view in the form of different kinds of meanings. Therefore, the individual's world view is the 'place' in the consciousness in which the competence is stored.

Core competencies arise from collective learning in organizations, especially from the co-ordination of skills and the integration of technologies. Management and the development of core competencies give a company a sustainable competitive advantage.

One of the normative advices for project team members is that emotionally competent project team members express emotions appropriate to the situation and they do not seek to suppress emotions in others.

Organizational memory concerns the knowledge-base of the organization and the attendant processes that change and modify that base over time. In this formulation, organizational memory is the means by which knowledge from the past is brought to bear on present activities, thus resulting in higher or lower levels of organizational effectiveness.

All project-based companies that pursue intellectual capital management should understand that intellectual capital defines the future capabilities of the company.

7
Evolution and Learning

Evolutionary theories are a class of theories, models, or arguments that explain how companies evolve and why successful companies differ from each other. They explain the generation and renewal of variation by random elements and winnowing. Internal forces provide continuity to whatever survives the winnowing. Many of the economic evolutionary theories assume that individual learning, organizational adaptation, and the environmental selection of organizations are processes going on at the same time (Nelson and Winter, 1982; Nelson, 1994, 1995).

An important aspect of the classical theory of evolution is the idea that in the course of evolutionary change and under the pressure of natural selection, organisms will gradually adapt to their environment until they reach a state that is good enough for survival and reproduction. However, in the new systemic view, evolutionary change is seen as the result of life's inherent tendency to create novelty, which may or may not be accompanied by adaptation to changing environmental conditions.

Evolutionary theories can also be regarded as learning theories (Dodgson, 1993). Foss et al. (1995), attempt to explain technological evolution and competition through a set of variables that change over time, as well as the dynamic process behind the observed change. These theories are process-oriented and they are based on routines that preserve and stabilize organizational behaviour. They focus primarily on intangible resources, whereas resource-based theory focuses in principle on all resources.

Evolutionary theories are consistent with the Schumpeterian evolutionary view of economic process and change. They focus on the dynamic process of social construction, and on the transformation of alternative forms within and across generations of competing organizational routines, forms, and institutions (Nelson, 1994). Evolutionary theories are explanatory process theories, not predictive ones (van de Ven, 1992). Their level of analysis has conventionally been an industry and the main emphasis has been on company populations. However, Foss et al. (1995) do not agree with this view, and according to them, an evolutionary theory of the company has been largely lacking. Fortunately, the new evolutionary literature is sensitive to intra-organization, organization, population, and community evolution (Baum and Singh, 1994a, b; Aldrich, 1999).

Baum and Singh (1994a) write that since the 1960s the open system model, where the environment locates outside the system, has been the prominent view of organization theory. However, the environment can be treated as exogenous only if the system of variables is in equilibrium. In different conditions, it is more useful to take a co-evolutionary approach and view each variable as influencing the others.

To conclude, it is natural to think of the history of organizations in evolutionary terms, for each organization competes with the others for scarce resources, and their fates must consequently by decided by some combination of natural selection and rational adaptation (e.g. Simon, 1993).

Intuition

Scholars often assume that learning, whether it is at the individual, group, or organizational level, is a conscious, analytical process. However, Underwood (1982) suggests that the links between experience, knowledge, and consciousness are more complex than generally assumed. The subconscious is critical to understanding how people come to discern and comprehend something new, for which there was no prior explanation. A theory of learning needs to explain how this occurs.

At its most basic level, individual learning involves perceiving similarities and differences – patterns and possibilities. Although there are many definitions of *intuition*, most involve some sort of pattern recognition (Behling and Eckel, 1991). An expert functions intuitively, on the basis of mental models which are derived from experience. These models are often founded on both experience and a deep understanding of explicit knowledge. The elements of knowledge which form a store of knowledge for the expert are so internalized and have been thought about so often from so many perspectives that the expert is no longer able to separate them again into individual details. For example, experienced designers have rich intuitions about complex systems which they cannot explain. Their intuition tells them that cause and effect are not simply in a reason-consequence dependency relationship, that obvious solutions will produce more harm than good, and that short-term fixes produce long-term problems. They cannot, however, explain their ideas in simple, linear cause-effect language. They end up saying: 'Just do it this way. It will work'.

Expert intuition provides insight into the important process of pattern recognition, while entrepreneurial intuition has more to do with innovation and change. No two situations are the same, and patterns, while similar, are never identical. The ability to make novel connections and to discern possibilities are key to intuiting. Entrepreneurs are able to make these novel connections, perceive new or emergent relationships, and discern possibilities that have not been identified previously. Expert intuition may be best pattern oriented, while entrepreneurial intuition is future possibility oriented.

According to Reber (1989), tacit knowledge acquisition in its different forms represents the epistemic core of intuition. Intuition is, according to Reber, a perfectly normal and common mental state/process that is the end product of tacit knowledge acquisition. In other words, intuition is a cognitive state that emerges under specifiable situations, and it operates to assist an individual to make choices and to engage in particular classes of action. 'To have an intuitive sense of what is right and proper, to have a vague feeling of the goal of an extended process of thought, to "get the point" without really being able to verbalize what it is that one has gotten, is to have gone through an implicit learning experience and have built up the requisite representative knowledge base to allow for such judgement' (Reber, 1989, p. 233).

Consequently, intuitive problem solving is not based on linear cause-consequence thinking. The result of this is that a person's intuitive skills are dependent on context and situation, and they can only be roughly evaluated by looking at his or her experience base.

Interpreting and mental models

Whereas intuiting focuses on the subconscious process of developing insights, *interpreting* begins picking up on the conscious elements of the individual learning process. Through the process of interpreting, individuals develop *mental models* about the various domains in which they operate (Johnson-Laird, 1987; Huff, 1990; Klimoski and Mohammed, 1994). Language plays a pivotal role in the development of these mental models, since it enables individuals to name and begin to explain what were once simply feelings, hunches, or sensations. Further, once things are named, individuals can make more explicit connections between them.

Interpreting takes place in relation to a domain or an environment. The nature or texture of the domain within which individuals and organizations operate, and from which they extract data, is crucial to understanding the interpretive process. The precision of the language that evolves will reflect the texture of the domain, given the tasks being attempted (Crossan et al., 1999).

Kim (1994) observes that mental models include explicit and tacit knowledge. According to him, the mental models provide the context in which to view and interpret new material, and they determine how stored knowledge is relevant to a given situation. They represent more than a collection of ideas, memories, and experiences. Kim uses colourful metaphors, describing mental models as analogous to the source code of a computer's operating system, the manager and arbiter of acquiring, retaining, using, and deleting new information. But they are much more than that because they are also like the programmer of that source code with the know-how (tacit knowledge) to design a different code as well as know-why (explicit knowledge) to choose one over the other.

Argyris (1989) argues that although people do not always behave congruently with what they say, they do behave congruently with their mental models. In other words, mental models are subtle but powerful. Subtle, because people are usually unaware of their effect. Powerful, because they determine what people pay attention to, and therefore what they do. That is why mental models are strongly conservative: left unchallenged, they will cause people to see what they have always seen: the same needs, the same opportunities, the same results. And because individuals see what their mental models permit them to see, they do what their mental models permit them to do.

According to Senge (1990), new insights often fail to get put into practice because they conflict with deeply held internal images of how the world works. These images limit us to familiar ways of thinking and acting. Developing an organization's capacity to work with mental models involves both learning new skills and implementing institutional innovations that help to bring these skills into regular practice:

- The organization must bring key assumptions about important business issues to the surface. Those models, if unexamined, limit an organization's range of actions to what is familiar and comfortable

- The organization must develop face-to-face learning skills. This is of special concern when an enterprise wants to be skilful with mental models.

Moreover, Senge (1990, p. 175) asks: 'Why are mental models so powerful in affecting what we do?' He answers his own question by stating, 'In part, because they affect what we see'. Because they've looked at different details, two people with different mental models can observe the same event and describe it differently.

In the opinion of Cannon-Bowers et al. (1993) and Mathieu et al. (2000), all tacit knowledge within a project is within the mental models of its team members. The result of this is that in the use of tacit knowledge in a project, what is critically important is how well the mental models of the personnel are known within the project. These authors also conclude that the mental models of the personnel within a project can be both helpful and harmful in their various functions. From this it follows that the benefit/harm of the personnel's mental models is always dependent on the context and situation, that is, their impact to a project varies.

People bring many deep-rooted assumptions, strategies, ways of looking, and guiding ideas (i.e. mental models) to whatever they do. 'Mental' because they exist in people's minds and drive their actions, 'models' because people construct them from their experiences. Mental models are what have worked in the past and therefore what people expect to work in the future. In short, individuals' mental models guide all their actions.

In sum, everyone continuously develops his or her mental models. They are a natural part of human life and a natural consequence of experience. For example, in an engineering project, which is, to a large extent, about the creation and combination of knowledge, the participants share their explicit and tacit knowledge with others and at the same time develop their own personal mental models.

Learning

Learning begins with perception (de Geus, 1997). Neither an individual nor a company will ever begin to learn without having seen something of interest in the environment. That is why surviving and thriving in a volatile world requires, first of all, management that is sensitive to its company's environment. Continuous, fundamental changes in the external world – a turbulent business environment, for example – require continuous management for change in the company. This means making continuous fundamental changes in the internal structures of the company. For many psychologists, this principle represents one important aspect of learning. A successful company is one that can learn effectively.

Some researchers claim that learning only occurs when a change in behaviour can be identified. However, the relationship between learning and change is not self-evident. According to Hildén (2004), change improves organizational functionality and may have broad implications for organizational processes, networks, and individual working conditions. However, frequent change may also reduce learning capability. An organization may create adaptation mechanisms that help to implement frequent changes, but that also neglect the intentions of managers.

According to Doz and Prahalad (1993), analysis of current organization theories shows a gap between the highly abstract theories and concrete, descriptive, and empirical research. In other words, there is a lack of knowledge concerning the structures, forces, and dynamics that influence a company's ability to learn, and its evolution. In the opinion of these writers, only organizational learning theory and part of institutional theory focus primarily on change and development.

A model of a learning process that is widely used is the Lewinian experiential learning model (Kolb, 1984) (Figure 7.1). This model has appeared in a variety of management guises: Deming's (1986) plan-do-check-act cycle, Schein's (1987) observation-emotional reaction-judgement-intervention cycle, and Argyris and Schön's (1978) discovery-invention-production-generalisation cycle.

Another model, namely Argyris and Schöns's (1996) model of single-, double-, and deuteron-loop learning was originally developed for explaining the learning processes of individuals, but it is useful in the context of organizations as well. Single-loop learning reflects the behaviour of a thermostat. If an error occurs, it will be corrected. The governing variables, such as goals, values, plans, rules, and strategies, are taken for granted and only action strategies that will work within the governing variables are considered. This means that the governing variables are operationalized rather than questioned. Double-loop learning causes changes in the governing values. Deuteron-loop learning (learning to learn, triple-loop learning) indicates that an organization knows how to carry out single-loop and double-loop learning. Learning takes place only when new knowledge is translated into new and different behaviour that is replicable. In Dodgson's (1993) words, single-loop learning involves adding to the knowledge base, firm-specific competences, or routines

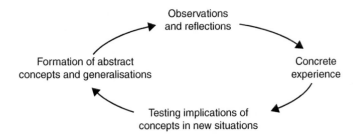

Figure 7.1   The Lewinian experiential learning model.

without altering the nature of the activities. Double- and deuteron-loop learning involve a consideration of why and how to change, and they imply that cognitive strategies and attitudes change.

To sum up, learning is the acquisition of new knowledge, behaviours, skills, values, preferences, or understanding. An individual's learning may occur as part of education or personal development. It may be goal-oriented and may be aided by motivation.

Learning organization

There is clear distinction between *learning organization* and *organizational learning* (Maula, 2006). Learning organization emphasizes structural and other aspects that make learning processes possible. Organizational learning deals with the learning process and its stages and characteristics. According to Garvin (1993), learning organization is an organization skilled at creating, acquiring, and transferring knowledge, and at modifying its behaviour to reflect new knowledge and insights.

In the opinion of Maula (2006), learning organization has become a relevant concept among large organizations. However, according to her, there is no consensus about how to define a learning organization: should it be defined as a learning entity as such, or through its individual members? Kim (1993) assumes that organizations learn via their individual members, and that the learning process is fundamentally different at individual and organizational levels. Here, because the focus is on an organization as a system, an organization is regarded as a learning entity. A learning organization facilitates the learning of all its members and continually transforms itself.

According to Boisot (1995), there are two kinds of theories about learning organizations. The neoclassical theories explain the 'war of position' and the Schumpeterian theory explains the 'war of movement'. Neoclassical theories of learning favour retentive strategies and lead the firm to accumulate its technological assets. Learning is based on the codification and diffusion of knowledge about objective reality. Schumpeterian learning is based on the subjective apprehension of reality. Innovations occur through creative destruction. The interpretations of reality are not fully shared. Schumpeterian learning emphasizes the absorption of knowledge (learning by doing and using, internalizing of tacit knowledge) and scanning (integrating codified and un-codified knowledge). A learning organization is 'a Schumpeterian animal, a creative destroyer that is forever destabilizing markets'. Here, the basis is on the 'war of movement'. This approach can be identified in an extreme form in D'Aveni and Gunther's (1994) idea of 'strategic maneuvering'. It involves disrupting the market and status quo, and eroding and destroying an opponent's advantage by making it obsolete, irrelevant, or non-unique. It implies that companies should abandon the objective to establish fit between environment, mission, strategy, and organizational characteristics, because fit implies permanence and predictability that is easy to read by competitors.

According to Senge (1990, p. 3), learning organizations are: 'organizations where people continually expand their capacity to create the results they truly desire, where new and expansive patterns of thinking are nurtured, where collective aspiration is set free, and where people are continually learning to see the whole together'. The basic rationale for such organizations is that in situations of rapid change only those organizations that are flexible, adaptive, and productive will excel. For this to happen, it is argued, organizations need to 'discover how to tap people's commitment and capacity to learn at all levels' (Senge, 1990, p. 4).

While all people have the capacity to learn, the structures in which they have to function are often not conducive to reflection and engagement. Furthermore, people may lack the tools and guiding ideas to make sense of the situations they face. Organizations that are continually expanding their capacity to create their future require a fundamental shift of mind among their members. 'When you ask people about what it is like being part of a great team, what is most striking is the meaningfulness of the experience. People talk about being part of something larger than them, of being connected, of being generative. It becomes quite clear that, for many, their experiences as part of truly great teams stand out as singular periods of life lived to the fullest. Some spend the rest of their lives looking for ways to recapture that spirit' (Senge, 1990, p. 13).

Indeed, for Senge, real learning gets to the heart of what it is to be human. We become able to re-create ourselves. This applies to both individuals and organizations. Thus, for a 'learning organization it is not enough to survive. "Survival learning" or what is more often termed "adaptive learning" is important – indeed it is necessary. But for a learning organization, "adaptive learning" must be joined by "generative learning", learning that enhances our capacity to create' (Senge, 1990, p. 14).

According to Raivola and Ropo (1991), the learning taking place in companies can be divided into three parts: informal, formal, and non-formal learning. Informal learning consists of all that is related to the work process itself, to the doing of the work. At all levels and sectors of the work new things are learned that affect the work processes one way or another either directly or indirectly. Informal learning is often not noticed or realized (e.g. Day, 1998). Therefore, it can be called tacit knowledge and know-how accumulation. Tacit knowledge and know-how have a central significance for professional identity and they form a part of qualifications that cannot be taught. In addition to work experience, professional training is required. More formal training can be acquired as updating, continuation, and/or additional training (formal learning). Non-formal learning means learning that takes place outside the daily routines of the company.

Sarala (1993) proposes small team activity as a means towards learning organization. According to him, the efficiency of working life today is increasingly based on a smooth and innovative co-operation of parties working together. The results are monitored in more detail, and this concerns teams and individuals as well, not only whole organizations. The payment of wages, salaries, and bonuses are often connected to results, calling for an increased need to develop one's own work. An operating system can only be efficient if its parts are efficient. This calls for the co-operation, planning, and realization of operation in teams, and furthermore, for the development of creativity and increased efficiency. According to Sarala (1993), the learning organization has a structure which is depicted in Figure 7.2.

Companies as learning organizations are, therefore, autopoietic cognitive systems that are autonomous with respect to knowledge, the creation of knowledge, and the application of distinctions and norms (von Krogh and Vicari, 1993; Parboteeah and Jackson, 2007). Instead of being merely the end result of a knowledge creation process, knowledge is a component of the autopoietic process (Maturana and Varela, 1987) and an essential component in a continuous organization-wide learning and renewal process that aims at survival and evolution. In this sense, an organization can be regarded as a stream of knowledge that drives a continuous re-creation of knowledge (von Krogh et al., 1996b). Autopoiesis therefore requires

Figure 7.2 Construction of a learning organization.

theories of knowing rather than theories of knowledge, and concepts of a system of knowing activity rather than notions of applications of abstract knowledge (Blackler, 1995; Spender and Grant, 1996).

A learning organization is, therefore, an organization skilled at creating, acquiring, interpreting, transferring, and retaining knowledge, and at purposefully modifying its behaviour to reflect new knowledge and skills (cf. Garvin, 1993).

Organizational learning

Organizational learning is a source of competitive advantage (e.g. Levitt and March, 1988; Sense, 2008). Learning is a dynamic concept that emphasizes the continually changing nature of organizations (Leroy and Ramanantsoa, 1997). For example, on one day when a manager figures out a new way to achieve efficiency, his or her company must somehow learn this knowledge so the company can start to use it. Organizational learning is also important because loyalty between companies and their employees is often low. Employees who move on to other opportunities may take critical knowledge and skills with them.

According to Dodgson (1993), organizational theory often regards learning as an adjustment to external stimulus. The management and innovation literature regards it as an attempt to retain and improve competitiveness, productivity, and innovativeness in uncertain technological and market circumstances. However, most economists' research about organizational learning is limited to descriptive analyses of the outcomes of cumulative experience. Dodgson (1993) claims that it is necessary to progress beyond static views of organizations as bundles of resources. According to him, learning is a dynamic concept that is defined as enhanced organizational capability and has thereby broad analytical value. It emphasizes the continually changing nature of organizations. It is an integrative concept that can unify various levels of analysis: individual, team, and company.

The outcome of learning may include quantifiable improvements in activities, sustainable, comparative, and competitive efficiency, or improved innovative efficiency. Learning can also be defined as a 'change in the state of knowledge' within an organization (Lyles et al., 1996). On the other hand, learning can be defined as a process that changes the state of knowledge of an individual organization. Learning also changes the level of mastery at which a company knows and applies its knowledge (Sanchez and Heene, 1997).

Indeed, learning improves an organization's efficiency and its capability to adapt to a changing environment (e.g. Scarbrough et al., 2004), thus increasing the probability of survival. Successful learning is generally measured by useful outcomes: new and better ways to perform. Several factors in the environment, such as rapid and turbulent technological change, increasing complexity, and the shortening of product life cycles, increase the need for organizational learning. The rate of environmental change influences an organization's ability to compete, especially when the changes are related to the market situation and the technological base of production.

According to Burns and Stalker (1994), a turbulent environment may favour organizational forms that have the capacity to respond quickly to new opportunities. A changing environment contributes to organic management, such as the constant alteration of a company's expectations and resetting the decision framework, while a relatively stable environment leads to a mechanistic and bureaucratic management system. However, the ability of a company to recognize significant changes in the environment may vary between companies. Rapid industrial transformations require managers to learn how to change their dominant logic and the recipes they have grown with (Prahalad and Hamel, 1994).

To conclude, organizational learning is an area of knowledge within organizational theory that studies models and theories about the way an organization learns and adapts.

A characteristic of organizational learning is the ability of an organization to adapt to its environment, that is, an organization is able to sense changes in signals from its environment (both internal and external) and adapt accordingly.

Expansive learning seen through activity theory

Activity theory distinguishes between temporary, goal-directed actions and durable, object-oriented activity systems (Vygotsky, 1986; Engeström, 2000). According to activity theory, the use and utilization of knowledge is not a spontaneous phenomenon in the development process of an organization. This means that there is a triggering action, for example, such as a conflicting questioning of the existing practices in the organization, in order to generate *expansive learning* (Engeström, 2000). Expansive learning produces culturally new patterns of activity. In this context, 'activity' has a broader meaning than simply 'action' or 'operation', that is, the activity is, for instance, a project-based company as a whole. As used in activity theory, the concept of activity links events to the contexts within which they occur (Blackler et al., 1999).

The object of expansive learning is the entire organization (e.g. a project-based company) in which the learners (i.e. project team members) work (Engeström, 2001). The work context forms the learning environment. Figure 7.3 illustrates the systemic structure of collective activity. Technologies used and language (instruments in Figure 7.3) mediate the relationship between a worker and the working community. The division of labour mediates the relationship between community members and shared activity (Blackler et al., 1999; Engeström 2000). Together this constitutes the learning environment, that is, the infrastructure through which individuals' 'action learning' (Revans, 1982) takes place.

Triggering an action, that is, causing an expansive learning activity, can grow from tension between the people working in a company. Therefore, a tense working atmosphere is not necessarily a negative feature. However, a feeling of ease can be problematic if nothing is seen to be worthy of development in the organization. Furthermore, people also fail to act intelligently. This is not because they, as individuals, lack intelligence, but because they are following this or that organizational ruler or practice (rules in Figure 7.3). Organizational context determines, to a great extent, whether people are allowed or encouraged to use their intelligence, for instance, by pointing out inadequacies in existing practices.

Thus, in order to meet customer requirements, a company has to make necessary changes (Aramo-Immonen, 2009; Aramo-Immonen et al., 2009). This means that a company has to learn in parallel with doing. Traditional learning theories such as single-loop and double-loop learning (Argyris and Schön, 1978) have little to offer in such

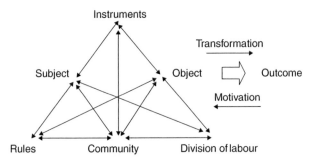

Figure 7.3   System of collective activity applying.

a situation. Expansive learning at work produces new forms of work activities (Engeström, 2001). An essential component of expansive learning is shared knowledge. This accumulates in explicit form, such as rules and instruments (artefacts and tools), and in tacit form, such as cultural, historical, and experience-based knowledge. This collective type of contemporary learning requires knowledge-sharing arenas as a field of growing. Therefore, face-to-face contacts and opportunities for mutual discussion have to be emphasized in the age of computer-aided communication.

Learning is associated with organizational tools, methods, and practices that facilitate the dynamic development of expertises, the sharing of knowledge, cognitive achievements, and the creation of knowledge and innovation (Vygotsky 1986; Engeström 2000). This means that the challenge is to create an atmosphere and culture of learning in companies. Heavy workloads, a constant sense of rushing, and tensed working atmospheres, which are typical situations in project-based companies, are not supportive factors for a learning environment.

To conclude, the relation between learning and knowledge may seem to be simple; knowledge is conceived as something that exists, learning as the way in which this 'something' can be acquired. But the relation is more complicated than it might seem at first. Knowledge is not self-created; it is created by people, and the creation of knowledge occurs simultaneously with learning. The two merge into one another.

Organizational ecology

Organizational ecology is a theoretical and empirical approach in the social sciences that is especially used in organizational studies.

Organizational ecology utilizes insights from biology, economics, and sociology, and tries to understand the conditions under which organizations emerge, grow, and die (e.g. Gupta and Govindarajan, 2000).

Organizational ecology aims to explain how social, economic and political conditions affect the relative abundance and diversity of organizations and to account for their changing composition over time. Research in organizational ecology is grounded in three observations. First, aggregates of organizations exhibit diversity. Second, organizations have difficulty devising and executing changes fast enough to meet the demands of uncertain, changing environments. And, third, organizations arise and disappear continually. Given these observations, ecological analyses formulate organizational change and variability at the population level, highlighting the differential creation of new and the demise of old organizations and populations with heterogeneous attributes. This formulation contrasts adaptation approaches, which explain organizational diversity in terms of ongoing organizations' leaders cumulative strategic choices. Changes in organizational populations reflect the operation of four basic processes: variation, selection, retention, and competition (Aldrich, 1999). Variations result from human behaviour. Any kind of change, intentional or blind, is a variation. Individuals produce variations continuously in their efforts to adjust their behaviour to others in the organization and to adjust the organization's relationship to the environment.

The approach of organizational ecology holds that organizations that are reliable and accountable are those that can survive. However, a negative by-product of the need for reliability and accountability has a high degree of inertia and resistance to change. A key prediction of organizational ecology is that the process of change itself is so disruptive that it will result in an elevated rate of mortality.

Theories about inertia and change are, therefore, fundamental issues to the organizational ecology, which seeks a better understanding of the broader changes in the organizational landscape. Given the limits on company-level adaptation, most of these broader changes thus come from the entry and selective replacement of organizations. Hence, organizational ecology has spent considerable effort on understanding the mortality rates of organizations.

The theory of niche width distinguishes broadly between two types of organizations: generalists and specialists. Specialist organizations maximize their exploitation of the environmental and accept the risk of experiencing a change in that environment. On the other hand, generalist organizations accept a lower level of exploitation in return for greater security (Hannan and Freeman, 1977). Niche theory shows that specialization is generally favoured in stable or certain environments. However, the main contribution of the niche theory is probably the finding that 'generalism is not always optimal in uncertain environments' (Hannan and Freeman, 1977, p. 958). The exception is produced by environments which 'place very different demands on the organization, and the duration of environmental states is short relative to the life of the organization' (Hannan and Freeman, 1977, p. 958). Thus, the niche theory explains variations in industrial structure in different industries. The theory shows how different structures in different industries (generalist vs specialist organizations) are shaped by relevant environments.

The relationship between generalists and specialist organizations is further developed in the resource-partitioning model which includes predictions about the founding and mortality rates of both specialists and generalists as a function of market concentration.

The theory can be illustrated by describing two environments. Environment A stands for an un-concentrated mass market and environment B represents a concentrated mass market. In environment B, generalists will always attempt to address the centre of the market where most resources peak. After all, in the centre of the market these generalists can thrive by exploiting economies of scale. Carroll (1985) claims that 'in environment B, despite the very concentrated generalists market, the resource space outside this market is larger than in environment A, where the generalist market is less concentrated' (Carroll, 1985, p. 1272). The abundance of resources in the periphery can then become hospitable to specialist organizations, and the market becomes effectively partitioned. Carroll concluded that 'more available resources should translate into better chances of success for specialist when they operate in the more concentrated market' (Carroll, 1985, p. 1272).

Organizational ecology also predicts that the rates of founding and the rates or mortality are dependent on the number of organizations in the market. The two central mechanisms here are legitimation and competition. Legitimation generally increases with the number of organizations, but so does competition. The result is that legitimation processes will prevail at low numbers of organizations, while competition at high numbers.

The founding rate will therefore first increase with the number of organizations (due to an increase in legitimation) but will decrease at high numbers of organizations (due to competition). The reverse holds true for mortality rates. Thus, the relationship of density to founding rates has an inverted U-shape and the relationship of density to mortality rates follows a U-shaped pattern.

Thus, organizational ecology refers to the social system in which people operate. It drives an organization's formal and informal expectations of individuals, defines the types of people who will fit into the organization, shapes individuals' freedom to pursue actions without prior approval, and affects how people interact with others both inside and outside the organization. The determinants of organizational ecology are culture, structure, information systems, reward systems, processes, people, and leadership. The word ecology suggests that the organizational system should be viewed not as a random collection of disparate elements but as a comprehensive whole (i.e. system) in which the various elements interact with one another.

Socio-cognitive engineering

Socio-cognitive engineering refers to a multi-disciplinary research field, involving biology, psychology, sociology, artificial intelligence, linguistics, management, and ethics, aiming at studying and reproducing the conditions from which knowledge can emerge among the agents (biological or not) of an autopoietic society (Cassapo and Scalabrin, 2004). From a socio-cognitive perspective, knowledge cannot emerge without the existence of a society, and a society cannot be stable without the emergence of knowledge fluxes. Knowledge emergence is then seen as the fundamental glue which allows for a stable society. Therefore, if in a given society, cognitive coupling links disappear between individuals, the society will not be autopoietic any more (i.e. it will not be able to continue producing itself in a stable way), and will then disappear.

According to Luhmann (1982), social systems are auto-referenced systems based on meaningful communication. They use communication in order to constitute and connect events, which construct themselves as a system. In that sense, they are autopoietic. They exist only for reproducing the events which serve as components for themselves. The 'meaningful communications' described by Luhmann, are what will be technically called here 'semiotic enacts'. These semiotic enacts are, for example, natural language communication, body language interactions, or chemical exchanges between autonomous beings. It is important to emphasize that from such a perspective, natural language cannot be seen as a tool designed for accessing to the word 'the way it is'. It has to be contemplated as a particular coupling device, the purpose of which is to provide stable auto-maintenance of a system's unity.

In order to engineer the conditions from which specific knowledge will be able to emerge, socio-cognitive engineering will pursue the following approaches:

- direct approach will consist of creating direct face-to-face-related ad hoc societies
- The allopoietic-artefact-mediated approach will consist of mediating the relationships between the cognitive agents of a society with heteronomous semantic-carrier artefacts like books and intranets
- The autopoietic-artefact-mediated approach will consist of mediating relationships with autopoietic artificial artefacts like cognitive artificial agents
- The mixed approach will consist of creating a complex socio-cognitive environment by combining the three previous approaches.

Knowledge, from a socio-cognitive perspective, is not something that can be stored in order to be retrieved later; it is actually to be produced by emergence anytime it is needed. This emergence can only occur inside an autopoietic society, which means that when a society no longer exists, knowledge no longer exists either. The notion of society has to be understood in the same way as Maturana and Varela define autopoietic systems. For example, a team of software engineers relate themselves in the context of a project as an autopoietic society.

The first and most intuitive method socio-cognitive engineering investigates in order to describe how social conditions can be produced to allow knowledge to emerge, is the 'direct approach'. This approach consists of creating the conditions which allow individuals – like project team members – to meet directly and share ideas through natural language. The direct approach can be compared with Nonaka and Takeuchi's (1995) concept of socialization. For example, by organizing meetings, brainstorming, or playing simulation games, people can be gathered to form an ad hoc community from which different ideas will emerge. At the same time, unmediated storytelling techniques fall in this direct-approach, socio-cognitive category. Concerning a company's client-satisfaction problem, the direct approach would then consist of meeting directly with the client in order to create trustful relationships, and to let the knowledge of the client's satisfaction emerge from these social interactions.

The second and classic method for companies that have successfully implemented some computer-based knowledge-management practices, is the 'allopoietic-artefact-mediated approach'. Because it is not always possible to gather people together directly, it is often possible to try to mediate the relationships of a given society's individuals with some allopoietic artefacts. The most trivial one is a document. It is completely heteronomous, as it needs someone to lend a semantic in order to make sense. Nevertheless, it still represents a semantic connection between an author and a reader from which a society can be formed, and from which knowledge can then emerge. Further, more evolved artefacts can also be used to form allopoietic connections between individuals. For example, chats, groupware, workflow systems, audio and video-conferences devices, and the general information portals are some media in common use. All these mediators possess the common property of being heteronomous semantic-carriers: a cognitive being has to access and interpret them to allow knowledge to emerge. That is, computers used in this way are not machines that think, but machines that provide food for thought. The allopoietic-artefact-mediated approach of socio-cognitive engineering is a technological genesis of meaning. Regarding a company's client-satisfaction problem mentioned above, the allopoietic-artefact-mediated approach would then consist of socializing the client's knowledge through synchronous and asynchronous computer-supported collaboration tools.

The third method of knowledge emergence engineering is the 'autopoietic-artefact-mediated approach'. Its most trivial proposition would consist of gathering together only biological autopoietic beings to allow knowledge to emerge, but this would lead the situation back to the direct approach. Therefore, it is defined here that the autopoietic-artifact-mediated approach is an introduction inside of biological societies of non-biological autopoietic artefacts like artificial cognitive agents. A good introduction to the concept of artificial agents is found in Bradshaw's (1997) 'Introduction to software agents'.

According to Franklin and Graesser (1996), the main characteristics of a software agent are:

- Autonomy, social skills, pro-activity and persistence
- Possessing sensors, executors, personal objectives, proper agenda, and knowledge about its environment
- Being able to plan, dialogue, negotiate, coordinate, and collaborate.

Reducing all these characteristics to the essential elements implied by their autopoietic nature, it is possible more simply say that an agent exhibits:

- Self-regulated autonomy
- Emergent intentionality
- Emergent embodied identity.

As a consequence, virtual autopoietic artefacts do not need any beneficiate ad-hoc semantics: they have their own objectives they can guide and anticipate users' needs they can introduce thoughtfully themselves inside social networks and provide active supports to social processes (like communication and negotiation). Concerning a company's client-satisfaction problem, the autopoietic-artefact-mediated approach consists of creating an autonomous software agent whose self-regulated autonomy results in the emergent intentionality of:

- Introducing itself inside societies where knowledge about the client can emerge
- Introducing itself inside a society in which an individual participates, and where knowledge about the client is required.

The fourth proposal of socio-cognitive engineering is the 'mixed approach'. This mainly consists of applying rationality (taking into consideration risks, complexity, costs, and time issues) to the three previous approaches in order to create a socially integrated human-and-agents environment where knowledge emergence's probability can be maximized.

Thus, socio-cognitive engineering can be seen as a branch of general system engineering, integrating the paradigms of physics, systemic theory, engineering, and the cognitive and social sciences.

Summary

There is a growing need in project-based companies and the project teams within them to move beyond solving problems at hand to continuously improving knowledge and skills in the face of changing conditions and situations. Learning has emerged as the most important activity of project-based companies and, moreover, the ability of a company to learn faster than its competitors is the only sustainable form of competitive advantage. Therefore, this chapter has explored concepts of evolution, learning, and socio-cognitive engineering. Some of the key claims and suggestions include the following:

Evolution is not a goal-seeking process. Its causes are accidental; they are not appropriate means to produce a result.

Intuitive problem solving is not based on linear cause-consequence thinking. The result of this is that a person's intuitive skills are dependent on context and situation, and they can only be roughly evaluated by looking at his or her experience base.

Learning is creating results – the only way people and organizations have of changing themselves and becoming more of who they want to be. Learning creates and recreates individuals' mental models.

Mental models are deeply held internal images of how the world works, images that limit individuals to familiar ways of thinking and acting. Very often people are not consciously aware of their mental models or the effects they have on their behaviour.

Learning organization is organization that facilitates the learning of all its members and consciously transforms itself and its context, reflecting the fact that change should not happen just for the sake of change, but should be well thought out.

Learning arises from a company's accumulated knowledge. Consequently, learning depends on the continuous creation of conflicts between old and new knowledge. New knowledge that does not fit existing knowledge challenges productivity and facilitates learning. Organizational learning is interconnected to individual learning.

Knowledge has the characteristic that it accumulates and depletes over time. This means that the rate at which a project-based company can learn depends critically upon the knowledge that it already holds. Organizational learning then becomes an expression of a company's effectiveness at building characteristics of learning organization.

Long-term change in the diversity of organizational forms within a population occurs through selection rather than adaptation. Most organizations have structural inertia that hinders adaptation when the environment changes. Those organizations that become incompatible with the environment are eventually replaced through competition with new organizations better suited to external demands.

Organizations have institutional capabilities that allow them to integrate and protect knowledge. The organization is an entity of knowing activity rather than an entity of applied abstract knowledge. It is essentially organic and inherently inexplicable. Organizations are increasingly communications-intensive adhocracies and knowledge-intensive entities.

Socio-cognitive engineering is a subjective perspective based on the explicitly involved distinguished positions of the intelligent problem observers/solvers. They are a part of the problem with all their goal-oriented cognitive properties, motivations, competences, and social constraints.

8
Components of the Project-Based Company When it is Regarded as an Autopoietic Knowledge System

A project-based company as an autopoietic knowledge system consists of 12 different non-physical components. The properties of and relationships among these components determine the interacting processes of autopoietic self-production. Their interactions maintain a project-based company's functioning, learning, renewal, and co-evolution with its environment. However, although the components can be identified in project-based companies, there can be a significant variation among them, depending on the environment type in which the company operates (e.g. a mechanical, organic, semi-mechanical, or semi-organic project work environment). Drawing primarily on the general characteristics of systems thinking, autopoiesis theory, and autopoietic system, the following 12 components have been identified as constituting the autopoietic project-based company:

1. *Identity* means that a project-based company maintains the integrity of its 'structure' and can be distinguished from the other types of companies.
2. *Perception of the environment* means that the project-based company creates knowledge about its environment according to its own speciality.
3. *Strategy* helps the project-based company to operationalize visions and objectives into internal standards and processes. It is based on identity, perception of the environment, and other relevant aspects.
4. *Knowledge management* facilitates and regulates a project-based company's self-production process.
5. *Knowledge sharing* is necessary to achieve the consistent planning objectives in a project-based company.

6. *Boundary elements and perturbations* include various embedded roles and functions that enable reciprocal interaction between a project-based company and its environment. Boundary elements enable sensing by identifying triggers by reciprocal interaction. Perturbations may lead to compensations in a project-based company's structure. Perturbations are not inputs to the company, per se. A company can also be triggered internally.

7. *Interactivity* includes the processes and artefacts used to communicate reciprocally with the environment and to influence co-evolution with clients, sub-contractors, and so on. It also includes social coupling that refers to communication among individuals both internally and externally.

8. *Boundary objects* are objects that serve as an interface between different individuals and/or organizations. They serve as a point of mediation and negotiation around intent.

9. *Commitment and motivation* of the project-based company's personnel assists the acquisition and sharing of knowledge between different project stakeholders.

10. *Information and communication systems* may include a variety of more or less structured information systems.

11. *Organizational climate and organizational/project culture* are important factors in encouraging people working for a project-based company to share knowledge.

12. *Trust* is an individual's reliance on another person under conditions of dependence and vulnerability. When the relationship between a project-based company and its customer is based on trust, many benefits are achieved by both parties.

The relationships between components enable the functioning of a project-based company. For example, boundary elements, interactive processes, and knowledge management influence each other. In the project business, interaction with clients and sub-contractors is crucially important.

Identity

One of the main principles underlying the concept of autopoietic systems is that of structural determinism (Maturana, 1991). Structural determinism refers to the relations between the components that give a system its *identity*. For example, a project-based company is, as outlined earlier, a system in which the majority of products are made according to bespoke designs for customers, a feature that gives a company its identity. If the structure (i.e. organization) of a project-based company changes, so does its identity. In other words, if the majority of a company's production is not based on projects, the company is not a project-based company.

In considering change, all companies are structure-determined. This means that the actual changes that the company undergoes depend on the structure itself at a particular instant. Any change in a project-based company must be structural change – that is, it must be a change in the number and quality of projects and individuals or their relations – and as such, must be determined by the properties of the projects and individuals. Changes occur in response to both internal dynamics and to interactions with the environment. But even in external interactions the resulting change is determined internally; it is only triggered by the environment. This is a very important conclusion, for it means that there can be no 'instructive interactions'. It is never the case that an environmental action can determine its own effect on a structure-determined system – namely, a project-based company.

Indeed, the perturbations in the environment only trigger structural changes or compensations in project-based companies. It is the structure (e.g. knowledge and competencies) that determines both what the compensation will be and even what in the environment can or cannot act as a trigger. In total, the structure (i.e. organization) at any point in time determines:

- All possible structural changes within the project-based company that maintain the current organization, as well as those that do not, and
- all possible states of the environment that could trigger changes of state and whether such changes would maintain or destroy the current organization.

Thus, the identity of an autopoietic system, like a project-based company, means that a system maintains the integrity of its structure and can be distinguished from the background and other units (i.e. other types of companies). Autopoietic systems have an identity because they are composite systems, characterized, for example, by a strategy and an organizational culture. Such a system subordinates all perturbations and changes, including the controlling inputs from its environment, to the maintenance of its identity (Varela, 1979). Consequently, identity refers also to the way the organization defines itself, its history, mission, and essential characterizing features.

All companies – including project-based companies – have four components (cf. de Geus, 1997):

- Sensitivity to the environment represents an ability to learn and adapt
- Cohesion and identity are aspects of a company's innate ability to build a community and an identity for itself
- Tolerance and its corollary, decentralization, are both symptoms of a company's awareness of ecology: its ability to build constructive relationships with other entities, within and outside itself
- Conservative financing, a company's ability to govern its own growth and evolution effectively.

Furthermore, the identity represents body and soul together, and it has several key characteristics:

- The identity is goal-oriented. It wants to live as long as possible and to realize the development of its potential from its talents and its aptitudes
- It is conscious of itself. An identity can perceive itself as 'I' or 'we' although it is composed of parts and elements, which are personae in their own right. In its turn, it can be a part of a larger entity, as the soldier is part of a platoon, the platoon is part of a company, the company part of an army, and the army part of a nation's armed forces
- It is open to the outside world. Elements from the outside constantly enter the human system. But human individuals and their ideas also constantly enter higher-order personae such as a company. At the same time, an identity is at all times related to the outside world, in the sense that every experience represents one more exchange in a lifelong dialogue with the forces of the world around it
- It is alive, but it has a finite lifespan. One day it is born, and one day it will pass away.

(cf. de Geus, 1997)

There is no ambiguity about who belongs and who does not. At the level of introspection, a company's members know who is prepared to live with the company's set of values. Whoever cannot live with those values should not be a member. Whoever is not a member does not need to share the values. However, they can share the values of some other institution, like a church parish, and still be an employee-non-member of the company. Of course, these non-members are likely to act as non-members, putting the needs of some other entity before the needs of the company. Members must share a set of institutional values that exist at the core of the company's persona.

Knowledge of a member of the organization hinges on the making of at least two fundamental distinctions (von Krogh and Roos, 1995a). First, there is a distinction between self and the organization. A cognitive system reproduces its own processes, and these processes distinguish it from its environment. Autopoiesis is necessary for the awareness of identity (Varela et al., 1991). Von Krogh and Roos (1995a) name this distinction 'identity–organization' distinction. The second type of distinction refers to the isolation of the domain of organization from the environment of the organization. Subsequently, many distinctions are made pertaining to this distinction, such as, this is a part of activities that belong to the organization, these norms are the norms of the organization, and so on.

In sum, a project-based company is open to the outside world: there is tolerance for a high entry of new individuals and ideas. It is, in fact, expected that new concepts and knowledge will flow through the company's 'stream of activity' on a daily basis. At the same time, however, the company maintains its cohesive identity. Members know 'who we are', and they are aware that they hold values in common. In a very real sense, they belong to each other. The values of the company coexist with the values of individuals within the company – and every member is aware of this coexistence. Further, a project-based company has a collective sense of the answer to the definitive question about company identity: Who belongs? Who is considered part of 'us'? Conversely, who does not belong, and thus is part of the surrounding world?

Perception of the environment

According to Meyer and Scott (1983), it is useful to distinguish broadly between two types of organizational environments: technical and institutional. *Technical environments* are those in which organizations produce a product or service that is exchanged in a market such that they are rewarded for effective and efficient performance. These are environments that foster the development of rationalized structures that efficiently coordinate technical work. Most types of manufacturing and service organizations operate in technical environments. By contrast, *institutional environments* are characterized by the elaboration of rules and requirements to which individual organizations must conform in order to receive legitimacy and support. In institutional environments, organizations are rewarded for utilizing the correct structures and processes, not for the quantity and quality of their outputs. Organizations operating in institutional environments include schools and hospitals, whose resources do not depend primarily on evaluations of their outputs in a competitive market.

According to Koskinen (2004), by identifying the knowledge gap between the existing knowledge base that is owned by the project-based company and the target knowledge base that is acquired by the company, it is possible to identify different knowledge-related project work environments. The discussion that follows describes four different knowledge-related project work environments, illustrating circumstances and situations where project work processes take place in project-based companies (see Figures 8.1 and 8.2).

The mechanical project work environment

In a mechanical project work environment (left lower part of Figure 8.1, and left lower part of Figure 8.2) a team tries to reach predetermined single-minded interpretations, that is, the utilization of explicit knowledge is abundant. Moreover, in a mechanical project work environment, knowledge utilized is often additive in nature (Hall and Andriani, 1999, 2002). Success in a mechanical project work environment requires that team members are skilled in adapting instructions. The tasks are precisely defined and a large proportion of the relevant knowledge is transferred in written form, that is, utilization of information technology in knowledge transfer is usually abundant. In a mechanical project work environment, knowledge moves from project management to individual team members. In other words and strictly speaking, knowledge is not sent for discussion but only to be obeyed. Because knowledge in a mechanical project work environment is, to a large extent, in explicit

	Explicit knowledge	Tacit knowledge
Substitutive knowledge	**Semi-mechanical PW environment** (e.g. investments)	**Organic PW environment** (e.g. product development)
Additive knowledge	**Mechanical PW environment** (e.g. house building)	**Semi-organic PW environment** (e.g. investments)

Figure 8.1   Four knowledge-related project work environments.

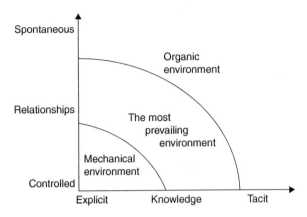

Figure 8.2   Knowledge-related project work environments.

form, it can be sent to the people involved over vast distances. The mechanical project work environment fits in projects in which quality criteria must be met precisely in advance.

For example, in fully standardized house building projects, the handling of knowledge is seen as processing knowledge primarily in a written form, and every problematic situation is met by more processing of knowledge. In these types of projects the potential for multiple interpretations is not usually taken into account. This means that a new standardized house is a manifestation of explicit and additive knowledge. Consequently, the implementation of a standardized house building project takes place in the environment which is described here as a mechanical project work environment.

Organic project work environments

In an organic project work environment (right upper part of Figure 8.1, and right upper part of Figure 8.2) the ambiguity of knowledge is significant. Projects involve inconsistent situations, and the changes that they produce and the challenges produced by circumstances do not necessarily have immediate answers. In the organic project work environment, solutions to problems are directed by non-linear thinking (e.g. in research and development projects). People act on the basis of world views born of their intuition and experience. Elements of knowledge consist of the multidimensional knowledge stores of the project participants, which mean that knowledge is often created with the help of face-to-face interactions.

Knowledge in an organic project work environment is, to a large extent, of a more difficult and multidimensional form than in a mechanical project work environment. A lot of the knowledge and know-how of a project team is based on experience-based tacit knowledge. Moreover, in an organic project work environment, the knowledge created is substitutive in nature (Hall and Andriani, 1999, 2002).

For example, when a manufacturer produces a concept for a new machine, then the concept is, to a large extent, a manifestation of tacit and substitutive knowledge. The creation of the concept may begin with team members discussing a variety of personal experiences, but as it proceeds, the expressions should converge through the understanding of individuals into one concept that becomes their common focus. Team members may apply creative techniques that make their insights and experiences more explicit, helping to bundle them into key words that finally form a concept. The crystallization of a concept is achieved when all team members feel that the concept corresponds with what they know tacitly. The implementation of a product development project can then take place in the environment which is described here as an organic project work environment.

Semi-mechanical and semi-organic project work environments

Semi-mechanical (left upper part of Figure 8.1) and semi-organic (right lower part of Figure 8.1), project work environments are probably the most prevalent. Knowledge is created with the help of both face-to-face communication and information technology. However, the utilization of information technology in knowledge creation and utilization is more abundant in the semi-mechanical project work environment than in the semi-organic project work environment, and, vice versa, face-to-face interaction-based knowledge creation and utilization is more abundant in the semi-organic project work environment than in the semi-mechanical project work environment.

For example, project delivery practices have a lot in common in paper and pulp and steel industries, but there is a great deal of difference between house constructing and product development projects. The same project management methods do not fit all. There are obvious practical differences. The learning culture varies considerably; some practices are more authoritarian and have more formal procedures than others; some are specialist while others are diverse, and so on. All these differences have implications for knowledge management.

To take another example, in many investment projects information technology-based document management is an important foundation for knowledge sharing. Engineers can access data on past projects, including plant designs. They can also use information technology for accessing reports from sales people and a directory of in-house experts. However, this explicit knowledge can often serve only as a basis for deciding what tacit knowledge to apply. This means that explicit knowledge is also subject to alternative interpretations, because everybody understands knowledge in a subjective way. Therefore, it is very difficult to know how to use this knowledge in an actual problem-solving situation.

To conclude, perhaps the most commonly held conception of the environment of organizations is that of the *task environment* (e.g. Dill, 1958, p. 410). This concept is broadly defined as all aspects of the environment 'potentially relevant to goal setting and goal attainment', but is typically narrowed in use to refer to sources of inputs, markets for outputs, competitors, and regulators. The conception of a task environment emphasizes that most organizations are created to achieve goals, and to perform some type of work. It also emphasizes that no organization is self-sufficient; all must enter into exchanges with the environment. Managers are viewed as ensuring adequate supplies of resources and markets, designing efficient work arrangements, and coordinating and controlling technical activities. The project-based company's structure is viewed as being closely linked to external technical requirements and to internal work systems.

Strategy and strategic management

Strategy is a pattern or plan that integrates an organization's major goals, policies, and action sequences in a cohesive whole (Quinn, 1996). The objective of a strategy is to help to operationalize visions and objectives into internal standards and processes. It is based on an organization's identity, perception of the environment, and other relevant aspects.

The essence of *strategic management* is the development and maintenance of meaningful assets and skills, and the selection of strategies and competitive arenas such that those assets and skills form a sustainable competitive advantage. Indicators of the strength of the assets and skills are thus required to measure performance and guide programmes needed to improve assets and skills. The ability to produce high-quality products (e.g. project deliveries) is a skill that could be monitored by quality goals such as a defect ratio to customer problem index. The asset of brand loyalty might be measured by a customer satisfaction index. Clearly, such measures suggest that assets and skills go beyond simply stating that a company is a 'high-quality' company or a 'low-cost' business, although such statements of strategic thrusts or culture can be helpful.

In general, the strategic value of a company's resources is enhanced the more difficult they are to buy, sell, imitate, or substitute (Amit and Schoemaker, 1993). For example, invisible assets such as tacit knowledge or trust between management and labour cannot be traded or easily replicated by competitors since they are deeply rooted in the organization's history (Liebeskind, 1996). Such company-specific and often tacit assets accumulate slowly over a period of time (cf. intellectual capital described in chapter 6 of this book).

Indeed, the key question in strategic management is how companies can achieve and sustain their competitive advantage. One response to this question is to suggest that it is a company's resources that lead to competitive advantage, arising from a 'resource-based theory of the firm' (Barney, 1991; Wernerfelt; 1984). Resources are the tangible and intangible assets a company uses to choose and implement its strategy (Barney, 2001). A seminal paper in this area (Barney, 1991) suggests a number of characteristics of resources by which to achieve competitive advantage:

- Resources are distributed heterogeneously across firms
- Resources have a 'stickiness' and cannot be transferred from firm to firm without a cost
- Resources are rare – not widely held
- Resources are valuable – they promote efficiency and effectiveness
- Resources are not imitable and cannot be replicated easily by competitors
- Resources are not substitutable – other resources cannot fulfil the same functions
- Resources are not transferable and cannot be bought in resource markets.

Furthermore, in the strategic management literature it has been suggested that a wide variety of resources that follow these conditions will lead to sustainable competitive advantage. Additionally, strategic management of a company also includes concepts of strategic planning, human resource management, top management skills, trust, information technology, and organizational culture (Priem and Butler, 2001). One of the highly influential concepts arising from the resource-based view is the notion of core competence, which is briefly described in chapter 6 of this book (Prahalad and Hamel, 1990).

However, according to Morecroft (2007), the traditional resource-based view seeks to explain superior company performance and competitive advantage in terms of unique configuration of company resources that rivals find difficult to acquire or imitate. Companies are seen as complex bundles of resource endowments. In other words, there is a lack of a clear or agreed basis for selecting which of a company's resources are those that contribute most critically to performance. Part of the difficulty arises from the fact that this sort of resource-based thinking seeks to identify idiosyncratic resources solely from a static analysis of resource endowments.

Therefore, Morecroft (2007) suggests that competitive advantage and superior performance stem not only from the uniqueness and variety of a company's current resources but also from the ways resource endowments change over time as a result of management policies. This view shifts attention from static comparisons of resource endowments to dynamic analyses of resource accumulation and the dominant logic of policies and feedback processes that control accumulation processes and drive the evolution of resource stocks over time. Such an approach allows for the discovery of company idiosyncrasies in approaches to managing the dynamic complexity of a resource system rather than in the composition of a company's resource stocks at a single point in time.

One outcome of the resource-based view of the company is the development of the 'knowledge-based view' of the company, which assumes that knowledge (know how and know what) is the company's most important resource (Grant, 1996; Spender, 1996a). This view revisits many of the principles of individual knowledge (Ryle, 1949; Polanyi, 1966), organizational learning (Huber, 1991), learning organization (Boisot, 1995), conversion of one form of knowledge to another (Nonaka, 1991), and organizational routines and culture (Levitt and March, 1988) as potential sources of competitive advantage. Learning and knowledge sharing are thus seen as vital to this perspective, and there is a recognition of the difficulty of sharing tacit knowledge which may be crucial to competitive advantage. The principal role of the company is to integrate an individual's knowledge into their goods and services (Grant, 1991). Hence, the primary task of management is to coordinate the process of knowledge integration. One potential aid in this integration process is to treat the company as a dynamic socio-technical and self-regulating system (Spender, 1996a).

In sum, knowledge assets do not appear by magic. In other words, orienting a company towards knowledge assets entails a major decision and commitment. Large, initial investment requirements combined with knowledge uncertainties may cause the half-hearted to stumble. Successful strategies are bold, comprehensive, and risky. The criteria for resources to provide sustainable competitive advantage are well-established (Wernerfelt, 1984; Barney, 1991; Mahoney and Pandian, 1992; Peteraf, 1993). They must be durable, should not be mobile or tradeable, should not be easy to replicate, and should also be difficult for others to substitute with alternatives. Moreover, they should be complementary, that is, capable of working well together.

Knowledge management

Knowledge management comprises a range of practices used by organizations to identify, create, represent, and share knowledge for reuse, awareness, and learning. Knowledge management is typically tied to organizational objectives and is intended to achieve specific outcomes, such as shared understanding, improved performance, competitive advantage, or higher levels on innovation (e.g. Davenport et al., 1997; Hansen et al., 1999; Huang and Newell, 2003; Walker et al., 2005). One aspect of knowledge management, knowledge transfer, has always existed in one form or another. Examples include on-the-job peer discussions, formal apprenticeship, and mentoring programmes. However, with computers becoming more widespread in the second half of the twentieth century, specific adaptations of technology such as databases, expert systems, and knowledge repositories have been introduced to further simplify the processes.

Knowledge management programmes attempt to manage the processes of knowledge creation, accumulation, and application across organizations (e.g. Leseure and Brookes, 2004). Therefore, knowledge management programmes attempt to bring under one set of practices various strands of thought and practice relating to:

- The idea of the learning organization
- Conscious knowledge sharing within the organization
- Various enabling organizational practices, such as boundary brokering and storytelling
- Various enabling technologies such as knowledge bases and company intranets.

According to Nonaka and Takeuchi (1995), creating new knowledge and making it available to others is a central activity for organizations, and is the defining characteristic of the phenomenon of knowledge management. Knowledge management at its heart involves the management of social processes at work to enable sharing and the transfer of knowledge between individuals. Sveiby (1997) asserts that business managers need to realize that, unlike data, knowledge is embedded in people, and knowledge creation occurs in the process of social interaction.

Systematic and explicit knowledge management covers four areas (Wiig, 1997):

- Top-down monitoring and facilitation of knowledge-related activities
- Creation and maintenance of knowledge infrastructure
- Renewing, organizing and transforming knowledge assets
- Leveraging (using) knowledge assets to realise their value.

Of particular importance are the activities related to fostering individual behaviours that lead to knowledge creation and improved knowledge utilization. According to Wiig (1997), there are eight operational areas on which knowledge management should focus:

- Survey, develop, maintain, and secure the intellectual and knowledge resources of the company
- Promote knowledge creation and innovation by everyone
- Determine the knowledge and expertise required to perform effectively, organize it, make the requisite knowledge available, 'package' it (e.g. in training courses, procedures manuals or knowledge-based systems), and distribute it to the relevant points-of action
- Modify and restructure the company to use knowledge most efficiently, take advantage of opportunities to exploit knowledge assets, minimise knowledge gaps and bottlenecks, and maximise the value-added knowledge content of products and services
- Create, govern, and monitor future and long-term knowledge-based activities and strategies – particularly new knowledge investments – R&D, strategic alliances, acquisitions, important hiring programmes, etc., based on identified opportunities, priorities, and needs
- Safeguard proprietary and competitive knowledge and control use of knowledge to ascertain that only the best knowledge is used, that valuable knowledge does not atrophy, and that knowledge is not given away to competitors
- Provide knowledge management capabilities and a knowledge architecture so that the company's facilities, procedures, guidelines, standards, and practices facilitate and support active knowledge management as part of the company's practices and culture

- Measure performance of all knowledge assets and account for them – at least internally – as capitalised assets to be built, exploited, renewed, and otherwise managed as part of fulfilling the company's mission and objectives.

However, according to Snowden (2002), some of the basic concepts underpinning knowledge management described above are now being challenged: knowledge is not a 'thing', or a system (Rubenstein-Montano et al., 2001), but an ephemeral, active process of relating. In the opinion of Stacy (2001), if one takes this view then no one, let alone a company, can own knowledge. Knowledge itself cannot be stored, nor can intellectual capital be measured, and certainly neither of them can be properly managed. Stacy accurately summarizes many of the deficiencies of common thinking, and is one of a growing group of authors who base their ideas on the science of complex systems. However, this new understanding does not require the abandonment of much of which has been valuable.

To sum up, there is no final solution in knowledge management. The patterns of knowledge are always changing. The best approach or solution for the moment is one that keeps things moving along while keeping options open. Flexibility in approach and in thinking is a must. There are always different approaches to try. In fact, the ongoing conversation about knowledge is more important than coming up with the right answer.

Knowledge sharing

According to Lee and Bai (2003), to achieve the consistent planning objectives, *knowledge sharing* is necessary in organizations. However, many authors have defined the concept of knowledge sharing in slightly different ways. Lee (2001) defines knowledge sharing as activities of transferring or disseminating knowledge from one person, group, or organization to another. Bartol and Srivastava (2002) define knowledge sharing as individuals sharing organizationallyrelevant information, ideas, suggestions, and expertise with one another. Connelly and Kelloway (2003) describe knowledge sharing as a set of behaviours that involves the exchange of information or assistance to others. They make it clear that knowledge sharing is different from information sharing, which typically involves management making information about the organization (e.g. financial statements) available to employees at every level. Knowledge sharing contains an element of reciprocity; information sharing can be unidirectional and un-requested.

Ruuska and Vartiainen (2005) mention two types of challenges in knowledge sharing that often arise in project organizations. Firstly, how to prevent the 'reinvention of the wheel' and share knowledge accumulated in one project with others because project teams are temporary and a lot of learning may be lost when they disband. They further elaborate that first challenge gives rise to the second challenge: how to enhance the communication of peers working in dispersed projects, as relationships in project organizations are maintained cross-functionally. This may increase knowledge sharing yet at the same time isolate people from peers.

Connelly and Kelloway (2003) have described four predictors of employees' perceptions about knowledge sharing cultures in organization:

- Management's support for knowledge sharing
- Positive social interaction culture
- Technology
- Demographics.

They further elaborate that uncertainty about leadership commitment to knowledge sharing is the key challenge. This support, of course, must be encouraging rather than coercive; employees can receive suggestions on what and how much to share with their colleagues, but the final decision is always up to them. In an organization with a positive social interaction culture, both management and employees socialize and interact frequently with each other, with little regard for their organizational status. Certain demographic variables may also influence whether an employee will choose to share his or her knowledge. An organization's size may also be related to its knowledge sharing culture. Employees in smaller organizations are more likely to rely on each other and to interact with each other socially. Employees' ages and career stages may also affect their knowledge sharing behaviours. Through the size and utility of their social networks, experienced employees may simply be more able to share their knowledge because they know more, and they know the right people in the organization.

Knowledge sharing initiatives can be positive for an organization because there are clear benefits within an organization from sharing knowledge (e.g. Huemann and Winkler, 1998). However, once knowledge is codified and articulated, the organization risks the knowledge being imitated outside the organization, which could damage competitive advantage (Winter, 1987). Husted and Michailova (2002) argue that knowledge is inequitably disseminated in any organization and that knowledge sharing depends on the willingness of individuals to hint at the ownership of knowledge and share it when asked for. They further propose that efficient knowledge sharing involves direct contact and commitment on both sides of the exchange but as in practical terms, monitoring of knowledge sharing where it takes place in an efficient manner is difficult. In addition, Nonaka (1994) highlights that efficient knowledge sharing depends on the motivation of individuals to discover the knowledge they possess and to share it when required.

Knowledge-sharing mechanisms can be categorized as formal and informal mechanisms for sharing, integrating, interpreting, and applying know-what, know-how, and know-why embedded in individuals and groups that will aid in the performance of project tasks. Thus, in project-based companies, to enable effective sharing of knowledge across projects, knowledge-sharing mechanisms are the means by which individuals access knowledge from other project sources. Table 8.1 shows notions of know-what, know-how, and know-why concepts which can be also called as knowledge levels.

Furthermore, Boh (2007) presents a framework that classifies the knowledge-sharing mechanisms used by project-based organizations. He describes different dimensions of knowledge sharing mechanisms like (i) personalization versus codification, and (ii) individualization versus institutionalization. Personalization mechanisms are often assumed to be more ad hoc and informal, and codification mechanisms are assumed to be formal and involve the use of electronic databases. Individualization versus institutionalization distinguishes between mechanisms that enable the sharing of knowledge at the individual level, or at a collective level. The institutionalization dimension describes socialization tactics that are collective and formal in terms of the contexts in which organizations provide information to newcomers, while the individualization dimension describes socialization tactics that are individual and informal. Figure 8.3 gives a snapshot of different dimensions of knowledge-sharing mechanisms.

To sum up, knowledge sharing is an activity through which knowledge, skills, and expertise are exchanged among people, members (e.g. project team members), and/or an organization. Nowadays, many organizations have recognized that knowledge constitutes a valuable intangible asset for creating and sustaining competitive advantage. Knowledge-sharing activities are generally supported by knowledge management systems. However, it is important to realize that technology constitutes only one of the many factors that affect knowledge-sharing organizations. Knowledge sharing, therefore, constitutes a major challenge in the field of project implementation because some team

Table 8.1   Knowledge levels

Knowledge Level	Features	Practical Examples
'know-what' It specifies what action to take when presented with a set of stimuli. For instance, a salesperson who has been trained to know which product is best suited for various situations.	Least sophisticated variety Easy to apply Incorporated in many computer-systems	In the insurance and banking industries customer service representatives who use database systems to address customer questions about products ranging from dishwashers to the latest digital TV sets.
'know-how' It is knowing how to decide on an appropriate response based on a diagnostic process, whether in sales, medicine, or any other area. It permits a professional to determine which treatment or action is best.	Sophisticated variety Not easy to apply	In the above mentioned example, when customer service representatives suggest the appropriate available option that is most suitable/appropriate for the customers according to their requirements.
'know-why' It involves an understanding of the underlying theory and/or a range of experience that includes many instances of interactions and exceptions to the norms and conventional wisdom of a profession.	Most Sophisticated variety Complicate to apply	Knowing that an unusually high level of sales might be due to an interactive effect – an influence of one factor that only operates at certain levels of another factor – would also represent such 'know-why' knowledge.

Source: King, (2007).

members often tend to resist sharing their knowledge with the rest of the project team.

Storytelling

Many authors (e.g. Gabriel, 2000; Laufer and Hoffman, 2000; Denning, 2001, 2004; Simmons, 2002; Walsh, 2003) have recognized the importance of stories and storytelling as a means of knowledge acquisition and sharing. Stories stimulate the imagination and offer reassurance (Bettelheim, 1976), they provide moral education (MacIntyre, 1981),

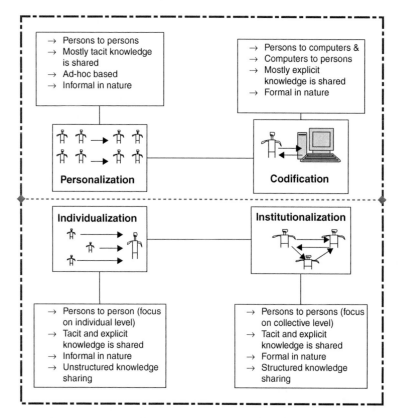

Figure 8.3 A snapshot of different dimensions of knowledge sharing mechanisms.

they justify and explain (Kemper, 1984), they inform, advise, and warn (van Dijk, 1975). Bruner (1990) claims that the story is the main mode of human knowledge, and according to Fisher (1987), the story is the main mode of communication.

Boden (1994), Drew and Heritage (1992), and Sachs (1995), have stressed the importance of informal conversations as well as storytelling and narratives. These ways of sharing knowledge are often framed in a community of practice which evolves around the sharing of experience related to work practice (e.g. Brown and Duguid, 1991; Wenger, 1998). This method of sharing experience relates to professional responsibilities, activities, and vocabulary. Since the actual work practice often differs from the canonical practice described in manuals and directive documents, the community of practice plays an important role for socializing and sharing the experiences of workarounds and trouble shooting.

By passing stories through communication networks, knowledge may be maintained for long periods of time even as organizational members come and go. Shared knowledge of norms and values emerge from these continuous processes of communication, contributing to the development of shared mental models (i.e. knowledge structures) and culture. However, it should be remembered that one of the critical aspects of storytelling through social networks is that knowledge embedded in a story must be validated as it is passed from one individual to the next. Duncan and Weiss (1979) argue that such validation is necessary if individual knowledge is to become organizational knowledge.

On stories

A story requires at least three elements: an original state of affairs, an action or an event, and the consequent state of affairs (Czarniawska, 1998). For example, in the story 'The project was about two weeks late, when the installation works started at the site. However, when a local contractor was hired, the project succeeded in catching up the time lag', the words 'The project was about ... started at the site' form an original state of affairs, the words 'However, when a local contractor was hired' form an action, and the last words 'the project succeeded in catching up the time lag' form a consequent state of the project. In addition to this, in order for these sentences to form a story, they require a plot, that is, some way to bring them into a meaningful whole. According to Czarniawska (1998), the easiest way to do this is by introducing chronology (as seen in the example earlier), which in the mind of the listener easily turns into causality.

Propp (1968) points out that the story has a double function: reporting on events, and putting these events into a meaningful whole. To bring an event into a whole, a plot is needed, for example, ordering the events chronologically or in some other sequence. A story may thus be seen as a way of making sense of new events by integrating them into the plot, making them understandable in relation to the context of what has happened.

According to Mangham and Overington (1987, p. 193), stories and experiences are linked together. 'If we listen carefully to the talk around, it is not difficult to think that storytelling goes on almost non-stop. People transform their lives and their experiences into stories with practiced ease.' A story emerges as the privileged form of sense making, as 'the primary form by which human experience is made meaningful' (Polkinghorne, 1988, p. 1).

A story may contain an explicitly formulated point, or else listeners are supposed to provide one. For example, the story 'The customer demands a better performance for the system we deliver' carries some ambiguity and therefore it leaves openings for meaning. But the story 'The customer demands 10 per cent better output for the system we deliver' is better, because it describes exactly the demand of the customer.

The success of individual projects entails gathering stories that embody knowledge (e.g. Laufer and Hoffman, 2000). However, it is important to understand that there are often many versions of the same stories. For example, Boddy and Paton (2004) talk about competing narratives, through which different people express different opinions about the objectives, progress, or success of projects. Thus, versions of stories vary according to who is telling them and who is listening to them. People remember different things, attach importance to different things, and view the projects from different viewpoints. For example, the literature mentions springboard stories (Denning, 2001) that communicate complex ideas and spark action, stories that lead people into the future (Simmons, 2002; Denning, 2004), and stories that share knowledge. In the next two sections the discussion deals with the latter type of stories, that is, knowledge-sharing stories in a project work context. Moreover, knowledge-sharing stories are divided into *project company stories* and *project implementation stories*.

Project company stories

Project company stories are stories which are commonly told by people in project-based companies. These stories are both inscriptions of past performances as well as scripts and staging instructions for future performances. However, it is important to note that they are highly charged narratives, not merely recounting 'events', but interpreting them, enriching them, enhancing them, and infusing them with meaning (cf. Gabriel, 2000, p. 31). Omissions, exaggerations, subtle shifts in emphasis, timing, and metaphors are some of the mechanisms which are used in the creation of project company stories. In other words, project company stories include a lot of tacit elements. This means that the responses invited by project company stories are not to challenge accurate facts, but to engage with their meanings (cf. Reason and Hawkins, 1988). However, this is not to deny the factual basis of project company stories, nor to reduce the stories to an elaboration of facts.

Project company stories are, for example, about how to make successful decisions regarding a tricky customer. These stories are often less about *what* to do and more about *how* to do.

When a project contract has been won, a kick-off meeting is often necessary to get things started. In this meeting the project manager explains the particular project organization, outlines the procedures that will apply, and answers questions about these issues. This meeting also gives team members an opportunity for storytelling. The team members, who are familiar with the customer, may tell illustrating stories about the customer's key persons, organizational culture, and circumstances which are not otherwise known. Furthermore, at the conclusion of the assignment, project team members contribute to the project-based company's organizational memory what they think they have learned when carrying out a particular assignment on a particular project.

Knowledge encoded in project company stories may be partly lost when existing patterns of interaction are repeatedly broken up or are not allowed to form. Companies that fail to reinforce storytelling may experience a loss of knowledge as relationship atrophy. On the other hand, organizational memories may be purposely eliminated to cope with change and to promote learning. Stories about difficult situations do not always flow easily, not only because of the fear of repercussions from admitting past mistakes but also because, in the flush of success, people tend to forget what they learned along the way. As a result, project company stories cannot be compelled, they have to be teased out.

Project implementation stories

Project implementation stories are problem-oriented and they are told in the course of project implementation. These stories provide ideas about whether the project is on the right track, and about possible changes related to the implementation of the project (e.g. Amtoft, 1994). Project implementation stories are, for example, about finding solutions to technical problems. This means that project implementation stories are often accurate and explicit descriptions focusing on problems and they include explanations for solutions. These stories often lack a detectable plot. They are about problems and how they got – or did not get – resolved and why. In other words, project implementation stories typically contain the context, the solution, and the explanation, which explains why the solution had the effect that it did. In Orr's (1990, 1996) ethnography of copy machine maintenance the war stories served as an important tool in the process of solving problems as well as in the distribution of the maintenance workers' experiences. The service technicians shared knowledge not covered in manuals but achieved through practical experience. In Orr's study, the stories were mainly distributed during lunch breaks and other informal occasions. That is, a project implementation story tells of the mechanism underlying the result.

Because project implementation stories are often about problems, they typically have a negative tone. Therefore much of the challenge in storytelling lies in creating settings that enable members to talk about what has gone wrong and how it can be fixed. However, irrespective of their form and content, project implementation stories can often give accurate explanations of the present problems of the project. This means that these stories are quite different from project company stories which are often inaccurate and in which the truth does not lie in facts, but in the meaning.

However, it should be remembered that neither of these two types of stories is ever a neutral, objective presentation, but rather a subjective indication of the significance of the project to an individual storyteller, project team, company, or other context in which stories are told. There are also rarely two different, pure forms of stories, but rather stories in which current and past experiences interact. It is, however, crucially important to hear many versions of the same stories. With this, performed storytelling entails a pervading ambivalence: on the one hand storytelling can subordinate people, adapting all to one grand story. On the other hand, storytelling practice in a project-based company can be liberating, by showing people that there are many stories, storytellers, and storytelling events (Boje, 1995).

Managers of project-based companies are in a key position to advance knowledge sharing with the help of storytelling. In practice this means, for example, that:

- They proclaim the usefulness of storytelling with the help of different means; keynote addresses, for example, or in the personnel bulletins of their companies
- They create company culture in which personal and informal face-to-face interaction – and thus also storytelling – is valued
- They equip the known storytellers with appropriate storylines.

To sum up, stories contain valuable knowledge about the various things like technology, customer, and organizational culture, which are often sources of problems. However, different stories create different understandings. For example, the project implementation stories are about problems and how they are solved, while the project company stories are more about meanings, including cultural issues within the company. In any case, narrative forms of knowledge sharing enrich an understanding of problems that exist in projects and project-based companies.

Writing

According to Olson (1977), there is a progression from oral language statements to written statements, both culturally and developmentally implying increasing explicitness. An important part of organized activity – like project-based business – is to produce texts for recording, directing, informing, inviting, entertaining, and so on (von Krogh and Roos, 1995a). The texts produced in organizations are many, and vary in style, form, and content: reports, memos, letters, procedures, vision and mission statements, value statements, strategic plans, job descriptions, contracts, and so on. These texts result from the knowledge of an individual, or a team in many instances. Being signs and marks, they are objections (Berger and Luckman, 1966; Berger, 1981) that lend themselves to further study and inquiry by organizational members.

As discussed earlier, according to autopoiesis theory, information does not equal knowledge, but information is a process which enables the creation of knowledge. In effect, the autopoietic system, whether at the organizational or individual level, does not import information (Luhmann, 1986). It continuously creates knowledge based on input data. This means that text belongs to the environment of the organization as the organization is an autopoietic knowledge system. It follows from the discussions of the relationship between *languaging* (cf. this notion later is this chapter) and organizational knowledge that text also belongs to the environment of conversations. Texts, produced by the organization, can be read at various times (i.e. observed) by the organizational members, project teams, and so on, and can be subject to conversations. As such, they become an input to the cognitive processes of individual organizational members, stimulating the creation of organizational knowledge.

However, sharing the assumptions of autopoiesis theory, text does not give an adequate representation of what the author knows (Calvino, 1990), not even to an observer of the processes of writing and reading. The two processes, writing and reading are distinct and belong to, at least in the case of textual dissemination, two different cognitive domains (Becker, 1991).

A particular type of text that is central to autopoiesis theory is *self-descriptions*. Luhmann (1990b, p. 253) defines self-descriptions as 'fix(ing) a structure or a "text" for possible observations which can now be made more systematically, remembered, and handed down more easily, and which can now be connected better to each other'. Elements of self-descriptions are covered in many organizational texts that result from self-observation of the organization. Some common self-descriptions found in organizations are as follows:

- Descriptions of organizational structure: the way the organization conceives of itself in terms of relations between tasks, people, positions, titles, and so on.
- Procedures and manuals: the way the organization proposes guidelines for the execution of functions within the organization.
- Policies: the various functions to be covered by the organization, and the possible products and markets it serves.
- Letters to stakeholders: the organization's way of describing important issues and events.
- Historical accounts: show the organization's conception of its own evolution into what it can currently describe as itself.

In sum, writing is the representation of language in a textual medium through the use of a set of signs or symbols. Project-based companies and project-teams produce numerous different texts: contracts, reports, memos, e-mails, plans, job descriptions, and so on. However, text does not give an exact representation of what the author knows (cf. autopoitic epistemology in chapter 5).

Boundary elements and perturbations

To be considered an autopoietic system requires that an organization has identifiable boundaries and that it is capable of continually producing a boundary, but does not require an explicit definition of the boundary or require specific *boundary elements*. For example, Mingers (1995) simply suggests that the components involved must create a boundary defining the entity, that is, a whole interacting with its environment.

Boundary can also be defined as the fundamental distinction between the system and its environment, although the nature of the distinction can vary with time and location. For example, in organizations as systems 'the boundary is created by individuals' knowledge pertaining to the organization-environment criterion. Each individual will form his or her own boundaries of the organization and recreate these dynamically as a part of their individual knowledge base' (von Krogh and Roos, 1995a, p. 57). In this sense, the autopoietic notion of boundary differs fundamentally from various atomistic notions of boundaries in the theories of company (Maula, 2006).

Indeed, an autopoietic system, like a project-based company, is a unity contained within and producing an identifiable boundary. It holds that in the context of the company the boundary consists of non-physical boundary elements that connect the company with its environment and enable interaction with it. They enable and maintain the reciprocal interaction and co-evolution between the project-based company and its environment. They enable sensing of the environment.

According to this definition, the project-based company's learning and renewal is enabled by boundary elements that are defined as various *roles* and *functions*. They can be embedded in employees and other people, groups, units, or information and communication systems. They may also consist of other kinds of advanced socio-technical solutions embodied in roles and functions. For example, a project manager role can be embedded in various people within a project-based company. Project managers interact with clients, acquire experiences, and accumulate new knowledge about projects. Such roles – but not the physical persons themselves – are continually produced by self-producing, project-based companies. Thus, an organization like a project-based company can be connected to its environment in various ways, and therefore the term 'boundary element' includes many ways to constitute boundaries (cf. Sivula et al., 1997; Maula 2000).

Consequently, environmental change such as the evolution of a technological standard might depreciate and erode the usefulness of an existing knowledge-stock such as technical know-how. Other environmental changes like the opening of new business opportunities or the extinguishing of old ones could also stimulate adjustments in and orient the search behaviour of the company. Changes in the overall economic context of an industry may also have an immediate effect on a project-based company's performance (Mollona, 2008).

The potential for a system – for example a project-based company – to communicate with its environment creates the conditions for the emergence of new behaviour and evolution. As Burgelman (1983) points out, a company may react to environmental change by absorbing or mirroring exogenous disturbances, or by amplifying them. In the first case, a *homeostatic* tendency often brings a company's behaviour back to its original trajectory. In the second case, a company undertakes an increasing divergence from its original trajectory. This latter case might generate difficulty in governing the system, but might also give rise to *homeoresis* – that is, a condition that brings out the capacity of a system not merely to return to its state prior to the disturbances, but to seek out new developmental pathways through successive instabilities (Burgelman, 1983).

As outlined earlier, autopoietic system theory accepts *perturbations* (i.e. triggers) that may lead to compensations in its structure. It does not treat them as input to the organization. An organization can also be triggered internally. Further, it is important to realize that an autopoietic system treats all perturbations in relation to its own identity, survival, and evolution. In other words, an autopoietic system interprets all signals and other inputs from the environment as perturbations that can lead to compensations in their own system.

To sum up, the autopoietic organization as a project-based company interacts by boundary elements – roles and functions – with the environment, leading to an organization's capability to absorb and create new knowledge. Boundary elements act like connecting absorption surfaces between an organization and its environment. Further, perturbations facilitate change. They themselves are not reproduced by the system, but exposure to the perturbations and the capability to respond to them is. Project-based companies can increase the utilization of perturbations, for example, through interaction and communication with the environment, by improving exposure and sensitivity to perturbations, and by experimenting.

Interactivity

Interaction plays a ubiquitous role in project business. Individuals and organizations interact to find the right party with whom to communicate; to arrange, manage, and integrate the activities associated with this exchange; and to monitor performance. These interactions occur within companies, between companies, and all the way through markets to the end customer. They take many everyday forms – management meetings, phone conversations, sales calls, problem solving, reports, memos – but their underlying purpose is always to enable the exchange of goods, services, or ideas. However, the literature handles the terms 'interaction' and 'knowledge sharing' more or less interchangeably. Here, knowledge transfer means communication without the exact object (e.g. person, team, or organization), and the notion interaction means communication with a more exact object.

Interactions include the methods used to communicate reciprocally and to co-evolve with the environment, for example, with clients. It also includes social coupling that refers to communication with individuals in the external environment of the organization. This means that knowledge flows connect a company's units and employees, and facilitate interaction with its environment (e.g. Gupta and Govindarajan, 1993; Hedlund, 1993).

According to Luhmann (1986), both individuals and organizations (e.g. project teams and project-based companies) use *meaning* as their basic form of interaction, that is, the kinds of knowledge an autopoietic system acquires and understands, is represented in the form of meanings. However, people use their *consciousness*, and organizations utilize *communication* as the basic mode of knowledge creation.

Consciousness

Numerous experiments with human beings have shown that *consciousness* is composed of many dimensions. It is created by many different brain functions, and yet it is a single coherent experience. For example, when the smell of a perfume evokes a pleasant or unpleasant sensation, one experiences a single, coherent mental state composed of sensory perceptions, memories, and emotions. The experience is not constant, and may be extremely short. Mental states are transitory, continually arising and subsiding. However, it does not seem possible to experience them without some finite span of duration. Another important observation is that the experiential state is always embodied. That is, embedded in a particular field of sensation. In fact, most mental states seem to have a dominant sensation that colours the entire experience.

Psychical-mental activities constitute, in the form of recurring processes, the consciousness of an individual. An object in the situation of an individual, for example a customer's requirement, provides the consciousness with a meaningful content. A meaning emerges in the consciousness as this content becomes referred to the object located in the situation in such a manner that a person understands what the object implies (Pihlanto, 2000, 2002, 2009). This means that an individual can understand an object only in terms of meaning. The network of all meanings accumulated in the consciousness is called the world view of an individual. The world view is recurrently redefined as new meanings emerge (i.e. meanings from perturbations which trigger information processes) on the basis of new contents from one's situation.

Everything in this process occurs in terms of understanding, which means that a person knows, feels, believes in, and dreams about phenomena and objects located in his or her situation in terms of their 'being something'. Understanding is complete only after a meaning is generated. Meanings are components from which the world, as people experience it, is constructed. In the consciousness, a continuous restructuring of meanings occurs as a person actively acquires or passively receives perturbations from a situation, that is, observes and creates new knowledge. Meanings are often forgotten, fading into unconsciousness and perhaps retrieved into the consciousness anew.

What an individual project team member brings to the knowledge creation situation has an important influence on what he or she can learn from another individual. This means that an individual's personal world view profoundly influences the way he or she experiences the situation at hand. '[A]lthough it is the individual who learns, this individual is one who has a language, a culture, and a history' (Usher 1989, p. 32). Thus, a project team member's personal world view affects, for example, how he or she commits to the project at hand, and what he or she can in the first place understand about the knowledge communicated. People always learn in relation to their world views or what they have learned before (cf. autopoietic epistemology in chapter 5).

To conclude, an individual understands an object only in terms of meaning. That is, a project team member's existing world view determines how a piece of data (i.e. perturbation) is interpreted. The information process may be influenced by his or her position within the project, previous experiences, other project team members, and the environment. To establish uniformity of shared interpretation, there needs to be uniformity in world views among the people of a project team. This is easier when new triggering perturbations are framed in a consistent and familiar manner. If a new perturbation is framed in a different manner around different people on a project team, it is likely that there will be a diversity of shared understanding of the perturbation.

Communication

According to autopoietic epistemology, knowledge *communication* means indirect transfer of knowledge between the world views of individuals (Pihlanto, 2000, 2002; Koskinen and Pihlanto, 2006). This transfer occurs under regulation of parties' personal situations in highly personally oriented ways. These personal world views are derived from the individuals' previous experiences, that is, they are acquired from social and cultural environments or situations, and they are partly forged by the individuals' own awareness and efforts. They contain pre-suppositions and assumptions that people have developed in the past. These world views are not something about which these people can readily give a comprehensive account. Parts of the contents of world views are even totally unconscious, but they can still influence behaviour.

According to Maturana (1988), communication is not a transmission of information, but rather a coordination of behaviour among living organisms (e.g. project team members) through mutual structural coupling. Such mutual coordination of behaviour is the key characteristic of communication for all living beings, and it becomes more and more subtle and elaborate with increasing complexity. Communication cannot be said to have occurred until the receiver has understood something, even if it was not what was intended (Mingers, 2002). This means that the very nature of communication remains undefined until it has been interpreted by the other.

Weick (1979) uses the term 'sense making' in that people justify their behaviour by making it meaningful and explicable. Their behaviour, Weick points out, is interlocking. That is, behaviour with one individual triggers behaviour with another, which again serves recursively to modify the behaviour of the first. Project-based companies and projects within them, then, are communication-oriented in the sense that they consist of people who interact and attribute meanings to their actions.

In sum, any communication generates meaning, whether intended or not. An autopoietic system determines what for it is relevant data, how it may be embodied, and how it may be interpreted. In doing this, it draws its own distinction as to what belongs to the system and what does not.

Absorptive capacity

According to autopoietic epistemology, the premise of *absorptive capacity* is that the company and the people working for it need prior related knowledge to assimilate and use new knowledge (Keller, 1996; Lane and Lubatkin, 1998; Tsai, 2001; Zahra and George, 2002). Also the research on memory development suggests that accumulated prior knowledge increases both the ability to memorize new knowledge, and the ability to recall and use it.

Badaracco (1991) claims that a human being cannot take advantage of new knowledge unless he or she has 'social software' connected to that knowledge. Also Cohen and Levinthal (1990), who introduced the 'absorptive capacity' concept, claim that an individual's ability to utilize new knowledge in problem solving purposes depends largely on his or her previous knowledge. For example, the chances that a project-based company will be successful in an engineering project can depend on the staff's experience of similar projects (cf. Koskinen, 2000). Therefore, when people in a project-based company solve problems, they are guided by the knowledge they have gained from similar previous problems.

With respect to the acquisition of knowledge, Bower and Hilgard (1981) suggest that a company's memory development is self-reinforcing in that the more objects, patterns, and concepts are memorized, the more readily new knowledge about these constructs is acquired, and the more adept the individual is in using them in new settings. The concept of self-reinforcing that may lead to the neglect of new knowledge provides insight into difficulties which companies and individuals face when, for example, the technological basis of an industry changes (cf. immunity reactions later in this chapter). In other words, for a project-based company, a discontinuity in knowledge means either adaptation or extinction for competitors. If a company has all its resources committed to the existing knowledge, and does not possess the absorptive capacity to develop the required new knowledge, it may find itself locked out of the market (Schilling, 1988). This means that the autopoietic system may disintegrate.

To sum up, absorptive capacity is a limit to the rate or quantity of knowledge that an individual or a company can absorb. Conceptually, it is similar to information processing theory, but at the company level rather than the individual level.

Media

In daily practice, knowledge is communicated through symbols with an efficiency that will vary depending on the characteristics of the channels used for such communication. According to Boisot (1983), the process of codifying a message for communication involves the loss of knowledge that can only be recovered in situations where the receiver associates the same cluster of meaning (i.e. there are similar parts in their world views) with the symbols chosen, as does the sender. Therefore the communication of knowledge, which may give rise to uncertain or ambiguous interpretations (e.g. tacit knowledge), requires either the simultaneous activation of several channels of communication in order to minimize the loss of knowledge caused by the use of a single channel, or a prior sharing of experiences out of which emerges a convention that reduces uncertainty for the use of certain symbols (Shannon and Weaver, 1949).

An instance of the first type of communication would be the transmission of behaviour patterns by, for example, sight and touch which are used together to convey a message, as when a music master demonstrates the application of a skill to his pupils (Boisot, 1983). An example of the second type would be the use of the cross by Christians to convey an intangible cluster of meanings to one another that mix values, norms, and expectations in inexplicable ways (Boisot, 1983).

According to Bengtsson and Eriksson (2002), projects must be linked to their context and such links develop if there is a flow of knowledge into and out of these projects. The flow can be characterized by both leakiness and stickiness (cf. Brown and Duguid, 1991; Szulanski, 1996). This means that some projects require an easy flow – that is, leakiness – of relevant knowledge into the projects. Stickiness is the opposite of leakiness and refers to mechanisms that hinder the flow, and, therefore, if stickiness hinders the knowledge flow among the stakeholders of a project, the stickiness is negative for that project.

The leakiness and stickiness in different projects is related to the type of knowledge that is utilized (Bengtsson and Eriksson, 2002). For example, Szulanski (1996) describes the difficulties of transferring tacit knowledge as the stickiness of knowledge. Hansen (1999) distinguishes between simple and complex knowledge, and argues that simple knowledge (e.g. explicit knowledge) can be transferred in relationships with weak ties, as this type of knowledge is more leaky, whereas complex knowledge (e.g. tacit knowledge) must be transferred in relationships with strong ties, as it is stickier.

The richness of a *communication medium* can be analysed in terms of two underlying dimensions: the variety of cues the medium can convey and the rapidity of feedback the medium can provide (Berger and Luckman, 1966; Daft and Lengel, 1984; Trevino, et al., 1987). That is to say, the media have varying capacities for resolving ambiguity, meeting interpretation needs, and sharing knowledge, and they can be placed along a five-step continuum: (1) face-to-face, (2) telephone, (3) written personal, (4) written formal, and (5) numeric formal (Daft and Lengel, 1984) (Figure 8.4).

Trevino et al. (1987) suggest that there is a link between the selection of media and the ambiguity of the message to be conveyed. In situations characterized by a high degree of ambiguity, no established scripts or symbols are available to guide behaviour. 'Meaning must

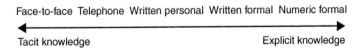

Figure 8.4   Media richness vs knowledge communicability.

be created and negotiated as individuals look to others for cues and feedback to help interpret the message' (Trevino et al., 1987, p. 557). Berger and Luckman (1966) argue that most experience of others takes place in face-to-face situations because the other person's subjectivity is available through a 'maximum of symptoms' – the here-and-now of each individual continuously impinges on the other, both consciously and subconsciously, as long as the face-to-face situation continues. The authors further argue that misinterpretation is less likely in face-to-face interactions than in less close mediums.

Given the strategic importance of face-to-face communication in project teams, one must carefully consider the effects of any social or team-related processes that could significantly affect the interaction patterns of project team members. Specifically, the actual communication activities of project team members are examined as a function of the length of time the members have worked and shared experiences with one another, that is, as a function of team longevity (Katz, 1982). As team longevity increases over time, a number of different but interrelated social processes begin to affect team behaviour. They cause members of long-tenured teams to become increasingly isolated from outside sources of knowledge and influence. Further, the research of many scientists (e.g. Allen, 1977; Katz, 1982) has consistently shown that interpersonal communication, rather than technical reports, publications, or other written documentation, are the primary means by which engineering professionals collect and transfer important knowledge into their project teams.

One of the important principles in organizational theory is that teams strive to structure their work environments to reduce the amount of stress they face by directing their activities towards a more workable and predictable level of certainty and clarity (Pfeffer, 1981). Based on this perspective, project team member interacting over a long period will develop standard work patterns that are familiar and comfortable, patterns in which routine and precedent play a relatively large part. Weick (1979), for example, discusses the strong tendency for groups to establish certain stable structures of interlocked behaviours and relationships simply because it keeps them feeling secure and confident in what they do.

To sum up, the knowledge utilization taking place in a project work context is not only about the processing of objective data but it also requires that the subjective views, intuitions, and inklings of the individual team members are presented, tested, and put into use. This is especially the case in an organic project work environment. These subjective views are largely shared through informal face-to-face interaction.

Language and languaging

'We human beings are human beings only in language. Because we have language, there is no limit to what we can describe, imagine, and relate. It thus permeates our whole ontology as individuals: from walking to attitudes to politics' (Maturana and Varela, 1987, p. 212). 'The language we use influences how we experience our world and thus how we know our world' (Sorri and Gill, 1989, p. 71).

Drucker (1954) was among the first to point out the relevance of *language* in management: according to him, managers have to learn to know language, to understand what words are and what they mean. Further, and perhaps most importantly, they have to acquire a respect for language as our most precious gift and heritage. The manager must understand the meaning of the old definition of rhetoric as the art which draws men's hearts to the love of true knowledge. In the opinion of Duncan and Weiss (1979, p. 91), 'frameworks exist within organizations and are to a large extent particular to a specific organization. That is, a given organization is characterized by a paradigm that is shared by organizational members in their socialization. Indeed, an organizational member must learn the system of concepts used within the organization if he or she is able to communicate and understand the actions they are to take and the actions taken by others'.

Pondy and Mitroff (1979) treat language as a kind of technology for processing data (i.e. perturbations or triggers) and meaning, and, as is the case with any production technology, language will also determine what inputs will be accepted and what transformations will be permitted. They identify four distinct roles for language in organizational behaviour:

- Control of perception: those events for which language expressions do not exist tend to be filtered out of consciousness.
- Attribution of meaning: by categorising streams of events, language gives meaning to our experiences.
- Facilitation of communication: old and new meanings can be communicated better.
- Provision of a channel of social influence: language is essential in the organization's power games.

The first of Pondy and Mitroff's four statements is, however, a little bit limited, because those expressions for which there is no language expression, may still be located in an individual's world view and also influence his or her behaviour. Of course, most important meanings are usually those which can be clearly expressed.

Indeed, language does not passively mirror the world. Instead, speech is a practical act that shapes and negotiates meanings (Blackler et al., 1998). This means, for example, that project team members operate within interpretative or discourse communities. The term 'project manager' only makes sense to members of a project team, who understand the deep meaning of it.

Our linguistic distinctions are not isolated but exist 'in the network of structural couplings that we continually weave through *languaging*' (Maturana and Varela, 1987, p. 234). Meaning arises as a pattern of relationships among these linguistic distinctions, and thus we exist in a 'semantic domain' created by our languaging. Self-awareness arises when we use the notion of an object and the associated abstract concepts to describe ourselves. Thus, the linguistic domain of human beings expands further to include reflection and consciousness.

Over time, organizations develop their own distinct domains of language (von Krogh and Roos, 1995a; Tannen, 1995). There are two explanations for this. First, the obvious explanation is that languaging may be understood as 'the stuff' that the organization is made of. By introducing the concept 'organization', people linguistically distinguish it from something else (i.e. the organization-environment distinction) (Fiol, 1989). Hence, the emergence of an entity/organization presupposes languaging (Bittner, 1974). Second, the broad linguistic distinction of organization-environment allows organizational members to make finer linguistic distinctions. This basic distinction allows them to coordinate their other linguistic distinctions given the concept of the organization. For example, the term 'customer' requires the environment-organization distinction. Following this, it is possible to understand a domain of language as tradition. In the process of languaging an organizational tradition is formed. This tradition will affect languaging, or in the words of Varela (1979, p. 268): 'Everything said is said from a tradition'.

Thus, given the variability of language, it is meaningful to speak of organizational languaging. Organizational languaging presupposes organizational knowledge and gives rise to distinctions that form an integral part of the concept of organization. Organization has its tradition from which new conversations can take place. It demands that its members continue to language about it on all scales in order for it to survive, or in other words, to continue its autopoiesis (von Krogh and Roos, 1995a).

Individual knowledge has self-referential properties since it stems from observation and distinction-making by the individual. As outlined above, the statement that everything said is said by an observer, is an illustration of this kind of self-reference. Languaging of organizations is also self-referential. Previous language and arguments form a tradition which is necessary for the production of new language and arguments. The organization, then, emerges as a self-referential system of knowledge, that, like any such system has self-knowledge and is able to describe and act on itself (von Foerster, 1972). It can, for example, produce arguments about its own argumentation processes; why they work or do not work, and how they should change. The organization can never step out of its own processes of argumentation (von Krogh and Roos, 1995a).

In sum, knowledge travels on language. Language is the verbal blueprint of our experience. Without a word or a language to describe our experience, we could not communicate what we know. Every mode of knowledge travels on a different language. Language initiates us into a particular world of experience. For example, traditional management uses the language of statistical control, inspection, and balance sheets. One is not 'initiated' into management ranks without learning this language. Expanding organizational knowledge means we must expand the languages we use to describe our work experience.

Metaphors

A *metaphor* is an assertion that A is B or that A is like B (Easton and Araujo, 1993). For example, one might say that 'life is just a bowl of cherries' or 'an atom is like the solar system'. It is important to recognize that a metaphor, as a figure of speech, is not simply an object, it expresses a relationship. To capture this relationship the individuals will use the terminology of base and target domains. A metaphor implies that the target domain 'is like' the base domain. The similarity between the domains is a crucial aspect of the process of using metaphors. Thus, metaphors in language are more than simply literary devices. They are central to research processes and ways of knowing as well as being ubiquitous in everyday language.

Linguists have proposed that words are introduced into a language whenever it becomes desirable to make functionally important distinctions in a given context of human endeavour (Bickerton, 1993). For example, externalizing tacit knowledge into explicit knowledge means finding a way (e.g. a word) to express the inexpressible. One of the means for doing this is through the usage of figurative language and symbolism – metaphor (e.g. Tsoukas, 1991). Using metaphors is a distinctive method of perception. It is a way for individuals grounded in different contexts and with different experiences to understand something intuitively through the use of imagination and symbols without the need for analysis or generalization (von Krogh and Roos, 1995b). Metaphors are special kinds of meanings in a person's world view. Through metaphors, people put together what they know in new ways and begin to express what they know but cannot yet say. As such, metaphor is highly effective in fostering direct commitment to the creative process in the early stages of knowledge creation.

To conclude, a metaphor can merge two or more different and distant areas of experience into a single, inclusive image or symbol, what Black (1962, p. 38) has aptly described as 'two ideas in one phrase'. By establishing a connection between different things that seem only distantly related, metaphors set up a discrepancy or conflict.

Boundary objects

Boundary object (e.g. Star, 1989; Star and Griesemer, 1989; Carlile, 2002, 2004; Bechky, 2003; Cacciatori, 2003; Koskinen, 2005a, b; Koskinen and Mäkinen, 2009) is a concept to refer to objects that serve as an interface between different individuals and/or organizations. It is an entity that is located in situations of the individuals concerned, and therefore shared by several different communities. However, it is viewed or used differently by each of them. As Star (1989) points out, the boundary object in an organization works because it necessarily contains sufficient detail to be understandable by the different parties, however, neither party is required to understand the full context of use by the other. Boundary object serves as a point of mediation and negotiation around intent.

Boundary objects are flexible in adapting to the local needs and constraints of all the parties sharing them. These objects are robust enough to maintain a common identity across different stakeholders and they can be abstract or concrete. Furthermore, they are often weakly structured in common use, and become strongly structured when they are used by individuals. Within a shared context (i.e. mutual knowledge, mutual beliefs, and mutual assumptions), 'perspective taking' occurs through boundary objects (Boland and Tenkasi, 1995). They are anything perceptible by one or more of the senses, that is, anything that can be observed consciously or subconsciously.

Boundary objects can be artefacts, documents and even vocabulary that can help people from different organizations to build a shared understanding. They are interpreted differently by different organizations and people, and it is the acknowledgement and discussion of these differences that enables a shared understanding to be formed. This means that the meanings formed on the basis of boundary objects may be different in different people's world views, but they are, however, to such a degree similar with each other, that there is the assumption of a shared understanding.

Boundary objects can serve as a co-ordinator of perspectives of various constituencies for a particular purpose. For example, a contract that is produced in project business negotiations translates the consultations of supplier and customer into a common understanding that can be processed. This boundary object serves as a kind of co-ordinating mechanism between supplier and customer, and, therefore, also between their different world views. According to Bowker and Star (2002, p. 297) 'the creation and management of boundary objects is a key process in developing and maintaining coherence across intersecting communities'.

People entering into a project-based relationship have to create shared understandings. This means that the interaction between the people involved in a project is a critical factor in enabling mutual understanding. Therefore, a boundary object may function as a fostering factor in designing knowledge communication systems in heterogeneous cultural project settings. Successful communication between different project participants starts with clarifying the semantic differences and commonalties, and then proceeds with the negotiated construction of coherence between the people involved (Harvey, 1996).

For example, a boundary object can be a helpful tool in combining the understandings of differently oriented project team members involved in the formation of a technology company's product development plan in an organic project work environment (Figure 8.5). While the business-oriented team members' view could include a plan which is based on the company's technological resources and capabilities, they do, however, tend to focus on products and markets to such an extent that the importance of technology is inevitably underestimated. Business-oriented team members are often lacking in experience and culture to establish and lead a technology company for a maximum return. Although they accept risk, which is more or less quantifiable, many are temperamentally and culturally uncomfortable dealing with what they perceive as uncertainty in technology. They see the occasional successful results from technology development (a new product or a reduction in costs), but they also know of multiple failures (cf. von Krogh and Roos, 1996b).

Moreover, when technology-oriented team members identify and select new or additional technologies which the company seeks to master, this analysis largely determines how technological resources

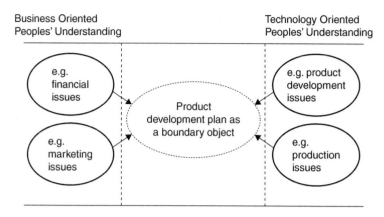

Figure 8.5   Product development plan as a boundary object.

are allocated toward product development. Because determining the directions in which the company intends to expand its technological capabilities is a major decision, it generally implies heavy investment, and thus such a decision has a decisive impact on the company's future. This, in turn, may mean that business-oriented team members do not understand all the technical jargon and the basis with the help of which technology oriented managers try to justify these investments. Consequently, the knowledge developed by the technology-oriented managers may be in conflict with the knowledge developed by the business-oriented managers. In other words, there is a great need to create a boundary object to coordinate differently oriented managers' understandings.

In this creation process, strongly structured boundary objects (the knowledge of business- and technology-oriented project people, represented by thick lines in Figure 8.5) are transformed into a weakly structured boundary object (the product development plan, represented by a thin line) when individuals collaborate to produce a plan. The plan emerges as more than an instrument for guidance: it becomes the individuals' interpretation of the project goal (i.e. the new product development plan) made into a collective reality. The intersectional nature of the individuals' shared work creates a weakly structured boundary object which includes multiple views simultaneously, and which must meet the demands of each other. Different views of particular business functions are included in this plan. Its boundary nature is reflected by the fact that it is simultaneously concrete and abstract. Thus, the developed boundary object (i.e. the project development plan) is often internally heterogeneous.

Crystallization of a boundary object is achieved when all the people involved feel that it corresponds to what they know tacitly. This means that the developed boundary object does not accurately describe the details of a project's goal. It is abstracted from all business domains, and may be fairly vague. Nevertheless, it is adaptable to an individual domain precisely because it is weakly structured; it serves as a means of communicating and co-operating symbolically – a good enough road map for all project stakeholders. In practice, a goal arises gradually with differences in the degree of abstraction. It results in the deletion of individual contingencies from the common object and has the advantage of adaptability.

Moreover, the creation of metaphoric boundary objects is a process whereby an organization develops and strengthens its knowledge domains. As a metaphoric boundary object strengthens, it becomes better able to support a company's innovation process. This means that the company develops a more accurate metaphor to describe a target idea. Strengthening signifies a movement from a global, undifferentiated naming to a more precise explication of constructs, where more coherent meaning structures are developed than preceding ones. Metaphoric boundary objects progressively clarify themselves over a period of time to successfully solve innovation problems. This means that the creation of metaphoric boundary objects is a process of posing and solving puzzles, thereby elaborating and refining the vocabulary that embody them. Agreement that knowledge is progressing is agreement that the metaphoric boundary object is strengthening.

Metaphors draw their power from being boundary objects. Once a company has found a metaphor particularly powerful, that metaphor serves to foster understanding between the people working for the company. However, not just any metaphor will do. The skill lies in finding the right metaphor – one that generates creative and co-ordinating responses among individuals. Indeed, crafting the right metaphoric boundary object is an organizational skill.

To sum up, when a boundary object is weakly structured, it may, however, play a significant role in the sharing of knowledge and understanding between project stakeholders. And in contrast, when a boundary object is strongly structured, it can function as a co-ordinating mechanism in the communication of knowledge. This is, what a boundary object gains in structure, it loses in creativity and tacit knowledge communication.

The creation of a metaphoric boundary object is a process whereby an organization (e.g. a project-based company or a project) develops and strengthens its knowledge domains, that is, a metaphor draws its power from acting as a boundary object.

Commitment and motivation

Commitment can be a powerful force for change (Burgess and Turner, 2000). Total commitment to an idea can provide individuals with the motivation and energy required to sacrifice everything in the pursuit of seemingly impossible goals. This power has been recognized by religious, political and military organizations for centuries, and more recently by business organizations.

An employee's lack of commitment to an organization (e.g. a project) and its goals has been identified as a major constraint on its performance, including its ability to change (Mullins, 2007). While project-based companies and projects would be unwise to expect individuals to sacrifice everything in pursuit of their goals, the ability to harness even a fraction of this power could provide them with a real impetus and focus for change (e.g. Burgess and Turner, 2000).

Motivation, in turn, is an internal psychological process, which starts, re-enforces, directs, and supports goal-directed behaviour. In engineering projects the question is often how to get people interested in the project and how to get them involved in dialogue. When, during a project, one speaks of motivation, one generally means how to keep a person's interest and how to keep him or her going ahead despite difficulties (cf. Buchanan and Huczynski, 1997).

Osterloh and Frey (2000) make a distinction between extrinsic (i.e. pay for performance) and intrinsic (i.e. undertaken for one's need for satisfaction) motivational approaches. They argue that the latter is crucial when tacit knowledge is to be transferred between teams and team members, as explicit motivation (i.e. pricing systems) is unlikely to work because the transfer of tacit knowledge cannot easily be observed or attributed to an individual. They further note that inappropriate organizational forms can hinder knowledge transfer. For example, extrinsic incentives may crowd out intrinsic motivation. Therefore, it is proposed that the tendency to hoard knowledge will be reduced if control mechanisms match the nature of the task and motivational factors (Figure 8.6).

Intrinsic motivation is a key driver of knowledge sharing. Extrinsic interventions such as rewards and evaluations may even adversely affect the knowledge sharing motivation because they appear to redirect

Motivation

		Extrinsic	Intrinsic
Control mechanisms	Social	Hoard	Share
	Mechanistic		Hoard

Figure 8.6 The propensity to hoard or share: control mechanisms and motivation.

attention from 'experimenting' to following rules or technicalities of performing a specific task. Furthermore, apprehension about evaluation can divert attention away from knowledge because individuals become reluctant to share or take risks in an environment where individual performance or failure may be negatively evaluated. In contrast, a sharing and learning environment (e.g. organic project work environment) allows individuals to be creative, allows freedom to take risks, play with ideas, and expand the range of considerations from which new innovative solutions may emerge.

According to Barkley and Saylor (1994), motivation is the behaviour of an individual whose energy is selectively directed toward a goal. Performance is the result of having both the ability and the motivation to do a task. These authors argue that motivation depends on satisfying the needs of individuals. Traditionally, motivation was equated with extrinsic rewards such as compensation, promotion, and additional benefits. The aim was to satisfy the basic needs of individuals for housing, food, and clothing (cf. Maslow's hierarchy of needs). 'Today, people need to be motivated by a higher order of needs, such as a sense of belonging, a feeling of accomplishment, improved self-esteem, and opportunities for personal growth' (Barkley and Saylor, 1994, p. 191).

Thus, rewards and recognition are essential to an individual to the promotion of his or her motivation (Robertson and Hammersley, 2000; McDermott and O'Dell, 2001). Intrinsic rewards are often sufficient to start implementing a task. Once an individual is established, he or she covets higher-level intrinsic rewards. In the opinion of Barkley and Saylor (1994), a good example of a reward that is effective in today's environment is an inclusion in personal development workshops. During personal development, recognition is particularly effective in reinforcing positive behaviour. An example of recognition could be the public announcement of a worker's achievements.

Badaracco and Ellsworth (1989), in turn, write that practitioners believe that people are motivated by self-interest and by a search for power and wealth. However, in the opinion of Senge (1990), if people are only interested in themselves, then the organization inevitably develops an atmosphere where they are no longer interested in common organizational objectives. In Senge's opinion, an alternative model could be one in which people want to be part of activities – like projects – which are greater and more significant than their personal and selfish goals. They want to contribute towards building something important, and they value doing it with others.

However, it is crucially important to understand that knowledge can be used to take action and to enforce spheres of influence, and then passing knowledge to colleagues brings about these potentials. Those who do not own this knowledge are deprived of the capacity to act or to influence respectively. From a project-based company perspective, this applies for instance to knowledge about procedures, methods, technology, suppliers, customers, and individuals from whom to ask. In this sense, an individual who passes his or her knowledge to another loses the exclusiveness of his or her influence, which might have created some job security and respect.

Indeed, 'knowledge is power' is a well-known phrase used to describe situations in which the person with the greatest knowledge has the highest reputation, and a monopoly on knowledge, and which causes knowledge to be hoarded instead of shared. Ego plays an important role in the knowledge sharing process (Brown and Starkey, 2000). According to Davenport and Prusak (1998), especially in situations where job security is low, knowledge as a power base becomes vital for an individual, and private knowledge might even be seen as a kind of insurance against losing one's job.

According to Hall (2003), people rarely give away anything without expecting something in return. He argues that knowledge is a private commodity and it is up to the owner to decide whether to share it or not. Thus, to entice project team members to share their knowledge as part of a social exchange transaction, team members need to be persuaded it is worth doing so. The stakeholders in a project work context expect mutual reciprocity that justifies their expense in terms of time and energy spent sharing their knowledge.

Thus, a lack of motivation to actively share knowledge across project boundaries leads to less than optimal project performance. Such a lack of sharing impedes the optimal development of projects (Pinto and Onsrud, 1995), and also hinders the development and utilization of a project technology's full potential (Frank, 1992). The impediments to sharing are both technological and cultural in nature, with the latter often being harder to overcome.

In special industries like engineering companies, employees often compete directly with each other through their special knowledge, gifts, and talents (cf. Disterer, 2001). It may be part of the individual culture of high performing employees that they voluntarily compete for a limited number of positions on the career ladder because they like to compete and to excel on principle (Quinn et al., 1996). But the drawback of the competition is obvious: people would be very cautious to share their knowledge openly with colleagues because it could mean giving up an individual lead. In these companies, competition and the corresponding incentives and rewards often encourage people to build a unique expertise in a certain area, and, in order to prove that expertise, for example, in relation to clients or whom to ask, they do not share it with colleagues.

Transferring knowledge may also be seen as additional work because communication takes time (cf. Disterer, 2001). Some individuals may not expect any reciprocal benefit from transferring their knowledge because they do not believe it would be beneficial, or they do not necessarily experience any benefit. And even if individuals do expect payback for their contributions, an answer to the natural question 'what is in it for me?' is often not clear for those people who suffer from a lack of motivation. According to Quinn et al. (1996), there is a need for employees to have some self-motivated creativity and some sense of 'care-why' in order to foster knowledge sharing.

However, in many cases, project team members can be motivated to share knowledge by money, promotion, travel opportunities, and so on. But, many researchers (e.g. Locke, 1984; Morris, 1988; Senge, 1990; Nonaka and Takeuchi, 1995; Leskinen, 1997) believe that genuine commitment and motivation derive from interesting content in the work and from the goals of the job being significant. 'If the work is valuable and the goals significant a person will endure dull stretches. In my opinion, it is not sufficient that the work is interesting, it must also be valuable' (Leskinen, 1997, p. 27).

Fortunately many projects offer significant goals (e.g. Ayas and Zeniuk, 2001). This means that when project team members work to create something new, the task at hand is clear, and there is pride and passion around what they create. This is especially true in the mechanical project work environment, but is also very applicable to projects implemented in organic project environments.

Moreover, the acquisition and sharing of knowledge within a project is assisted by a person's strong motivation to the goals of the project. The result of this is that external situational factors, such as management style and project culture, are often critically important to the success of knowledge sharing in project work. It is also important to remember that for knowledge sharing to occur, the motivation (i.e. both individual and organizational motivation) has to be positive and in this, the attitude of the project stakeholders in the sharing relationship is crucial. More intensive sharing of knowledge will come about when the people that are involved are committed to sharing, willing to negotiate, and work on the different issues related to sharing in a co-operative way. That is, the successful project-based company has a committed, motivated, and entrepreneurially-minded core personnel and management approach that strongly supports the working conditions of its personnel.

To sum up, commitment and motivation are factors that support project team members' goal-directed behaviour.

To achieve successful knowledge sharing, projects and project-based companies need to convince people to reject the old-fashioned thinking that they are being measured by what they know and do individually. Such thinking only perpetuates knowledge hoarding and the development of knowledge repositories from which little value-adding transfer takes place. One way by which this can be achieved is to build conscious knowledge sharing practice into daily work processes such as performance appraisals. Reward and appraisal systems can encourage people to participate in knowledge sharing activities in a way that can be seen to be valued by the company. They can reinforce and convey the desired culture by providing tangible evidence of what it values. The efforts of the company to reward those individuals and teams who share their knowledge in a spirit of collaboration and innovation are therefore congruent with creating the type of learning organization. The concurrent emphasis on rewarding team performance rather than just the excellence of the individual is also supportive in a project work context.

Creative tension

In an organic project work environment (Koskinen, 2004) the *creative tension* is the primary source from which individuals derive their power. One can compare creative tension to a bow and arrow. The bow is non-functional as a weapon until tension is applied. When the arrow is placed on the string and pulled, it increases the tension. The potential power of the weapon is then developed. Therefore, the power and effectiveness of the arrow lies in the tension exerted in the bow.

In the case of an individual project team member, there are three components of creative tension: the vision, current reality, and the gap. Identifying a clear vision of what an individual wants, and how that overlaps with an organization's (e.g. project's) vision is the first step. Vision must be clear enough that if the result occurred, one would recognize it (Fritz, 1989). However, it is important to realize that it is difficult for many people to separate what they want from what they think is possible.

The second component of creative tension is a clear understanding of the reality of the current situation. This includes a disarmingly simple and profound strategy: telling the truth (Senge, 1990). This means a relentless willingness to root out the way an individual limits himself or herself from seeing the truth.

The gap is the comparison of the vision that has been formulated, and the realistic perception of the current situation (e.g. Koskinen, 2005c). According to Fritz (1989), the gap creates tension, and most people have some level of tolerance for that tension. However, if an individual has intolerance for discrepancy, he or she will tend to resolve the tension in favour of continuing his or her present circumstances rather than working towards his or her vision. If the creative tension is perceived as real, there is adequate intrinsic motivation to reduce the tension.

In sum, creative tension describes the feeling people have when they recognize the difference (the gap) between where they are (their current scenario) and where they want to be (their preferred scenario). The gap creates a natural and healthy tension that seeks to resolve itself. This tension is the reason choices are made and actions are taken. It is the source of energy for change. Creative tension is a natural force.

Resistance to change and immunity reactions

Resistance to change – or the thought of the implications of the change – is a common phenomenon. It is the action taken by individuals and teams when they perceive a change that is proposed or is occurring as a threat to them. The threat need not be real or large for resistance to occur.

Resistance to change can take many forms and it is often difficult to pinpoint the exact reasons. The forces against change in companies include: ignoring the needs and expectations of people; when people have insufficient knowledge about the nature of the change; or if they do not perceive the need for change. Fears may be expressed over such matters as employment levels and job security, de-skilling of work, loss of job satisfaction, wage rate differentials, changes to social structures and working conditions, loss of individual control over work, and greater management control.

Some common reasons for individual resistance to change within organizations include (Mullins, 2007):

- *Selective perception:* people's interpretation of stimuli presents a unique picture or image of the 'real' world and can result in selective perception. This can lead to a biased view of a particular situation, which fits most comfortably into an individual's own perception of reality, and can cause resistance to change.
- *Habit:* people tend to respond to situations in an established and accustomed manner. Habits may serve as a means of comfort and security, and as a guide for easy decision-making. Proposed changes to habits, especially if the habits are well established and require little effort, may well be resisted. However, if there is a clearly perceived advantage, for example a promotion to act as a project manager, there is likely to be less, if any, resistance to the change.
- *Inconvenience or loss of freedom:* if the change is seen as likely to prove inconvenient, make life more difficult, reduce freedom of action, or result in increased control, there will be resistance.
- *Fear of the unknown:* changes which confront people with the unknown tend to cause anxiety or fear. Many major changes in a project and/or company present a degree of uncertainty, for example the introduction of new methods of working. A person may resist promotion to act as a project manager because of uncertainty over changes in responsibilities or the increased social demands of a higher position.

Indeed, although project-based companies have to couple their structures to their environment, they tend to feel comfortable operating within the policies and procedures which have been formulated to deal with a range of present situations. To ensure operational effectiveness, they often set up defences against change and prefer to concentrate on the routine tasks they perform well.

Resistance to change or path dependency (Teece et al., 1997) means that the previous history of an individual and/or company can limit their future behaviour. 'Our experiences are not like water in a glass which can be emptied and then refilled' (Flöistad, 1993, p. 73). This means, for example, that a person's knowledge is often bound to a specific context and era, and therefore it could be difficult to utilize in other times and situations. The path dependency also favours present technology (Steele, 1989). This means that the people whose careers are associated with a given field always see continued opportunities for improvement. They are slow to accept that a field may be maturing, because that threatens their own feeling of self-worth. This means that the people whose lives are intertwined with existing technology resist suggestions that the field is maturing.

Immunity reactions are thoroughly human and are usually not based on bad will (Otala, 1995). Instead, they are caused by a perceived threat from changes that may alter the balance of power within the organization, or modify the old tasks, thereby inflicting a need to change the way of thinking. They may also be based on the fear of an endless chain of changes, should one allow a first departure from the ingrained routines. Experience shows that fighting and anticipating immunity reactions takes at least as much effort as the whole restructuring process itself.

A considerable amount of time and effort must be used in avoiding immunity reactions. Preliminary rational reactions like 'We have no manpower or a budget' will often develop towards higher levels of sophistication such as 'I personally would of course agree, but my boss (or colleagues) would not' or 'It is strictly against our rules'. A dangerous reaction is the well-known 'Not-invented-here' syndrome, which usually takes highly innovative forms. The most dangerous immunity reactions are borne from concealed efforts to create or induce such organizational obstacles which would make a given proposal impracticable.

To conclude, most people do not like change because they do not like being changed. When change comes into view, fear and resistance to change follow – often despite the obvious benefits. People fight change for a number of reasons: because they fear the loss of something they value; because they do not understand the change and its implications; because they do not think that the change makes sense; or because they find it difficult to cope with either the level or pace of the change.

Information and communication systems

Information and communication systems may include a variety of more or less structured digital information systems. According to Hirschheim et al. (1995, p. 236), the current information and communication systems emphasize communication among people. 'For self-referential ... systems, either communication or action are the fundamental building blocks and this differs from the "elements" and sub-systems as typically defined in engineering and natural sciences. Recent systems theory makes clear ontological distinctions between machines, organisms, social and psychic systems.' The social autopoiesis interpretation is compatible with a language/action approach to information systems that is based on conversations and commitment (Lyytinen and Klein, 1985). A study of the information systems' discipline concludes that the importance of organizational behaviour and culture has been recently recognized, and there is a move toward interpretivism (Mingers and Stowell, 1997). Autopoiesis theory has contributed to the ideas and development of sophisticated technical solutions such as enabling network systems.

Databases require a special way of thinking (Allee, 1997). The way individuals organize data into separate tables or categories impacts how reports, forms, and queries are generated. These are all different processes for manipulating the data into representations of knowledge. Category mismatches make it difficult to integrate databases. Database design always reflects individuals' own thinking processes. The way they organize a database directly reflects their own mental models of how things work. The more individuals rely on data, the more they need to understand the way they conceptualize their world and co-create meaningful patterns of data.

Indeed, evolving technology allows people to reflect more and more on the creation of knowledge and the making of meaning. This means, for example, that databases are gradually becoming a mirror image of the larger mind of the organization. Data, ultimately, is what an individual uses to test the system, pumping various data cases through the system to see how well the system performs its various tasks. The tasks themselves, however, are derived from the knowledge needs of the people in the organization (cf. Allee, 1997).

According to McDermott (1999), new information and communication systems have inspired many companies to imagine a better way for staff to share knowledge and insight. Instead of storing documents in personal files and sharing personal insights with a small circle of colleagues, they can store documents in a common databases and use electronic networks to share insights with their whole community, even people scattered across the globe. However, according to these authors, most companies soon discover that leveraging knowledge is actually very hard and is more dependent on community building than information and communication technology. This is not because people are reluctant to use technology, rather it is because they often need to share knowledge that is neither obvious nor easy to document, knowledge that requires a human relationship to think about, understand, share, and apply appropriately. Thus, while information and communication technology has inspired the 'knowledge revolution', it takes building human communities to realize it.

Internet

The Internet is a worldwide, publicly accessible network of interconnected computer networks that transmit data. It is a 'network of networks' that consists of millions of smaller domestic, academic, and business networks which together carry various data and services such as electronic mail, online chat, file transfer, and the interlinked Web pages and other documents of the World Wide Web. The Internet is allowing greater flexibility in working hours and location, and it is these features that are especially useful for a project when its delivery installation takes place on a site far from home and in a different time zone.

Intranet

An intranet is a network that exists exclusively within an organization and is based on Internet technology. It can provide an e-mail system, remote access, group collaboration tools, an application sharing system, and a company communications network (Laudon and Laudon, 2000). It protects data from unauthorized use through a software mechanism called a firewall that blocks unwanted access from outside but allows internal users to gain access to the Internet. Some traditional applications of intranets are:

- Access to databases
- Forum for discussion
- Distribution of electronic documentation
- Administering payroll and benefits packages
- Providing online training
- Frequently asked questions to provide answers to commonly raised questions.

Most organizations have adopted 'firewall' technologies to prevent intruders from gaining access to their sensitive organizational data. The most important goals of firewall systems are (Loew et al., 1999):

- Access control at different levels
- Control at the application layer

- User rights administration
- Isolation of certain services
- Proof back-up and analysis of the log
- Alarm facilities
- Concealment of internal network structure
- Confidentiality
- Resistance of firewall against attacks.

Firewalls examine every packet of data between networks (using packet filters) and analyse their characteristics to decide whether to deny any unauthorized messages or access attempts. A high-level security firewall can be constructed using two packet filters. The weakness of one packet filter is supported by the other. Attacks on these servers will not endanger the internal network. However, there can never be any guarantee of total security. In the future, it is likely that encryption technologies will be used to strengthen the security of firewalls.

When building intranets, organizations need to be mindful of the dangers of developing large and sophisticated solutions that nobody visits. The technology needs to be user led to meet explicit needs. Another danger is the use of intranets to develop 'electronic fences' in organizations contrary to the espoused principle of knowledge sharing (Swan et al., 1999).

Thus, intranet supports sharing of documents, diagrams, and conceptual models that support thinking and decision-making. Increasingly a shared computer work space becomes the meeting place where project team members generate and share data. Intranet technology helps people forge working relationships with each other and pull together team members. However, it is crucially important to realize that the data communicated with the help of the intranet needs to be interpreted by human beings. As pointed out earlier, these interpretations may be crucially different, and consequently may cause misunderstanding and harm.

Text-based conferencing

There are a number of text-based conferencing channels through which individuals can share data. Usenet newsgroups are worldwide discussion forums on a multitude of topics where discussions take place on an electronic bulletin board, with individuals posting messages for others to read. Another public forum for sharing knowledge within predefined groups is discussion lists that individuals can subscribe to. These lists are generally moderated, in comparison with newsgroups which are not. An individual subscribes and joins a discussion group and receives e-mail messages sent by others concerning the topic. The individual can reply to the group and their offerings are distributed to all subscribers to the group (cf. Jashapara, 2004).

Various chat tools have been developed to allow two or more individuals on the Internet to hold live interactive conversations. If the number of contributors increases substantially, chat groups can be divided into different themes and topic areas. Some enhancements are providing voice chat capabilities. Individuals can arrange to meet at predefined times to share their knowledge and ideas, particularly in cases where the phone may not be the appropriate medium. Discussion groups can also be set on a variety of topics on an organization's intranet to enable knowledge sharing. Sensitivities relating to the membership of these groups need to be considered so that full, frank and open discussions and dialogues can be promoted. For example, in a work context, people may be guarded in their contributions if they are aware that their boss or senior management may be party to the conference (cf. Jashapara, 2004).

Groupware tools

The raison d'être behind groupware is to encourage collaboration between people to enhance knowledge sharing. In commercial terms, the assumption is that greater collaboration will lead to increased productivity, lower costs and higher quality through better decision-making. Groupware, as a concept, tends to be applied to information communication technologies that support collaboration, communication, and co-ordination of activities over space and time as well as shared information spaces (Robertson et al., 2001). Two common technologies used in groupware are e-mail and Lotus Notes discussion databases. Lotus Notes is generally considered as the first groupware product to provide discussion databases, e-mail with attachments, shared databases, workflow automation, and applications development. Other systems have included (Williams, 1996):

- Group decision systems with brainstorming, ideas generation and voting systems
- Collaborative writing and whiteboards
- Computer-based conferencing
- Schedule meetings and diary organisers
- E-mail-systems used proactively.

To sum up, advances in information technology have greatly simplified data sharing. Distributed databases, electronic reports, and communication technologies have augmented the ability of project stakeholders to access and share data. Sharing technologies, such as the Internet, and intranets, make it possible for people to self-organize around data sharing. Data mining tools and technologies help people working for projects to reach shared understandings of essential data. However, it is important to note, that data management is not the same as knowledge management. Being able to organize data is often a key organizational enabler for knowledge, but it is only one component.

Organizational climate and organizational/project culture

Few managers would dispute that the climate or atmosphere of an organization is likely to have some impact on its performance. However, there is less agreement about the ideal climate for optimum performance, and the influence managers can have in creating and maintaining it. *Organizational climate* may be summed up succinctly as 'what it feels like to work here'. There are certainly a number of elements which contribute to an individual's perception of what an organization 'feels like'. According to Gray (2001), some of those elements in project-based companies are:

- The management style at the organizational level within which the project work is done, with particular attention to the levels of threat or insecurity
- The management style at the project level
- The extent to which a team of behaviour characteristics collectively labelled 'voluntarism' is apparent. The components of voluntarism are: free expression of ideas and concerns, innovation, questioning, intrinsic satisfactions, and participation in defining goals
- The level of purposive threat directed at the informant himself or herself, or others. Purposive threat is defined here as any form of threat or coercion intended to cause someone to act in a certain way
- The level of environmental threat affecting the informant himself or herself, or others. Environmental threat is defined here as a threat arising from natural events, from societal forces which, for practical purposes are undirected by intelligence, or from macro-political causes or policies determined so remotely from the affected individuals that they may be regarded, again for practical purposes, as being undirected.

Furthermore, few concepts in organizational theory have as many different and competing definitions as *organizational culture* (e.g. De Long and Fahey, 2000). Smircich (1983), for example, has cited five classes of such definitions in her review of the literature on organizational cultures. Rather than attempt to resolve the numerous and subtle definitional conflicts, here organizational culture is defined as a component of the project-based company's members' situations, which is also embedded in their world views – in case they have adopted and understood the culture.

Thus, organizational culture contains the basic, taken-for-granted assumptions and deep patterns of meaning shared by organizational participation and manifestation of these assumptions (Slocum, 1995). The failure of many knowledge management systems is often the result of cultural factors rather than technological oversights. This is especially the case in organic project work environments. However, culture, by its very nature, is a nebulous subject with a variety of perspectives and interpretations (Ajmal and Koskinen, 2008).

Studies of organizational culture – and project culture, too – have been able to shed light on project teams and project-based companies as a whole, as epistemological systems. In addition, they have underscored the importance of such human factors as values, meanings, motivations, symbols, and beliefs, and paved the way for more elaborate research on knowledge management in a project work context. A culture that is able to harness knowledge as a transferable asset which can be used to enhance future projects, can and should be created. Thus, continuous learning at individual, team, and company levels should nowadays be embedded within the project-based company's culture (Brown and Duguid, 1991).

The importance of culture has also been emphasized by organizational theorists such as Burns and Stalker (1994) who present a case for organic structures as opposed to mechanical structures. In popular thought there are many arguments that suggest that in order to facilitate knowledge sharing, work environments must be simultaneously tight and loose. There appears to be a high dependency on knowledge with the development and maintenance of an appropriate context within which knowledge sharing occurs. The key distinguishing factor between projects that are successful in managing knowledge and those that are not, is the ability of management to create a sense of community in the workplace. Highly successful projects behave as focused communities, whereas less successful projects behave more like traditional bureaucratic departments. Therefore it is possible to conclude that project culture refers to underlying values and principles that serve as a foundation for project management (Denison, 1990). In a socio-historical context, project culture is created in a situation where new concepts of the 'right' and 'wrong' ways of operation are born within mutual experience. The culture stabilizes the project's ways of operation, and at its best supports the initiative and efforts of an individual at his or her daily work.

Project culture may determine individual behaviour, but it is also concurrently constituted through human behaviour (Swieringa and Wierdsma, 1992). Culture awareness increases the likelihood of learning becoming a natural process in the project. This requires surfacing the hidden, basic assumptions and beliefs embedded in the project and developing the ability to engage in double-loop learning, using the inquiry processes that Argyris and Schön (1978) suggest. This means that for a project design to be effective for learning, there needs to be a context in which team members can question institutional norms (Ayas and Zeniuk, 2001). Project culture based on motivation to truth and inquiry starts at the level of individual team members as they reflect on their actions and how they contribute to their problems, feel the necessity for change, and see their own part in the process of change (Senge, 1990).

Because project culture and organizational culture as a whole are such difficult concepts to capture and describe, it is important to identify the basic elements of predominant cultures within them. According to West (1997), the two fundamental dimensions of organizational culture are flexibility versus control, and internal versus external orientation. High flexibility is characterized by flatter organizational structures, decentralized decision-making and low specialization of jobs (cf. the organic project work environment earlier in this chapter), while high control cultures tend to be very hierarchical in their structures, with centralized decision-making and many specialized jobs with a proliferation of job titles (cf. the mechanical project work environment earlier in this chapter).

Project managers often engage in transactions with several different cultures simultaneously. They typically work within their own base organization's core culture, with the sub-cultures of other departments within the organization (research and development, marketing and sales or manufacturing), or with an external customer's core culture. Each has their own inherent 'ways of doing things around here to succeed' (Suda, 2006, p. 52). This means, for example, that understanding and speaking the language of the immediate culture is critical for project success. Effectively communicating with the surrounding culture can help to develop plans and strategies that will be recognized and time-honoured by the project – while avoiding practices that violate the beliefs and values of the client organization. Thus, project managers have many opportunities and duties to create and shape a project culture in purposeful ways. Very often project culture must be in alignment with the organization's lead culture. This is an important part of both project team development and a healthy team climate, and sets the stage for ensuring project success.

Internal forces like a project's structure and management style affect the project culture. Rigid, formal, and command and control structures, for example, can promote functional efficiency at the expense of collaborative and innovative activities. Moreover, sub-cultures typically exist within the overall structure of a project, and they grow out in different locations, occupations, and the provision of services. Sub-cultures may be very different from the base organization's culture, even within the same organization. External forces often shape project culture and are very powerful since projects reflect national, trans-national, regional, industrial, and occupational ideologies. These may take the form of religions, political ideologies, and environmental concerns. The substance of a project's culture may reflect many beliefs, only some of which originate within the project.

Since the final product of a project delivery consists of the work of several experts in various fields, the cultures of the basic organization and of the various professional groups meet. Different professions typically have their own cultures and ways of working which are not necessarily in harmony with the rules of the project (Ruuska, 1999). When various cultures are effectively joined, the result is a project organization which is able to mediate the message to many and get everyone working for a common goal. A good project culture therefore requires a directing whole which consists of an organizational culture and a strong professional culture (Figure 8.7). What is in question is the synthesis of cultures. One should not even attempt to unite the various professional cultures but rather seek appropriate modes of co-operation and communication for the project at hand.

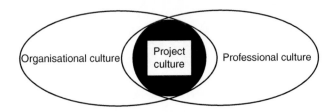

Figure 8.7   Project culture.

In the opinion of Brown and Eisenhardt (1997), culture is important in encouraging team members to share knowledge, and according to them, successful project organizations appear to be good places to work and share knowledge. In these types of atmospheres, interpersonal communication tends to be non-problematic. Furthermore, according to these authors, the basic challenge in project organizations may not be the transfer of tacit knowledge into explicit knowledge, but the 'bumping up' of knowledge one level so that it becomes part of the decision-making process of the project team and/or project-based company.

To conclude, understanding the culture of a project is critical to running successful projects. Culture resides in every fold of a project, influencing the dynamics of how people perform, relate, and perceive the project's impact on their lives. However, individuals, project teams, and organizations seldom fit one particular type of organizational culture because they represent complex social systems and mixtures of many cultural patterns.

Cultural differential applies to the project-based company as a whole. It incorporates the habits, attitudes, values, and beliefs which permeate the individuals and teams which comprise a company. When a company's culture results in, for example, a perception of high quality standards, an ability to react to change, an ability to change, an ability to put the customer first, and so on, then that culture is a contributor to competitive advantage.

Values

Values are abstract concepts and they are very general. They refer to various personal goals like status or power, and to the means of attaining these goals. Values are thought to exert a broad influence on society and over any related activity. They can help to explain behavioural differences among various project teams (Gudykunst, 1988).

Here it is again accentuated that the values individual team members follow in their work must be understood by them, that is, these values must be in their world views in the form of meanings. The clearer these meanings are, the better the team members behave in accordance with them.

Values may determine 'how things ought to be in the team' (e.g. Lord and Brown, 2001). If the values of different project teams are similar, the behaviour has the potential to be similar (Lachman et al., 1994). Values can be considered in a framework where some values are more important than others (Figure 8.8). Values higher in the hierarchy are

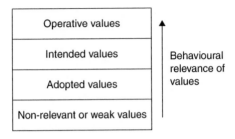

Figure 8.8   Value framework.

more enduring and resistant to change, and have more power to control social behaviour.

Organizational values fall into four categories and it is important to avoid confusion between them (Lencioni, 2002):

- Core values are deeply ingrained principles that guide a company's actions. They are never compromised for convenience or economic gain and often reflect the values of the company founders
- Aspiration-based values are values to support a new strategy. They are values that the company needs to compete in the future but currently lacks
- Permission-to-play values are the minimum behavioural and social standards required of people in the company
- Accidental values are values that arise spontaneously over time. They reflect the common interests or personalities of personnel. They may be positive, such as the inclusion of employees, or negative, such as the ingrained mistrust of management.

Core values guide every action and decision that a company makes. They form the fabric underlying every recruitment, selection, appraisal, and rewards policy. If the core values are poorly implemented, they can lead to the mistrust and cynicism of the motives of senior management (Jashapara, 2004). Core values require constant vigilance to make explicit what a company stands for and to act as a rallying call to guide people's actions. They can reinforce individual commitment and willingness to give energy and loyalty to a company. Individuals may make sacrifices and investments based on company values.

Hofstede (1991) argues that values are unconscious to those who hold them. For example, this means that project team members cannot articulate these meanings but may still behave according to them. Therefore, they cannot be discussed, but only understood by others by observing the way people act under various situations. This is contrasted by other accounts as values influence behaviour through either behavioural channelling or perceptual screening, or both. In contrast to values, the culture is claimed to be an entirety made up of beliefs, needs, and cognitive processes. Beliefs reflect how people construct their social reality. They are composed of an object and associated attributes. Thus, they can be discussed.

The value agendas of managers and project leaders of project-based companies can be organized under three broad imperatives: *orienting*, *institutionalizing*, and *sustaining* company values (Goodpaster, 1989). The first two deal with placing value considerations in a position of authority alongside considerations of profitability and competitive strategy in the company mindset. The third imperative (sustenance) has to do with passing on the spirit of this effort in two directions: to future leaders of the company and to the wider network of organizations that make up the social system as a whole.

Orienting

Managers and leaders must first identify and then, where needed, attempt to modify their organizations' (e.g. project-based companies' and projects') shared values. Such a prescription cannot be followed without first performing a kind of value inventory. What is needed is a sounding process sophisticated enough to get behind the natural cautions, defences, and espoused values of people. Managers and leaders must listen to and understand their organizations in ways that reach its character strengths and defects. Such a process is relatively easy in a small organization (e.g. in small project teams) because behaviour is observable daily and communication is direct. But in large companies, the task is much more complex, and almost of a different kind.

Institutionalizing

Once managers and leaders have identified characteristic values and value conflicts – and have clarified the direction they want to take in whole or in part – the process of institutionalization becomes paramount. Possible acts could be, for example, decisive actions, a statement of standards with regular audits, and appropriate incentives.

Since 'actions speak louder than words', a major factor in the process of institutionalizing company/project values is leadership activity that has both wide visibility and clear ethical content. Such actions serve as large-scale demonstrations to the rank and file of the seriousness and importance that management attaches to needed values.

Every company and project addresses values somewhat differently. Nevertheless, certain elements will be common to the process of institutionalization in any company and/or project. A statement of norms along with a monitoring process is one of those common elements.

Sustaining

To sustain values is to communicate them to all the project stakeholders as well as to the wider social system. The objective is to find congruence between the mindsets of the people working in a company and its projects. Without some degree of 'value fit' or congruence, the company mindset simply cannot survive or replicate itself.

Project values have considerable potency as they tend to link the social, cognitive, and behavioural dimensions of a company. The social aspects characterize the history of experiences and understandings of teams within the company. The cognitive aspects draw on the history and experiences of individuals within these teams and the behavioural aspects show how these values affect individual actions and interactions (Ashkanasy et al., 2000).

To conclude this section, a personal and cultural value is a relative ethical value, an assumption upon which implementation can be extrapolated. Values are considered subjective, vary across people and cultures, and are in many ways aligned with belief and belief systems. Types of values include ethical/moral values, doctrinal/ideological (religious, political) values, social values, and aesthetic values. It is debatable whether some values are intrinsic or not.

Norms

Norms are expectations of appropriate and inappropriate behaviour. These may be norms about dress code or issues such as expectations surrounding performance and handling conflict. Norms attach approval or disapproval to holding certain beliefs and attitudes, and acting in particular ways. They can vary along two dimensions (O'Reilly, 1989):

- Intensity of approval or disapproval attached to an expectation
- Degree of consistency with which a norm is shared.

At the team-member level, norms are a part of a team member's world view, and therefore, norms are more or less individually understood. Also a project team's norms are like fingerprints – each is unique. Yet there are still some common classes of norms that appear in most teams (Goodman et al., 1987):

- Probably the most common class of norms in 'performance norms'. Project teams typically provide their members with explicit cues on how hard they should work, how to get the job done, their level of output, appropriate levels of tardiness, and the like (Blau, 1995). These norms are extremely powerful in affecting an individual team member's performance – they are capable of significantly modifying a performance prediction that was based solely on the team member's ability and level of personal motivation.
- A second category encompasses 'appearance norms'. This includes things like appropriate dress, loyalty to the project team or company, when to look busy, and when it is acceptable to goof off. Some companies have formal dress codes. However, even in their absence, norms frequently develop to dictate the kind of clothing that should be worn to work. Similarly, presenting the appearance of loyalty is important, especially among professional employees and those in the executive ranks. So it is often considered inappropriate to be openly looking for another job.
- Another category concerns 'social arrangement norms'. These norms come from informal work groups and primarily regulate social interactions within a team. With whom team members eat lunch, friendship on and off the job, social games, and the like are influenced by these norms.
- A final category relates to 'allocation of resources norms'. These norms can originate in the team or in the company, and cover things like pay, the assignment of difficult tasks, and the allocation of new tools and equipment.

To conclude, norms are the behavioural expectations and cues within a project-based company or a project team. Norms are used by a team for appropriate and inappropriate values, beliefs, attitudes, and behaviours. Norms may be explicit or implicit. Failure to follow the norms can result in severe punishments, including exclusion from the team.

Beliefs, attitudes and assumptions

Beliefs are a manifestation of culture embedded in project members' world views. Beliefs concern what people think to be true. For example, some project leaders may believe that adaptive learning (i.e. single-loop learning) is more likely to lead to greater company-wide performance whereas other project leaders may believe it is generative learning (i.e. double-loop learning). Sometimes values and beliefs may be hard to distinguish, especially where these are closely related (learning styles, for example). Values could be considered as enduring beliefs where certain actions are considered socially more appropriate than others (Rokeach, 1973).

Attitudes of people connect their beliefs and values with feelings (Brown, 1998) in their world views. They are a learnt predisposition to act in a favourable or unfavourable manner to a given circumstance and situation, and involve evaluations based on individuals' feelings. Attitudes are, according to Jashapara (2004), more enduring than opinions and have an impact on an individual's motivation. They can result in prejudices and stereotypes, such as the negative attitudes towards projects' 'after action reviews'. All these complicated processes are realized in the world views of project team members in terms of dynamics between different kinds of meanings.

Basic *assumptions* are the taken-for-granted solutions to particular problems (Brown, 1998). They are the 'theories-in-use' (Argyris and Schön, 1978) that perpetuate organizational routines and single-loop learning. Assumptions are unconsciously held, making them difficult to confront or make explicit. They are highly complex interpretations based on individuals' beliefs, values, and emotions. One typology of basic assumptions considers five dimensions (Schein, 1985):

- Whether an organization dominates the external environment or is dominated by it
- Whether truth and reality are received dogma, rules, and procedures, a consequence of debate on what works
- Whether people are inherently lazy or self-motivated
- Whether 'doing' and work are more primary than 'being' and valuing employees' private lives
- Whether human interaction is based on individualism or collectivism.

In the opinion of Flannes and Levin (2001), many project team members join a new project team with a certain amount of 'baggage' located in their world view. Baggage can be feelings, attitudes, beliefs, assumptions, or expectations that have a negative tone and are the result of previous negative personal or professional experiences of the team member. In essence, baggage becomes an impediment to the team member's active, positive engagement with the work of the current team. The residual feelings that make up a person's baggage become a 'chip on the shoulder' that can hinder a team member's learning and knowledge sharing. Sources of baggage are located in a person's world view and include:

- Previous or ongoing organizational problems, such as reductions in workforce
- Industry changes
- Health issues
- Career stalling
- Personal problems.

To conclude, the clearer one is about what he or she values and believes in, the happier and more effective he or she will be. Beliefs are the assumptions individuals make about themselves, about others in the world, and about how they expect things to be. Beliefs are about how people think things really are, what people think is really true, and therefore what they expect the likely consequences of their behaviour will be.

Trust

In the knowledge economy, the most important work is conversation – and creating *trust* is a manager's most important job (Webber, 1993).

Indeed, knowledge and trust share several properties and characteristics (e.g. Huemer et al., 1998). Knowledge is history-dependent and context-sensitive (von Krogh et al., 1996a), just like trust. Consequently, neither trust nor knowledge can be universally defined, but must be dealt with according to history, relationship, and context. Both knowledge and trust reduce uncertainty and complexity. 'Trust cannot reasonably exist without knowledge, i.e. we might hope or even be ignorant, but we cannot trust' (Huemer et al., 1998, p. 140).

When the relationship between a project company and a customer is based on trust, many benefits are achieved by both parties (see Table 8.2). According to Huemer et al. (1998) and Kadefors (2004), in a project-based company – customer relationships, single sourcing, outsourcing, early supplier involvement, and the just-in-time philosophy are different phenomena that all have bearings on trust. This means that when parties recognize that they have common interests, cooperative relations more readily ensue. In situations of high probability of future association, however, parties are not only more likely to

Table 8.2 Benefits of trust in the project company – customer relationships

With trust	Without trust
Long-term contracts, repeat business, and sole-source contracts	Continuous competitive bidding
Minimal documentation	Massive documentation
Minimal number of customer-project company meetings	Excessive customer-project company meetings
Team meetings without documentation	Team meetings with documentation
Sponsorship at middle-management levels	Sponsorship at executive levels

Source: Kerzner (1997).

co-operate but they are also increasingly willing to punish defectors (e.g. Powell, 1996).

The assumptions of self-interest seeking with guile and opportunism seem unjustifiable (e.g. Huemer et al., 1998). But so do assumptions of trustworthiness (e.g. Ring and van de Ven, 1994). In other words, the idea of trust depends on assumptions that allow uncertainty and diversity in human behaviour. The claim resonates well with Ghoshal and Bartlett's (1994) view, which reflects a relativistic perspective on personal attributes, and more a view on human behaviour.

Some authors (e.g. Baier, 1986; Meyerson et al., 1996; Rousseau et al., 1998) define trust as an individual's reliance on another person under conditions of dependence and vulnerability. Dependence means that one's outcomes are contingent on the trustworthy or untrustworthy behaviour of the other, and vulnerability means that one would experience negative outcomes from the other person's untrustworthy behaviour. For example, Meyerson et al. (1996) define vulnerability in terms of the goods or things one values and whose care one partially entrusts to someone else, who has some discretion over him or her. Because self-sufficiency is rare in a project work context, vulnerability is common. This means that trust includes approved vulnerability to another's possible, but not anticipated, ill will toward one (Baier, 1986).

Most conceptions of how trust develops emphasize that personal trust is a history-dependent process (e.g. Lindskold, 1978). This means that personal trust builds incrementally and it accumulates. Furthermore, many conceptions of trust refer to expectations (e.g. Luhmann, 1979; Ring and van de Ven, 1994; Rousseau et al., 1998), which are in turn based on the trustor's perception of the motives and the abilities of the trustee. Ring and van de Ven (1994) argue that expectations are the bases for an explanation of the development of inter-organizational relationships, which in turn are grounded in the motivational and cognitive pre-dispositions of individuals to engage in sense-making and bonding processes. Thus, expectations are also crucial aspects of trust in a project work context.

This all means that trust is a structure of meanings embedded into a team member's world view. It is rather permanent, but can be destroyed rather quickly, when something negative happens in a person's situation, which puts an end to expectations concerning the other party's behaviour.

It is likely that if trust is violated, then distrust between the parties ensues rather than a continued state of trust, especially if such violations are viewed as deliberate rather than due to circumstances beyond the control of the violating party (Luhmann, 1979). Furthermore, in a crisis situation, incorrect allocations of resources based on trust violations could be fatal for project implementation. In other words, the vulnerability aspect of trust is even greater in crisis situations than in more common non-crisis situations.

Lewis and Weigert (1985) suggest that various qualitative mixes of cognitive, emotional, and behavioural contents make it possible to categorize different types of trust. Furthermore, they argue that trust in everyday life is a mixture of feelings and rational thinking. Excluding one or the other leads to pure faith. According to Moorman et al. (1993), the practical significance of trust lies in the social attitudes and actions it underwrites. This means that trust takes different forms depending on what its bases are and how it is communicated and manifested (e.g. Lewicki and Bunker, 1996; Huemer et al., 1998; Rousseau et al., 1998). In other words, trust is formed from different components. Both technically competent performance and fiduciary responsibility in fulfilling contracts are needed in different mixtures of work settings. That is, both components of trust are always present in a successful project implementation (cf. Barney and Hansen, 1994).

Researchers have generally argued that different forms of trust vary considerably in their 'thickness'. For example, the trust associated with close personal relationships has generally been characterized as a thick form of trust which is relatively resilient and durable (e.g. Janoff-Bulman, 1992; Powell, 1996). Other forms of trust, in contrast, have been characterized as thin forms of trust because they are negotiated in a cautious manner and withdrawn easily. Therefore within these forms of trust, expectations are high, but so are reservations.

Deterrence-based trust (i.e. calculus-based trust)

The most fragile relationships are contained in deterrence-based trust (a thin form of trust) (e.g. Shapiro et al., 1992; Gulati, 1995; Lewicki and Bunker, 1996; Sheppard and Tuchinsky, 1996; Greenberg and Baron, 2003). One violation or inconsistency can destroy a relationship. This is based on the fear of reprisal if the trust is violated. Individuals who are in this type of relationship do what they promise because they fear the consequences of not fulfilling their obligations. In other words, deterrence-based trust emphasizes utilitarian considerations that may also lead to a belief that a partner will behave in a trustworthy manner. Potential sanctions such as the loss of reputation and of repeat business, which are perceived to be more costly than any potential benefits of opportunistic behaviour, may cause deterrence-based trust.

Deterrence-based trust will work only to the extent that punishment is possible, the consequences are clear, and that punishment is actually imposed if the trust is violated. To be sustained, the potential loss of future interaction with the other party must outweigh the potential profit that comes from violating the expectations. Moreover, the potentially harmed party must be willing to introduce harm to the person acting untrustingly.

If one party violates the deterrence-based trust, the other party can either renegotiate the relationship to better ensure the desired outcomes, or seek another relationship. Repairing of deterrence-based trust assumes that both parties would prefer to do so relative to best-alternative relationships for having the same need met (Lewicki and Bunker, 1996).

Role-based trust

There is not always time in temporary project teams to engage in the usual forms of trust-building activities. Therefore the people in project teams often deal with each other more as roles than as individuals. This means that trust manifests itself in impersonal form and trust bases on categorical assumptions until personal contacts are made. But, although role-based trust is a thin form of trust, it is, however, a thicker form of trust than deterrence-based trust.

Expectations of ill will or good will develop in project teams just as they do in other forms of organization. However, because project teams do not have enough time for these expectations to be built from zero, they are imported from other settings and applied in project teams in categorical forms. Expectations defined in terms of categories are especially likely because people have little time to judge each other (Fiske and Taylor, 1991).

If people in project teams deal with one another more as roles than as individuals, which is probable because the project is often built of strangers interacting to achieve set objectives, then expectations should be more stable and defined in terms of professions than personalities. As Dawes (1994, p. 24) noted: 'We trust engineers because we trust engineering and believe that engineers are trained to apply valid principles of engineering'. For example, in an engineering project it is assumed that a civil engineer knows things regarding construction, and an electricity engineer knows things regarding electrification (Koskinen and Pihlanto, 2003).

If one party violates the role-based trust, the other party can try to repair it in the same way as described earlier in the case of deterrence-based trust.

Knowledge-based trust

Most organizational relationships are rooted in knowledge-based trust (a thick form of trust) (e.g. Shapiro et al., 1992; Gulati, 1995; Lewicki and Bunker, 1996). That is, trust is based on the behavioural predictability that comes from the history of interaction. It exists when an individual has adequate knowledge about someone to understand him or her well enough to be able to predict considerably accurately his or her behaviour. According to Shapiro et al. (1992, p. 369), mutual trust results from predictability, for it produces a 'self-fulfilling prophecy' effect. That is, people often act co-operatively towards those they expect to be co-operative, and this action encourages the receivers of co-operative gestures to reciprocate in kind.

The repair of violated knowledge-based trust is problematic, because the violation presents a direct threat to the victim's self-image and self-esteem. According to Lewicki and Bunker (1996), violation of knowledge-based trust suggests that the victim has been very wrong about the violator (i.e. he or she does not know that person as well as previously thought).

Identification-based trust

The thickest form of trust is identification-based (e.g. Lewis and Weigert, 1985; Shapiro et al., 1992; Lewicki and Bunker, 1996; Robbins, 2003). It is achieved when there is an emotional connection between the parties. This means that identification-based trust allows one party to act as an agent for the other and substitute for that person in interpersonal transactions. Trust exists because the parties understand each other's intentions and appreciate each other's wants and desires. This mutual understanding is developed to the point where each person can effectively act for the other. This form of trust once again underlines the relevance of feelings in communication between people.

The repair of violated identification-based trust is even more problematic than the repair of violated knowledge-based-trust. This means that a restoration of trust to its former state is not often possible.

As noted earlier, project teams often lack the requisite history on which incremental and accumulative trust-building measures could be asserted. There is in many projects neither enough time nor the opportunity for the sort of experience necessary for a thick form of trust to emerge. Therefore a 'hedge' may be used in order to reduce the perceived vulnerability of trust by reducing interdependence between the parties involved. Hedges minimize the dangers of misplaced trust, when the goods dealt with are of high value (Baier, 1986). Hedges imply an attitude that one trusts the other, but only partly. The existence of a hedge allows one to enter a vulnerable activity because the worst-case outcome is covered.

For example, most customers buying new software are very reluctant to trust the supplying company with the sole copy of the software. Creating a backup of the software as a hedge (a contract regarding after sales services) enables the customer to trust the supplying company, even though it has had little or no prior experience with the supplying company. Hedges imply an orientation that resembles the attitude of wisdom described by Meacham (1983) as a stance of simultaneously believing and doubting, understanding and questioning.

Due to the fact that it is possible that the project team does not achieve the set objectives, the members entrust their reputations. This means that there exist vulnerabilities in terms of the loss of reputations and grounds for expectations of good will in terms of the reality of interdependence. However, the realities of project work interdependence can forestall intentional harm-causing to those reputations. Team members know that their specialities are crucial and worthless without links to other team members. They also know of the implicit threat imposed on their own reputations if they do not perform. A well-known saying 'We all are in the same boat' describes well the situation.

As outlined earlier, an approach to deterring untrustworthy behaviour is to provide possibilities for interactions. This means that the more the project stakeholders have opportunities for mutual communication, the more they can improve trust. For example, project team members may begin their interactions with a series of social messages (e.g. Pinto and Kharbanda, 1995; Kerzner, 1997). They then increase knowledge-based trust by introducing themselves and providing some personal background before focusing on the work at hand.

By clarifying the roles for each project team member, it is possible to improve trust among the project team. This clarification makes clear to team members that they are dependent on a variety of expertise. In other words, assigning each member a particular task enables all of them to identify with one another, forging a foundation for identification-based trust. Especially at the outset of the project, dependency is strongly forged when ambiguous knowledge drives the team, whether it is constructing a new building or developing a new product. The issue of identification is a critical one in all project work environments.

Different authors (e.g. Thamhain and College, 1993; Pinto and Krarbanda, 1995; Kerzner, 1997; Tuckman and Jensen, 1977; Järvenpää et al., 1998) have reported that the project teams with the highest levels of trust tend to share the following traits:

- They meet deadlines. If an individual promises to get something done on time, it is essential to meet that deadline. Although a few incidents of lateness may be overlooked, people who are chronically late in meeting deadlines, rapidly gain a reputation for being untrustworthy (Greenberg and Baron, 2003)
- They spend time sharing personal values and goals. Identification-based trust requires a keen understanding and appreciation of others
- The hallmark of the trusting team is the right attitude: the project team members consistently display eagerness, enthusiasm, and an intense action orientation in all their communication. According to Järvenpää et al. (1998), one pessimist has the potential to undermine an entire project team.

Indeed, trust is critical to successful knowledge management in a project work context. Despite its value, trust continues to intangible: difficult to create and maintain. This is especially the case in large project-based companies. Once it is properly embedded into a company and maintained within the company politics that make sense for knowledge management, it has the potential to have a lasting effect. However, because there is not always time in a project work context to develop thick forms of trust, project teams often have to make do with thin forms of trust.

Moreover, trust is based on understanding, with which people try to understand their partners' behaviour, states of mind, and motives. The development of relationships directs the process. When a feeling of trust becomes established, it affects the perceptions of a partner's motives more than behaviour does. Thus, trust has an indirect effect on the efficient transfer of knowledge. The greater the level of trust, the greater the level of openness, and the better the opportunities for knowledge to be transferred.

To sum up this section, trust develops only with time as the result of interpersonal relations. One result of this is that in temporary organizations like project teams, the trust of individual project team members is often based on the roles of the other team members, and therefore the utilization of tacit knowledge within a project team may be a problematic one. The shared experiences of project team members, experiences that are derived from previous jointly implemented projects, improve the potential for sharing all types of knowledge.

Summary

The project-based company is composed of 12 components that are produced as simultaneous tracks in an interacting pattern. They are:

- Identity
- Perception of the environment
- Strategy
- Knowledge management
- Knowledge sharing
- Boundary elements and perturbations
- Interactivity
- Boundary objects
- Commitment and motivation
- Information and communication systems
- Organizational climate and organizational/project culture
- Trust.

Numerous components support the view of project-based companies as complex dynamic systems. The components and relationships among them enable the two major knowledge flows in the functioning of these companies.

9

Two Major Knowledge Flows

As a system, an organization must continuously replenish its stock of knowledge and competencies necessary to use different resources effectively. This is because an organization's operations are determined by the specific activities or organizational routines an organization can perform in using its resources (Nelson and Winter, 1982). The market's responses to the company's products (e.g. project deliveries) generate flows of revenues as well as data about its markets. Data about an organization's products, operations, and resource stocks also flow to decision makers within the organization's management processes. From an organization's management processes emanate the specific decisions, policies, procedures, budgets, and norms that direct the flows of the organization's financial and other resources to maintain or increase resource stocks in the organization's operations, tangible assets, intangible assets, or management processes (Maula; 2006; Sanchez and Heene, 2008).

Thus, knowledge flows have a crucial role in the reproduction of an organization's knowledge structure (Tuomi, 1996). This chapter will elaborate on the idea that maintaining a project-based company requires processes of *sensing* (a condition for interactive openness) and *memory* (a feature of self-referentiality), each of which constitutes a major knowledge flow (cf. Maula, 2006). This means that an autopoietic system (i.e. a project-based company) incorporates two major knowledge flows: sensing and memory. Sensing means, in practice, that the project-based company interacts, co-evolves, and coordinates its activities with its changing environment. For example, a project-based company creates new knowledge by using various kinds of *boundary elements*, such as roles (e.g. project manger) and functions (e.g. projects) through which it interacts reciprocally with its environment. Memory, in turn, means that the system (i.e. the project-based company) has access to its own accumulated knowledge. The company is, therefore, internally closed in the sense that it utilizes its existing knowledge resources and may thereby operate efficiently. Sensing and memory help the project-based company make distinctions that then become embedded in its internal knowledge structure.

Sensing

In order to survive, adapt, learn, and renew itself, a project-based company needs the ability to co-evolve reciprocally with its environment. Boundary elements influence a company's learning and renewal capability by enabling two kinds of sensing activities:

- Exposure or awareness of the company to triggers – perturbations in its environment that elicit compensation reactions
- Interactive processes and communication with clients, suppliers, and other entities.

(Maula, 2006)

In other words, these two activities enable a project-based company to maintain openness. In this way, autopoietic boundary elements function as connecting and absorbing mechanisms, rather than as separating elements.

Sensing means that a project-based company interacts with its environment by being aware of, and compensating for, perturbations, by improving its knowledge and by changing internally. In other words, a company interacts with its environment through structural coupling, that is, through recurrent interactions, each of which triggers changes in the company. However, it is crucially important to realize that the environment only triggers changes; it does not specify or direct them (cf. Maturana and Varela, 1987).

Indeed, structural coupling establishes a clear difference between the ways in which living systems (e.g. project-based companies) and non-living systems (e.g. machines) interact with their environments. As Bateson (1972, 1979) has pointed out, kicking a stone and kicking a dog are two very different stories. The stone will react to the kick according to a linear chain of cause and effect. Its behaviour can be calculated by applying the basic laws of mechanics. The dog will respond with structural changes according to its own nature and non-linear pattern of behaviour. The resulting behaviour is generally unpredictable.

To conclude, as a project-based company responds to environmental influences with internal structural changes, these changes will in turn alter its future behaviour. This means that a structurally coupled, project-based company is a learning system. As long as a company remains functioning, it will couple structurally to its environment. Its continual structural changes in response to the environment – and consequently its continuing adaptation, learning, and development – are key characteristics of the behaviour of project-based companies.

Memory

Psychological research makes a distinction between learning and memory (e.g. Postman, 1976). Learning has more to do with acquisition, whereas memory has more to do with retention of whatever is acquired. In reality, however, separating these two processes is difficult because they are tightly interconnected. 'What we already have in our memory affects what we learn and what we learn affects our memory' (Kim, 1998) (cf. autopoitic epistemology in chapter 5). The concept of memory is commonly understood to be analogous to a storage device where everything we perceive and experience is filed away.

While sensing helps the company coordinate its functions within the changing business environment and to create new knowledge, memory maintains the company's daily functioning and utilization of accumulated knowledge. According to Maula (2006), this self-referentiality means that:

- The accumulated knowledge affects the company's mode of operation
- The mode of operation affects the creation and acquisition of new knowledge.

According to Hofstadter (1979), different organizational levels collapse, which makes it possible to understand the phenomenon of self-reference. These levels should be interpreted at the same time in terms of being separated and tangled, hierarchized and non-hierarchized. According to Hofstadter, this helps us understand 'strange loops', which threaten the stability of hierarchy and may even lead to its destruction. Every objective takes the place of another in a process of 'oscillation' that cannot be stopped (cf. Bakken and Hernes, 2002). Hence, self-referentiality can be a resource, but it can also be a constraint, depending on the implementation.

Thus, memory provides access to accumulated experience and knowledge. Knowledge is stored in the company's internal knowledge structure – such as a company's shared culture, strategies, rules, and practices. It can be stored in the competence of the company and the expertise of its individuals. Knowledge can also be stored in explicit form in databases.

Because there is a variety of knowledge, and the needs of project-based companies vary widely between each other, it is important that knowledge management practices support the specific needs of the company. For example, a small project-based company with a high degree of tacit knowledge may reduce the need to accumulate explicit knowledge. On the other hand, a large company which operates globally often shares and reuses explicit knowledge with the help of information technology. This creates opportunities to save time in routine parts of an assignment, and to focus on those parts that require innovation and expertise.

In sum, project-based companies utilize two processes, one that provides new knowledge for the company and coordinates it with the environment (sensing), and another that provides access to existing knowledge and increases effectiveness (memory). The processes are interconnected, for example, through information and communication systems. This means a continual coordination of these flows is necessary so that new knowledge becomes a part of the existing knowledge structure, and the existing knowledge structure helps to find, create, and evaluate new knowledge (cf. Maula, 2006).

Recursivity

According to autopoiesis theory and autopoietic epistemology, the interaction between process (e.g. project implementation) and stable (e.g. a project-based company's organizational memory) takes place through the operation referred to as *recursivity* (Luhmann, 1995a). Recursivity is what permits the reproduction of interactions over time. Having a recursive view of a project-based company implies dealing with questions of how the company persists and develops. For example, recursivity takes place when knowledge and skills needed by the company are offset against a company's present knowledge and skills, which again enable new knowledge and skills to occur. This means that a project-based company's knowledge and skills are developed by projects which, in turn, influence future projects. According to Giddens (1984), recursivity occurs in the field of tension between structure and action – that is, between a project-based company's organizational memory and the implementation of its projects respectively. Hence, a project-based company's memory and projects become mutual media for one another in recursive processes.

Recursivity is pivotal to the idea of autopoiesis. Autopoietic systems (e.g. project team members, a project team, or a project-based company), in contrast to allopoietic systems (technical systems), exist through their own production and reproduction. Rather than analysing companies as entities existing on an input-output basis in relation to their environments, the emphasis is on understanding how systems reproduce themselves (Bakken and Hernes, 2002).

Although actions (i.e. project implementations) are recursive, we prefer to think that there is a level beyond actions (e.g. a project-based company's organizational memory) that provides a context for actions. This level is not a level unaffected by the actions in the system. Instead, this other level is both produced by actions and influences the actions in turn. Recursivity refers principally to the interaction between actions and the context for actions. For example, project-based companies' memories are created through actions, that is, they form contexts within which projects take place. In other words, although a companies' memories were created in the past, they are formative for future projects. It is therefore impossible to understand the future without understanding the past, as the past is written into the future. Seen in this way, a project-based company's memories may constitute constraints, partly because they are created in the past, partly because they put limits on the actions that may be taken. That is, when new projects are negotiated, there is a repertoire of possibilities open to people involved. This repertoire is shaped by the projects that have been completed earlier. Whether they are expected or unanticipated, they serve to inform new projects. Consequently, the idea of recursivity represents explanatory potential for relationships between project-based companies' organizational memories and project implementations within the companies in ways that are not possible with singular epistemologies. This takes place by considering these companies as wavering between change and no change and understanding relationships between past, present and future so that new insights may be gained (cf. Bakken and Hernes, 2002).

To conclude, the idea of recursivity represents explanatory potential for bringing new light to the relationships between change and stability. It is by considering a project-based company as wavering between change (i.e. project implementation) and no change (organizational memory) and understanding relationships between past, present, and future that new insights may be gained.

Summary

Boundary elements influence an organization's learning and renewal capability by enabling two kinds of sensing activities:

- Exposure or awareness of an organization to perturbations in its environment that elicit compensating reactions
- Interactive processes and communication with clients, suppliers, and other entities.

The maintenance of an autopoietic system is based on sensing and memory, each of which constitutes a major knowledge flow and is part of the core of the dynamic process of a project-based company. Sensing and memory are likely to be simultaneous and interconnected phenomena.

That is, sensing (a condition of interactive openness) means that an organization interacts with its environment by being aware of and compensating for perturbations, by improving its knowledge (distinctions), and by changing internally. As an organization is exposed to its environment, its boundary elements and components are engaged in a process of mutual co-evolution (structural coupling) with its environment. An organization interacts reciprocally with its environment, and compensates for perturbations by making specific compensations in its internal structure. Some degree of interactive openness is thus necessary for creating and accumulating new knowledge that helps an organization sense and respond to its evolving environment.

And, memory (self-referentiality) means that:

- The organization has access to its existing knowledge
- Old accumulated knowledge affects the organization's 'structure' and operation
- The organization's 'structure' and operation affect the acquisition of new data and the creation of new knowledge. This can occur, for example, through an organization's use of accumulated knowledge to interpret new signals in its environment. Self-referentiality facilitates access to and learning from earlier experience and knowledge. Here self-referentiality is also used to refer to organizational memory.

Linkage between sensing and memory (interactive openness and self-referentiality) means that they are simultaneous and interconnected phenomena in an autopoietic system. Sensing helps to coordinate the functioning of an organization within the environment, while memory maintains the organization's efficient functioning.

Having a recursive view of a project-based company implies dealing with questions regarding how the company persists and develops. This means that the idea of recursivity represents explanatory potential for relationships between project-based companies' organizational memories and project implementations within companies in ways that are not possible with singular epistemologies.

To sum up, what knowledge does or does not affects the project-based company, and the nature of any effect is determined by the company's knowledge structure. The project-based company brings forth its own world. It observes, talks about, and knows about events – in its own manner – and thereby, it is sustained as a coherent system of knowledge.

10
The Project-Based Company as an Autopoietic Knowledge System

As discussed *autonomous or controlled* (cf. chapter 4), autopoiesis theory is a *relational theory*. The focus and level of observation determine whether a project-based company should be regarded as *autonomous or controlled*. The control and autonomy approaches complement each other. A project-based company may be seen as an autonomous whole while simultaneously its projects may be seen as input-process-output systems from the control perspective (cf. Varela, 1979). This means that it is possible to regard a project-based company simultaneously as an autonomous, autopoietic system capable of self-production, and as a controlled system.

Indeed, certain organizational phenomena, such as knowledge creation (i.e. learning), may imply that the project-based company is regarded as autonomous and capable of self-production. This means that when the focus is on the project-based company's learning and renewal processes, the autonomy perspective may be appropriate. Seen from this angle, the project-based company is controlled by its internal knowledge structure. This means that an autonomy perspective is applicable when a project-base-company's internal knowledge structure directs its functioning and the company thereby controls its own behaviour. Environmental influences, including externally defined purposes, goals, schemes, plans, and orders become perturbations (i.e. triggers) rather than inputs. That is, the project-based company has properties (e.g. internal laws) that are not controlled from the outside, but the company can modify its objectives internally as part of its autonomous operation. The autonomy approach helps us understand learning and renewal processes that are motivated, for example, by a company's strategic choices.

Some other phenomena, such as the transformation of customers' orders into project deliveries, means that the outputs (i.e. project deliveries) are determined by the inputs and the company operates as a controlled system. So, when we describe a project-based company's production process, the control approach can be used. The control approach reduces a company to input-output behaviour in which the environment – like customers' orders – largely determines its functioning.

Evolution and learning in the project-based company

Various combinations of sensing and memory can describe a project-based company's potential to evolve (cf. Maula, 2006):

- When a project-based company systematically explores and accumulates knowledge it can learn effectively from perturbations from its environment and then it co-evolves with its environment. The company identifies new knowledge through its boundary elements and then also utilizes its earlier knowledge continually accumulating experiences.
- When a project-based company seeks new innovations it means that instead of responding to external perturbations, it utilizes its knowledge and other internal resources proactively, combines them in creative way, acts first, and then receives the response from its environment. In this way, a project-based company produces original, self-generated, and innovative outcomes with the potential to influence the environment with a time delay. A project-based company can facilitate endogenous development and originality and use accumulated knowledge creatively. Based on responses from the environment, a project-based company may react according to its internal rules.
- When a project-based company adapts to situations and circumstances means its efficient exploration and co-evolution with the environment and inefficient utilization of earlier experiences. This type of project-based company is 'double-open'. It uses its sensing but not its memory. The company continually seeks new experiences and changes itself at a rapid tempo. However, it cannot learn from its experiences and utilize them.
- When a project-based company isolates itself from its environment it means that it uses its memory but not its sensing capability. Interaction with its environment is weak or missing. Knowledge is based on organizational memory only. This type of evolution may result in endogenous, self-generated outcomes that lack viability.
- When a project-based company is passive, it means that it does not learn from the perturbations from its environment, i.e. it does not

have sensing capability. Moreover, it does not learn from its own accumulated experiences. Therefore, the company is not coordinated with its environment, it does not function in an efficient way, and it does not have the capability to co-evolve with its environment.

The link between the learning of individual project team members, project teams, and that of the project-based company, occupies a critical position in practice. Simon (1991, p. 125) has defined organizational learning as the insights and successful restructuring of organizational problems by individuals as reflected in the structural elements and outcomes of the organization itself. In other words, he rejected the notion that organizations as project teams and project-based companies themselves learn, claiming that 'all learning takes place inside individual human heads' and that organizations learn either through the learning of their members or by taking in new members with new knowledge.

In a detailed account of the links between learning at the individual (e.g. a project team member), group (e.g. a project team), and organizational (e.g. project-based company) levels, Argyris and Schön (1996, p. 4) represented individual knowledge as 'theories of action' which include strategies of action, the values that govern the choice of strategies, and the assumptions on which those strategies and values are based. These authors also posited the existence of group and organizational theories of action that account for the patterned way in which groups and organizations perform their tasks. On both the individual and organizational levels, Argyris and Schön made a critical distinction between 'espoused' theory, which represents what people or organizations say about their behaviour, and theories-in-use, which are implicit in that behaviour. Argyris and Schön not only found contradictions between the two kinds of theories they also found that individuals were unaware of the contradictions. Thus, according to this approach, one can understand a project-based company's learning only by examining the ways in which individual team members and interpersonal inquiries are linked to organizational patterns of both action and learning that are characteristic of project teams and the organization as a whole (Friedman, 2002).

Furthermore, according to the ethno-methodology framework of organizational learning, the knowledge creation of a project-based company is based on the juxtaposition between exploration and exploitation (Crossan et al., 1999; Bontis et al., 2002). This means that the renewal of the companies is based on their exploring and their creation of new knowledge at the same time as exploiting the knowledge they already have. This framework considers knowledge creation at three

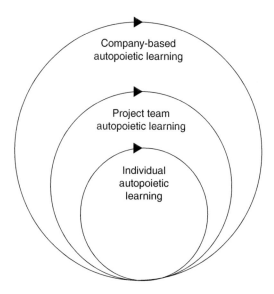

Figure 10.1 The three autopoietic learning levels.

levels, namely at the individual, team, and company levels. Therefore, we can conclude that knowledge creation (i.e. learning) takes place at various levels, that is, autopoietic knowledge creation at various organizational levels (Figure 10.1).

Besides knowledge creation from past experiences and establishing standard practices within the project-base company, some companies are noted for making conscious attempts to unlearn certain lessons from the past, and to engage themselves in a continuous process of 'creative destruction'. This process of unlearning is said to prevent development processes from becoming too rigid. This means that the challenge is to avoid learning myopia, and to retain some of the useful knowledge accumulated from the past, while at the same time discarding that part of knowledge which is no longer applicable. However, according to autopoietic epistemology, unlearning is not possible. This is due to the fact that what an individual learns is influenced by what he or she knows and has learnt before, that is, what kinds of knowledge are stored in his or her memory.

All in all, a project-based company can be described by sensing through boundary elements that coordinate the company with its environment, and by organizational memory that maintains the company's

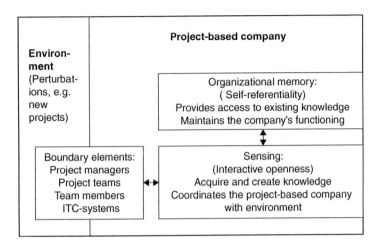

Figure 10.2 Project-based company as an autopoietic knowledge system.

functioning. These characteristics are interconnected and simultaneous. They are facilitated by the knowledge flows. This means that project-based companies compensate for environmental perturbations by changing internally whereby knowledge is accumulated with the help of the formation of new and different projects. Figure 10.2 visualizes the project-based company by presenting the relationship between sensing, memory, and boundary elements.

To sum up, the project-based company serves to bind projects over time. This means that it is nearly inconceivable that project-based company can exist without such binding. Company presupposes interaction around projects and provides essential stabilization of expectations among those who take part in these projects. It is equally inconceivable that project-based companies should exist without projects. In the absence of projects, there is nothing to inform companies hence they would not be able to reproduce themselves.

Improving a project-based company's potential to be an autopoietic knowledge system

According to the basic principles of autopoiesis, it is not possible to control a project-based company and the people working for it from outside. Instead, a company may implement changes that its people regard as relevant and in line with the company's identity, existing knowledge, and other relevant components. Therefore, it is important to plan a possible intervention so that it begins by strengthening awareness and clarifying the identity.

A project-based company seen as an autopoietic knowledge system helps in understanding how to create an infrastructure that enables learning and continuous renewal in a company. The core issue is to coordinate, clarify, and strengthen the components into a composition so that the two major knowledge flows – sensing and memory – function better. This may imply changes in individual components or more comprehensive changes in the whole 'puzzle'.

Therefore, in a project-based company it is necessary to create awareness and communicate the need for change. This is because the development process must be based on a shared understanding of strengths, problems, objectives, and methods. Consequently, it is important to ensure that there is sufficient awareness of the general principles of autopoietic knowledge creation.

A project-based company's 12 components largely determine its current capability to renew itself and to co-evolve with its environment. Therefore an analysis of these components and their relationships is needed. Their systematic analysis helps in depicting the system and communicating the specific development needs to a company, and helps individuals in different projects and positions to understand the strengths and weaknesses in the different components and their relationships.

The analysis of sensing benefits from the careful investigation of existing and potential boundary elements (i.e. roles and functions) and their functioning. The sensing activities – exposure to triggers and responding to them, interactive processes, and communication with the environment – also have to be mapped and evaluated. Organizational memory, especially the type and location of critical knowledge and access to it, is also a target for analysis.

There is no standard content for the components within the system to be implemented. Taking the current composition as a point of departure, the following task is to design improvements to the composition or to design a new composition, and to align the components so that the composition becomes a functioning entity. Sometimes better coordination of current individual components may be sufficient, and sometimes the composition may require a more thorough revision and alignment. This is the case, for example, in project-based companies that have resulted from mergers and acquisitions, because they may have two different organizational cultures that have to be coordinated and streamlined into a functioning entity.

One of the tasks is to prioritize the improvements to the system so that their systemic effects can be maximized. Communicating the improvement plans in the company may increase the systemic effects. The improvements may also cause systemic effects in the business environment. It may therefore be useful to test the systemic impact of the new composition, for example on a smaller scale before launching it on a larger scale.

Implementation of the changes to a system probably causes changes in organizational culture and attitudes of people. The current system may have evolved during a long period, and therefore the acceptance and development of the new enabling infrastructure may face some resistance and take a long time. Therefore, it is important to utilize the systemic effects and to build the process by accumulating successes. It is also important to communicate the commitment to long-term development of the enabling infrastructure.

Finally, in order to facilitate the evolutionary process properly, it is useful to create methods to measure the most critical aspects of its functioning and the impact of the composition of the project-based company's learning and renewal. Measurement should focus mainly on aspects that are systemically important, and should enable and facilitate development. It is also useful to continually improve the structure and functioning of the system and the co-evolution of the company with its business ecosystem.

Summary

Autopoiesis theory is a relational theory. Therefore, the focus and level of observation determine whether a project-based company should be regarded as autonomous or controlled. From this it follows that it is possible to regard a project-based company simultaneously as an autonomous, autopoietic system capable of self-production, and as a controlled system.

Various combinations of sensing and memory can describe a project-based company's evolutionary potential. For example, the company's evolution is effective when it systematically explores and accumulates knowledge. As a result, it learns from perturbations from its environment and co-evolves with its environment. The company identifies new knowledge through its boundary elements and then it also utilizes its earlier continually accumulating experiences.

The link between the learning of individual project team members, project teams, and the project-based company occupies a critical position in the practice of the project-based company's learning. The renewal of a project-based company is based on its exploration of new knowledge at the same time as it exploits the knowledge it already has. This means that autopoietic knowledge creation takes place at three levels, namely at the individual, team, and company levels.

The project-based company serves to bind projects over time. This means that it is nearly inconceivable that a project-based company can exist without such binding. A company presupposes interaction around projects and provides essential stabilization of expectations among those who take part in these projects. It is equally inconceivable that project-based companies should exist without projects. In the absence of projects there is nothing to inform companies, hence they would not be able to reproduce themselves.

According to the basic principles of autopoiesis, it is not possible to control a project-based company and the people working in it from outside. Instead, a company may implement changes that its people regard as relevant and in line with the company's identity, existing knowledge, and other relevant components.

Epilogue

Knowledge management is today an integral feature of project-based companies that try to exploit their knowledge resources to generate superior performance. More than ever the success of project-based companies is governed by their abilities to manage knowledge assets that can improve the efficiency and effectiveness of project management. Therefore, project-based companies can be seen as knowledge-intensive units, which can be approached in terms of systems. I have utilized systems thinking – the autopoietic approach in particular – in order to gain a better understanding of project-based companies as knowledge-producing systems.

Autopoiesis theory is a relational theory. Therefore, the focus and level of observation determine whether a system – the project-based company in our case – should be regarded as autonomous or controlled. From this it follows that it is possible to regard a project-based company simultaneously as an autonomous, autopoietic system capable of self-production, and as a controlled system.

In my view, the project-based company as an autopoietic knowledge-producing system consists of 12 different non-physical components. The properties of and relationships among these components determine the interaction processes of a company's knowledge production. Their interaction maintains a company's functioning, learning, renewal, and co-evolution with its environment. However, although the components can be identified in project-based companies, there can be a significant variation among them depending on the environment type in which the company operates.

The non-physical components and relationships among them enable two major knowledge flows: sensing and memory. Sensing means that the project-based company interacts, co-evolves, and coordinates its activities with its changing environment. Memory, in turn, means that the company has access to its own accumulated knowledge. Consequently, sensing and memory help the project-based company to make distinctions that then become embedded in its knowledge structure.

There are numerous ideas that have been used to advance knowledge management and production in project-based companies. In this book I have sought to offer systems thinking and autopoietic epistemology as the basis of a new understanding of knowledge, learning, and knowledge transfer in these companies. In other words, the choice is based on the idea of presenting a fresh – alternative – observational scheme for the understanding of knowledge management and production in projects and project-based companies.

Bibliography

Ahmed, K. P., Lim, K. K., and Loh, Y. W. (2002). *Learning through Knowledge Management*. Oxford: Butterworth-Heinemann.

Ajmal, M. M. and Koskinen K. U. (2008). 'Knowledge Transfer in Project-Based Organizations: An Organizational Culture Perspective'. *Project Management Journal*, 39(1), pp. 7–15.

Aldrich, H. (1999). *Organizations Evolving*. London: SAGE Publications.

Allee, V. (1997). *The Knowledge Evolution: Expanding Organizational Intelligence*. Boston: Butterworth-Heinemann.

Allen, T. J. (1977). *Managing the Flow of Technology: Technology Transfer and the Dissemination of Technological Information within the R&D Organisation*. Cambridge: MIT Press.

Amit, R. and Schoemaker, P. (1993). 'Strategic Assets and Organizational Rent'. *Strategic Management Journal*, 14, pp. 33–46.

Amtoft, M. (1994). 'Storytelling as a Support Tool for Project Management'. *International Journal of Project Management*, 12(4), pp. 230–3.

Ancori, B., Bureth, A., and Cohendet, P. (2000). 'The Economics of Knowledge: The Debate about Codification and Tacit Knowledge'. *Industrial and Corporate Change*, 9(2), pp. 255–87.

André, R. (2008). *Organizational Behavior: An Introduction to Your Life in Organizations*. Upper Saddle River: Pearson Education Inc.

Andrew, A. M. (1989). *Self-Organizing Systems*. New York: Gordon & Breach Science Publishers.

Anell, B. I. and Wilson, T. L. (2002). 'Organizing in Two Modes: On the Merging of the Temporary and the Permanent'. In: K. Sahlin-Andersson and A. Söderholm (Eds), *Beyond Project Management* (pp. 170–86). Malmö: Liber.

Aramo-Immonen, H. (2009). *Project Management Ontology: The Organizational Learning Perspective*. Tampere: Tampere University of Technology. Publication 836.

Aramo-Immonen, H., Porkka, P., and Koskinen K. U. (2009). 'The Role of Formal Training in Project-based Companies'. In K. Kähkönen, A. S. Kazi, and M. Rekola (Eds), *The Human Side of Projects in Modern Business* (pp. 695–708). Helsinki: Project Management Association Finland (PMAF) in collaboration with VTT Technical Research Centre of Finland.

Argyris, C. and Schön, D. A. (1978). *Organizational Learning: A Theory of Action Perspective*. Reading: Addison-Wesley.

Argyris, C. (1989). *Reasoning, Learning, and Action: Individual and Organizational*. San Francisco: Jossey-Bass.

Argyris, C. and Schön, D. A. (1996). *Organizational Learning II*. Reading: Addison-Wesley.

Artto, K., Heinonen, R., Arenius, M. Kovanen, V., and Nyberg, T. (1998). *Projektiliiketoiminta yrityksen menestystekijäksi* (Project Business for a Benefit to a Company). Helsinki: TEKES.

Artto, K. A. and Wikström, K. (2005). 'What is Project Business?' *International Journal of Project Management*, 23(5), pp. 343–53.

Artto, K. and Kujala, J. (2008). 'Project Business as a Research Field'. *International Journal of Managing Projects in Business*, 1(4), pp. 469–97.

Ashby, W. R. (1956). *An Introduction to Cybernetics*. London: Chapman and Hall.

Ashby, W. R. (1968). 'Principles of the Self-Organizing System'. In: W. Buckley (Ed.), *Modern Systems Research for the Behavioral Scientist* (pp. 108–18). Chicago: Aldine Publishing Company.

Ashkanasy, N. M., Wilderom, C. P. M., and Peterson, M. F. (2000). *Handbook of Organizational Culture and Climate*. Thousand Oaks: SAGE Publications.

Ayas, K. and Zeniuk, N. (2001). 'Project-Based Learning: Building Communities of Reflective Practitioners'. *Management Learning*, 32(1), pp. 61–76.

Badaracco, J. L. and Ellsworth, R. R. (1989). *Quest for Integrity*. Boston: Harvard Business School Press.

Badaracco, J. L. (1991). *The Knowledge Link: How Firms Compete through Strategic Alliances*. Boston: Harvard Business School Press.

Baecker, D. (1996). 'Kybernetik Zweiter Ordnung' (Second Order Cybernetics). In: H. von Foerster (Ed.), *Wissen und Gewissen: Versuch einer Brücke* (Knowledge and Conscience: Trial of a Bridge) (pp. 17–23). Frankfurt am Main: Suhrkamp.

Baier, A. (1986). 'Trust and Antitrust'. *Ethics* 96 (2), pp. 231–260.

Bakken, T. and Hernes. T. (2002), 'The Macro-Micro Problem in Organization Theory: Luhmann's Autopoiesis as a Way of Handling Recursivity'. In T. Bakken, and T. Hernes (Eds), *Autopoietic Organization Theory* (pp. 53–74). Oslo: Abstrakt.

Banathy, B. H. (2000). *Guided Evolution of Society: A Systems View*. New York: Kluwer Academic Publishers.

Barklay, B. T. and Saylor, J. H. (1994). *Customer-Driven Project Managements*. Boston: McGraw-Hill.

Barney, J. B. (1991). 'Firm Resources and Sustained Competitive Advantage'. *Journal of Management*, 17(1), pp. 99–120.

Barney, J. B. and Hansen, M. H. (1994). 'Trustworthiness as a Source of Competitive Advantage'. *Strategic Management Journal*, 15, Special Issue, pp. 175–90.

Barney, J. B. (2001). 'Is the Resource-Based "View" a Useful Perspective for Strategic Management Research? Yes'. *Academy of Management Review*, 26(1), pp. 41–56.

Baron, R. A. and Markman, G. D. (2000). 'Beyond Social Capital'. *Academy of Management Executive*, 14, pp. 106–16.

Bartol, K. and Srivastava, A. (2002). 'Encouraging Knowledge Sharing: The Role of Organizational Reward Systems'. *Journal of Leadership and Organization Studies*, 9(1), pp. 64–76.

Bateson, G. (1972). *Steps to an Ecology of Mind: Collected Essays in Anthropology, Psychiatry, Evolution, and Epistemology*. Chicago: University of Chicago Press.

Bateson, G. (1979). *Mind and Nature: A Necessary Unity (Advances in Systems Theory, Complexity, and the Human Sciences)*. New York: Hampton Press.

Batterman, R. (2001). *The Devil in the Details: Asymptotic Reasoning in Explanation, Reduction, and Emergence*. Oxford: Oxford University Press.

Baum, J. A. C. and Singh, J. V. (1994a). 'Organizational Hierarchies and Evolutionary Processes: Some Reflections on a Theory of Organizational Evolution'. In: J. A. C. Baum and J. V. Singh (Eds), *Evolutionary Dynamics of Organizations* (pp. 3–20). Oxford: Oxford University Press.

Baum, J. A. C. and Singh, J. V. (1994b). 'Organization-Environment Coevolution'. In: J. A. C. Baum and J. V. Singh (Eds), *Evolutionary Dynamics of Organizations* (pp. 379–402). Oxford: Oxford University Press.

Baumard, P. (2001). *Tacit Knowledge in Organizations*. London: SAGE Publications.

Bechky, B. (2003). 'Sharing Meaning across Occupational Communities: The Transformation of Understanding on the Production Floor'. *Organization Science*, 14, pp. 312–30.

Becker, A. (1991). 'A Short Essay on Languaging'. In: F. Steier (Ed.), *Research and Reflexivity* (pp. 226–34). Beverly Hills: SAGE Publications.

Behling, O. and Eckel, H. (1991). 'Making Sense Out of Intuition'. *Academy of Management Executive*, 5(1), pp. 46–54.

Bell, S. and Morse, S. (1999). *Sustainability Indicators: Measuring the Immeasurable*. London: Earthscan.

Bengtsson, M. and Erikson, J. (2002). 'Stickiness and Leakiness in Inter-Organizational Innovation Projects'. In: K. Sahlin-Andersson and A. Söderholm (Eds), *Beyond Project Management* (pp. 81–107). Malmö: Liber.

Berger, P. and Luckman, T. (1966). *The Social Construction of Reality*. New York: Penguin.

Berger, P. (1981). *The Sacred Canopy*. Garden City: Doubleday.

von Bertalanffy, L. (1968). *General System Theory*. New York: Braziller.

Bettelheim, B. (1976). *The Uses of Enchantment: The Meaning and Importance of Fairy Tales*. London: Thames & Hudson.

Bickerton, D. (1993). *Language and Species*. Chicago: University of Chicago Press.

Biggiero, L. (2001). 'Are Firms Autopoietic Systems?' In: F. Geyer and J. van der Zouwen (Eds), *Sociocybernetics: Complexity, Autopoiesis, and Observation of Social Systems* (pp. 125–39). London: Greenwood Press.

Bittner, E. (1974). 'The Concept of Organization'. In: R. Turner (Ed.), *Ethnomethodology* (pp. 267–311). Harmondsworth: Penguin.

Black, M. (1962). *Models and Metaphors*. Ithaca: Cornell University Press.

Blackler, F. (1995). 'Knowledge, Knowledge Work and Organizations: An Overview and Interpretation'. *Organization Studies*, 16(6), pp. 1021–46.

Blackler, F., Crump, N., and McDonald, S. (1998). 'Knowledge, Organizations and Competition'. In: G. von Krogh, J. Roos, and D. Kleine (Eds), *Knowing in Firms* (pp. 67–86). London: SAGE Publications.

Blackler, F., Crump, N., and McDonald, S. (1999). 'Managing Experts and Competing through Innovation: An Activity Theoretical Analysis'. *Organization Articles*, 6(1), pp. 5–31.

Blau, G. (1995). 'Influence of Group Lateness on Individual Lateness: A Cross-level Examination'. *Academy of Management Journal*, 38(5), pp. 1482–96.

Blomquist, T. and Söderholm, A. (2002). 'How Project Management Got Carried Away'. In K. Sahlin-Anderson and A. Söderholm (Eds), *Beyond Project Management* (pp. 25–38). Malmö: Liber.

Boddy, D. and Paton, R. (2004). 'Responding to Competing Narratives: Lessons for Project Managers'. *International Journal of Project Management*, 22, pp. 225–33.

Boden, D. (1994). *The Business of Talk*. Cambridge: Polity Press.

Boh, W. F. (2007). 'Mechanisms for Sharing Knowledge in Project-Based Organizations'. *Information and Organization*, 17, pp. 27–58.

Boisot, M. H. (1983). 'Convergence Revisited: The Codification and Diffusion of Knowledge in a British and a Japanese Firm'. *Journal of Management Studies*, 1, pp. 159–90.

Boisot, M. H. (1995). 'Is your Firm a Creative Destroyer? Competitive Learning and Knowledge Flows in the Technological Strategies of Firms'. *Research Policy*, 24, pp. 489–506.

Boisot, M. H., Lemmon, T., Griffits, D., and Mole, V. (1996). 'Spinning a Good Yarn: The Identification of Core Competencies at Courtalds'. *International Journal of Innovation Management*, 11(3/4), pp. 425–40.

Boje, D. (1995). 'Stories of the Storytelling Organization: A Postmodern Analysis of Disney as "Tamara-Land"'. *Academy of Management Journal*, 36, pp. 997–1035.

Bolman, L. G. and Deal, T. E. (1997). *Reframing Organizations: Artistry, Choice and Leadership*. San Francisco: Jossey-Bass.

Boland, R. J. and Tenkasi, R. V. (1995). 'Perspective Making and Perspective Taking in Communities of Knowing'. *Organization Science*, 6(4), pp. 350–72.

Bonner, J. T. (1969). *The Scale of Nature*. New York: Pegasus.

Bontis, N., Crossan, M., and Hulland, J. (2002). 'Managing an Organizational Learning System by Aligning Stocks and Flows'. *Journal of Management Studies*, 39(4), pp. 437–69.

Boulding, K. (1956). 'General Systems Theory: The Skeleton of Science'. *Management of Science*, 2(3), pp. 197–208.

Bower, G. H. and Hilgard, E. R. (1981). *Theories of Learning*. Englewood Cliffs: Prentice-Hall.

Bowker, G. C. and Star, S. L. (2002). *Sorting Things Out: Classification and Its Consequences*. Cambridge: MIT Press.

Boyatzis, R. E. (1982). *The Competent Manager: A Model for Effective Performance*. New York: John Wiley & Sons.

Bradshaw, J. M. (1997). 'An Introduction to Software Agents'. In: J. M. Bradshaw (Ed.), *Software Agents* (pp. 3–46). Cambridge: MIT Press.

Brady, T. and Davies, A. (2004). 'Building Project Capabilities: From Exploratory to Exploitative Learning'. *Organization Studies*, 25(9), pp. 1601–21.

Bresnen, M., Goussevskaia, A., and Swan, J. (2004). 'Embedding New Management Knowledge in Project-Based Organizations'. *Organization Studies*, 25(9), pp. 1535–55.

Briner, W., Geddes, M., and Hastings, C. (1990). *Project Leadership*. Aldershot: Gower.

Brown, J. S. and Duguid, P. (1991). 'Organizational Learning and Communities-of-Practice: Toward a Unified View of Working, Learning and Innovation'. *Organization Science*, 2(1), pp. 40–57.

Brown, S. and Eisenhardt, K. (1997). 'The Art of Continuous Change: Linking Complexity Theory and Time-paced Evolution in Relentlessly Shifting Organizations'. *Administrative Science Quarterly*, 42, pp. 1–34.

Brown, A. D. (1998). *Organisational Culture*. London: Pearson Education Ltd.

Brown, A. and Starkey, K. (2000). 'Organizational Identity and Learning: A Psychodynamic Perspective'. *Academy of Management Review*, 25(1), pp. 102–20.

Bruner, J. (1990). *Acts of Meaning*. Cambridge: Harvard University Press.

Bruner, J. S. and Anglin, J. M. (1973). *Beyond the Information Given*. New York: Norton.

Buchanan, D. and Huczynski, A. (1997). *Organizational Behaviour: An Introductory Text*. London: Prentice-Hall.

Buckley, W. (1967). *Sociology and Modern Systems Theory*. Englewood Cliffs: Prentice-Hall.

Burgelman, R. A. (1983). 'Corporate Entrepreneurship and Strategic Management: Insights from a Process Study'. *Management Science*, 29, pp. 1349–64.

Burgess, R. and Turner, S. (2000). 'Seven Key Features for Creating and Sustaining Commitment'. *International Journal of Project Management*, 18, pp. 225–33.

Burns, T. and Stalker, G. M. (1994). *The Management of Innovation*. London: Oxford University Press Inc.

Burt, R. (1987). 'Social Contagion and Innovation: Cohesion versus Structural Equivalence'. *American Journal of Sociology*, 92(1), pp. 1287–335.

Burton, R. and Obel, B. (1995). *Design Models for Hierarchical Organizations: Information and Decentralization*. Boston: Kluwer Academic Publishers.

Cacciatori, E. (2003). 'Organisational Memory in Innovative Project-Based Firms – A Boundary Object Perspective'. Paper presented at the DRUID Summer Conference 2003 on 'Creating, Sharing and Transferring Knowledge: The Role of Geographical Configurations, Institutional Settings and Organizational Contexts'. Copenhagen: Esinore.

Calvino, I. (1990). *Six Memos for the Next Millennium*. London: Cage.

Cannon-Bowers, J. A., Salas, E., and Converse, S. A. (1993). 'Shared Mental Models in Expert Team Decision Making'. In: N. J. Castellan (Ed.), *Current Issues in Individual and Group Decision Making* (pp. 221–46). Hillsdale: Elbraun.

Capra, F. (1996). *The Web of Life: A New Scientific Understanding of Living Systems*. New York: Anchor Books.

Carlile, P. (2002). 'A Pragmatic View of Knowledge and Boundaries: Boundary Objects in New Product Development'. *Organizational Science*, 13(4), pp. 442–55.

Carlile, P. (2004). 'Transferring, Translating, and Transforming: An Integrative Framework for Managing Knowledge across Boundaries'. *Organization Science*, 15(5), pp. 555–68.

Carroll, G. R. (1985). 'Concentration and Specialization: Dynamics of Niche Width in Populations of Organizations'. *American Journal of Sociology*, 90(6), pp. 1262–83.

Cassapo, F. M. and Scalabrin, E. E. (2004). 'Autopoietic Societies: A Hermeneutic Approach to Socio-Cognitive Engineering'. In *Proceedings of the Fifth European Conference on Organizational Knowledge, Learning, and Capabilities*. Innsbruck, Austria.

Chakravarthy, B. S. and Doz, Y. (1992). 'Strategy Process Research: Focusing on Corporate Self-Renewal'. *Strategic Management Journal*, 13, Special Issue, pp. 5–14.

Chan, R. and Rosemann, M. (2001). 'Managing Knowledge in Enterprise Systems'. *Journal of Systems and Information Technology*, 5(2), pp. 37–53.

Checkland, P. (1999). *Systems Thinking, Systems Practice: Includes a 30-Year Retrospective*. New York: John Wiley & Sons.

Checkland, P. and Scholes, J. (1990). *Soft Systems Methodology in Action*. Chichester: John Wiley & Sons.

Chia, R. (1994). 'The Concept of Decision: A Deconstructive Analysis'. *Journal of Management Studies*, 31, pp. 781–806.

Cicmil, S. (1997). 'Perspectives: Critical Factors of Effective Project Management'. *The TQM Magazine*, 6(6), pp. 390–6.

Cohen, W. and Levinthal, D. (1990). 'Absorptive Capacity: A New Perspective on Learning and Innovation'. *Administrative Science Quarterly*, 35, pp. 128–52.

Cohen, M. D. and Bacdyan, P. (1994). 'Organizational Routines are Stored as Procedural Memory: Evidence from a Laboratory Study'. *Organization Science*, 5(4), pp. 554–68.

Conklin, J. (2001). 'Designing Organizational Memory: Preserving Intellectual Assets in a Knowledge Economy'. http://cognexus.org, retrieved 31 October 2005.

Connelly, C. E. and Kelloway, E. K. (2003). 'Predictors of Employees' Perceptions of Knowledge Sharing Cultures'. *Leadership & Organization Development Journal*, 24(5), pp. 294–301.

Conroy, G. and Soltan, H. (1998). 'ConSERV, as a Continual Audit Concept to Provide Traceability and Accountability over the Project Life Cycle'. *International Journal of Project Management*, 16(3), pp. 185–97.

Cooper, R. (1986). 'Organization/Disorganization'. *Social Science Information*, 25, pp. 299–335.

Cowan, R., David, P. A., and Foray, D. (2000). 'The Explicit Economics of Knowledge Codification and Tacitness'. *Industrial and Corporate Change*, 9(2), pp. 211–53.

Cross, R. and Baird, L. (2000). 'Technology Is Not Enough: Improving Performance by Building Organizational Memory'. *Sloan Management Review*, (Spring 2000), pp. 68–78.

Crossan, M. M., Lane, H., and White, R. (1999). 'An Organizational Learning Framework: From Intuition to Institution'. *Academy of Management Review*, 24(3), pp. 522–37.

Cyert, R. M. and March, J. G. (1963). *A Behavioural Theory of the Firm*. London: Blackwell.

Czarniawska, B. (1998). *A Narrative Approach to Organization Studies*. Thousand Oaks: SAGE Publications.

Daft, R. L. and Lengel, R. H. (1984). 'Information Richness: A New Approach to Managerial Behavior and Organization Design'. *Research in Organizational Behavior*, 6, pp. 191–233.

Daft, R. L. and Weick, K. E. (1984). 'Toward a Model of Organizations as Interpretation Systems'. *Academy of Management Review*, 9(2), pp. 284–95.

D'Aveni, R. A. and Gunther, R. (1994). *Hypercompetition – Managing the Dynamics of Strategic Maneuvering*. New York: Free Press.

Davenport, T. H., De Long D. W., and Beers, M. C. (1997). 'Building Successful Knowledge Management Projects'. *Managing the Knowledge of the Organization*. Boston: Ernst & Young LLP.

Davenport, T. H. and Prusak, L. (1998). *Working Knowledge: How Organizations Manage What They Know*. Boston: Harvard Business School Press.

Davies, A. and Brady, T. (2000). 'Organisational Capabilities and Learning in Complex Product Systems: Towards Repeatable Solutions'. *Research Policy*, 29, pp. 931–53.

Dawes, R. M. (1994). *House of Cards: Psychology and Psychotherapy Built on Myth*. New York: Free Press.

Day, N. (1998). 'Informal Learning Gets Results'. *Workforce*, June, pp. 31–6.

Day, J. and Wendler, B. (1998). 'The Power of Knowledge'. *McKinsey Quarterly*, 3, pp. 22–8.

Deal, T. and Kennedy, A. (1982). *Corporate Cultures: The Rites and Rituals of Corporate Life*. Reading: Addison-Wesley Publishing Company.

DeFilippi, R. J. and Arthur, M. B. (1998). 'Paradox in Project-Based Enterprise: The Case of Film-Making'. *Californian Management Review*, 40, pp. 125–39.

De Long, D. W. and Fahey, L. (2000). 'Diagnosing Cultural Barriers to Knowledge Management'. *Academy of Management Executive*, 14(4), pp. 113–27.

Deming, W. E. (1986). *Out of the Crisis*. Boston: MIT Press.

Denison, D. R. (1990). *Corporate Culture and Organizational Effectiveness*. New York: John Wiley & Sons.

Denning, S. (2001). *The Springboard: How Storytelling Ignites Action in Knowledge-Era Organizations*. Boston: Butterworth-Heinemann.

Denning, S. (2004). *Squirrel Inc.: A Fable of Leadership through Storytelling*. San Francisco: Jossey-Bass.

Dickson, A. (1982). *A Woman in Your Own Right*. London: Quartet Books.

Dickson, A. (2000). *Trusting the Tides*. London: Rider.

Dierickx, I. and Cool, K. (1989). 'Asset Stock Accumulation and Sustainability of Competitive Advantage'. *Management Science*, 33(12), pp. 1504–13.

van Dijk, T. A. (1975). 'Action, Action Description, and Narrative'. *New Literary History*, 6, pp. 275–94.

Dill, W. R. (1958). 'Environment as an Influence on Managerial Autonomy'. *Administrative Science Quarterly*, 2, pp. 409–43.

Disterer, G. (2001). 'Individual and Social Barriers to Knowledge Transfer'. In *Proceedings of the Thirty-Fourth Annual Hawaii International Conference on System Sciences*, Hawaii.

Dodgson, M. (1993). 'Organizational Learning: A Review of Some Literatures'. *Organization Studies*, 14(3), pp. 375–94.

Dougherty, D. (1992). 'Interpretive Barriers to Successful Product Innovation in Large Firms'. *Organization Science*, 3, pp. 179–202.

Doz, Y. L. and Prahalad, C. K. (1993). 'Managing DMNCs: A Search for a New Paradigm'. In: S. Ghoshal and E. D. Westney (Eds), *Organization Theory and the Multinational Corporation* (pp. 24–50). New York: St. Martin's Press.

Drew, P. and Heritage, J. (1992). 'Analysing Talk at Work'. In: P. Drew and J. Heritage (Eds), *Interaction in Institutional Settings*. Cambridge: Cambridge University Press.

Drucker, P. F. (1954). *The Practice of Management*. New York: Harper & Row.

Drucker, P. F. (1993). 'The New Society of Organizations'. In: R. Howard (Ed.), *The Learning Imperative: Managing People for Continuous Innovation* (pp. 3–17). Cambridge: Harvard Business Review Press.

Druskat, V.U. and Wolff, S.B. (2001). Building Emotional Intelligence of Groups. *Harvard Business Review*, March.

Duncan, R. and Weiss, A. (1979). 'Organizational Learning: Implications for Organizational Design'. In: B. M. Staw (Ed.), *Research in Organizational Behavior* (pp. 75–123). Greenwich: JAI Press.

Dupeuy, J-P. (1988). 'On the Supposed Closure of Normative Systems'. In: G. Teubner (Ed.), *Autopoietic Law: A New Approach to Law and Society* (pp. 51–69). Berlin: Walter de Gruyter.

Easton, G. and Araujo, L. (1993). 'Language, Metaphors and Networks'. *Advances in International Marketing*, 5, pp. 67–85.

Edvinsson, L. and Malone, M. S. (1997). *Intellectual Capital: The Proven Way to Establish Your Company's Real Value by Measuring Its Hidden Brainpower*. London: HarperCollins Publishers, Inc.

Engeström, Y. (2000). 'Activity Theory as a Framework for Analyzing and Redesigning Work'. *Ergonomics*, 43(7), pp. 960–74.

Engeström, Y. (2001). 'Expansive Learning at Work'. *Journal of Education and Work: Towards an Activity Theoretical Reconceptualization*, 14(1), pp. 132–56.

Fiol, C. M. (1989). 'A Semiotic Analysis of Corporate Language: Organizational Boundaries and Joint Venturing'. *Administrative Science Quarterly*, 34, 2, pp. 277–303.

Fisher, W. R. (1987). *Human Communication as Narration: Toward a Philosophy of Reason, Value, and Action*. Columbia: University of South Carolina Press.

Fiske, S. T. and Taylor, S. F. (1991). *Social Cognition*. New York: McGraw-Hill.

Flannes, S. W. and Levin, G. (2001). *People Skills for Project Managers*. Vienna: Management Concepts.

Fleischaker, G. R. (1992). 'Autopoiesis in Systems Analysis: A Debate'. *International Journal of General Systems*, 21(2).

Flood, R. L. (1990). *Liberating Systems Theory*. New York: Plenum Press.

Flood, R. L. (1999). *Rethinking the Fifth Discipline: Learning within the Unknowable*. London: Routledge.

Flöistad, G. (1993). *Kunsten å omgås hverande* (The art of getting on with people). Gyldendal: Ad Notam.

von Foerster, H. (1972). 'Responsibilities of Competence'. *Journal of Cybernetics*, 2(2), pp. 1–6.

von Foerster, H. (1984). 'Principles of Self-Organization in Socio-Managerial Context'. In: H. Ulrich and G. J. B. Probst (Eds), *Self-Organization and Management of Social Systems* (pp. 2–24). Berlin: Springer.

Forrester, J. W. (1961). *Industrial Dynamics*. Cambridge: MIT Press.

Forrester, J. W. (1968). *Principles of Systems*. Cambridge: MIT Press.

Foss, N. J., Knudsen, C., and Montgomery, C. A. (1995). 'An Exploration of Common Ground: Integrating Evolutionary and Strategic Theories of the Firm'. In: C. A. Montgomery (Ed.), *Resource-Based and Evolutionary Theories of the Firm: Towards a Synthesis* (pp. 1–18). London: Kluwer Academic Publishers.

Frank, A. U. (1992). 'Telecommunication and GIS: Opportunities and Challenges'. In: P. W. Newton, P. R. Zwart. and M. E. Cavill (Eds), *Networking Spatial Information Systems* (pp. 235–50). London: Belhaven.

Franklin, S. and Graesser, A. (1996). 'Is It an Agent, or Just a Program?: A Taxonomy for Autonomous Agents'. In: *Proceedings of the Third International Workshop on Agent Theories, Architectures, and Languages*. Berlin: Springer-Verlag.

Friedman, V. J. (2002). 'The Individual as Agent of Organizational Learning. *California Management Review*, 44(2), pp. 70–89.

Fritz, R. (1989). *The Path of Least Resistance: Learning to Become the Creative Force in Your Own Life*. New York: Ballantine Books.

Frost, P., Moore, L. F., Louis, M. R., Lundberg, C. C., and Martin, J. (1990). *Reframing Organizational Culture*. Newbury Park: SAGE Publications.

Gabriel, Y. (2000). *Storytelling in Organizations: Facts, Fictions, and Fantasies*. Oxford: Oxford University Press.

Gaines, B. R. (1979). 'General Systems Research: Quo Vadis?' *General Systems Yearbook*, 24, pp. 1–9.

Gann, D. M. and Salter, A. I. (1998). 'Learning and Innovation Management in Project-Based, Service-Enhanced Firms'. *International Journal of Innovation Management*, 2(4), pp. 431–54.

Gann, D. M. and Salter, A. I. (2000). 'Innovation Management in Project-Based, Service-Enhanced Firms: The Construction of Complex Products and Systems'. *Research Policy*, 29, pp. 955–72.

Garvin, D. A. (1993). 'Building a Learning Organization'. *Harvard Business Review*, 71(A), pp. 78–91.

de Geus, A. (1997). *The Living Company*. Boston: Harvard Business School Press.

Ghoshal, S. and Bartlett, C. A. (1994). 'Linking Organizational Context and Managerial Action: The Dimension of Quality Management'. *Strategic Management Journal*, 15, Special Issue, pp. 91–112.

Giddens, A. (1984). *The Constitution of Society*. Cambridge: Polity Press.

Gilmore, R. (1981). *Catastrophe Theory for Scientists and Engineers*. New York: John Wiley & Sons.

Ginsberg, A. (1990). 'Connecting Diversification to Performance: A Socio-Cognitive Approach'. *Academy of Management Review*, 15, pp. 514–35.

Goguen, J. A. and Varela, F. J. (1979). 'System and Distinctions; Duality and Complementarity'. *International Journal of General Systems*, 5, pp. 31–43.

Goldman, A. I. (1986). *Philosophical Applications of Cognitive Science*. Cambridge: Harvard University Press.

Goleman, D. (1995). *Emotional Intelligence*. New York: Bantam Books.

Goodman, P. S., Ravlin, E., and Schminke, M. (1987). 'Understanding Groups in Organizations'. In: L. L. Cummings and G. M. Staw (Eds), *Research in Organizational Behavior*, 9 (p. 159). Greenwich: JAI Press.

Goodpaster, K. E. (1989). 'Ethical Imperatives and Corporate Leadership'. In: K. R. Andrews (Ed.), *Ethics in Practice: Managing Moral Corporation* (pp. 212–28). Boston: Harvard Business School Press.

Grabher, G. (2002). 'The Project Ecology of Advertising: Tasks, Talents and Teams'. *Regional Studies*, 36, pp. 245–62.

Grant, R. M. (1991). 'The Resource-Based Theory of Competitive Advantage: Implications for Strategy Formulation'. *California Management Review*, 33(3), pp. 114–35.

Grant, R. M. (1996). 'Toward a Knowledge Based View of the Firm'. *Strategic Management Journal*, 17, Special Issue, pp. 109–22.

Grant, R. M. (1997). 'The Knowledge Based View of the Firm: Implications for Management Practice'. *Long Range Planning*, 30(3), pp. 450–4.

Gray, R. J. (2001). 'Organisational Climate and Project Success'. *International Journal of Project Management*, 19, pp. 103–9.

Greenberg, J. and Baron, R. A. (2003). *Behavior in Organizations*. Upper Saddle River: Prentice-Hall.

Gudykunst, W. B. (1988). 'Culture and Intergroup Processes'. In: M. H. Bond (Ed.), *The Cross Cultural Challenge to Social Psychology* (pp. 165–81). London: SAGE Publications.

Gulati, R. (1995). 'Does Familiarity Breed Trust? The Implications of Repeated Ties for Contractual Choice in Alliances'. *Academy of Management Journal*, 38(1), pp. 85–112.

Gupta, A. K. and Govindarajan, V. (1993). 'Coalignment between Knowledge Flow Patterns and Strategic Systems and Processes within MNC's'. In: P. Lorange, B. Chakravarthy, J. Roos, and van de Ven (Eds), *Implementing Strategic Processes: Change, Learning and Co-Operation* (pp. 329–46). Oxford: Blackwell.

Gupta, A. K. and Govindarajan, V. (2000). 'Knowledge Management's Social Dimension: Lessons from Nucor Steel'. *Sloan Management Review*, (Fall 2000) pp. 71–80. (Spring 2000), pp. 68–78.

Haines, S. G. (1998). *The Manager's Pocket Guide to Systems Thinking & Learning.* Amherst: HRD Press.

Haldin-Herrgard, T. (2000). 'Difficulties in Diffusion of Tacit Knowledge in Organizations'. *Journal of Intellectual Capital*, 1(4), pp. 357–69.

Hall, A. D. and Fagen, R. E. (1968). 'Definition of System'. In: W. Buckley (Ed.), *Modern Systems Research for the Behavioral Scientist* (pp. 81–92). Chicago: Aldine.

Hall, R. and Andriani, P. (1999). 'Operationalising Knowledge Management Concepts: The Development of a Technique for Sharing Knowledge in New Product Development Projects'. *International Journal of Innovation Management*, 3(3), pp. 307–33.

Hall, R. and Andriani, P. (2002), 'Managing Knowledge for Innovation'. *Long Range Planning*, 35, pp. 29–48.

Hall, H. (2003). 'Borrowed Theory: Applying Exchange Theories in Information Science Research'. *Library and Information Science Research*, 25, pp. 287–306.

Hall, W. P. (2005). 'Biological Nature of Knowledge in the Learning Organization'. *The Learning Organization*, 12(2), pp. 169–88.

Hamel, G. and Prahalad, C. K. (1989). 'Strategic Intent'. *Harvard Business Review*, May–June, pp. 63–76.

Hamel, G. and Prahalad, C. K. (1994). *Competing for the Future.* Boston: Harvard Business School Press.

Handy, C. (1994). *The Age of Paradox.* Boston: Harvard Business School Press.

Hannan, M. T. and Freeman, J. (1977). 'The Population Ecology of Organizations'. *American Journal of Sociology*, 82(5), pp. 929–64.

Hannan, M. T. and Freeman, J. (1989). *Organizational Ecology.* Cambridge: Harvard University Press.

Hansen, M. T. (1999). 'The Search Transfer Problem: The Role of Weak Ties in Sharing Knowledge across Organizational Sub-Units'. *Administrative Science Quarterly*, 44, pp. 82–111.

Hansen, M. T., Nohria, N., and Tierney, T. (1999). 'What's Your Strategy for Managing Knowledge?' *Harvard Business Review*, March–April, pp.106–16.

Harvey, F. (1996). 'Improving Multi-Purpose GIS Design: Participative Design'. In: S. C. Hirtle and A. U. Frank (Eds), *Spatial Information Theory* (pp. 313–28). Berlin: Springer.

Hatchuel, A. and Weil, B. (1995). *Experts in Organizations: A Knowledge-Based Perspective on Organizational Change.* Berlin-New York: Walter de Gruyter.

Hedlund, G. (1993). 'Assumptions of Hierarchy and Heterarchy, with Applications to the Management of the Multinational Corporation'. In: S. Ghoshan and E. D. Westney (Eds), *Organization Theory and the Multinational Corporation* (pp. 211–36). New York: St Martin's Press.

Heene, A. and Sanchez, R. (1997). *Competence-Based Strategic Management.* Chichester: John Wiley & Sons.

Hildén, S. (2004). *Does Organizational Change Improve Organizational Functionality? Intentions and Experiences in a Frequently Changing Organization.* Tampere: Tampere University of Technology.

von Hippel, (1994). '"Sticky Information" and the Locus of Problem Solving: Implications for Innovation'. *Management Science*, 40(4), pp. 429–39.

Hirschheim, R., Klein, H. K., and Lyytinen, K. (1995). *Information Systems Development and Data Modeling: Conceptual and Philosophical Foundations.* London: Cambridge University Press.

Hobday, M. (1998). 'Product Complexity, Innovation and Industrial Organization'. *Research Policy*, 26, pp. 689–710.

Hobday, M. (2000). 'The Project-Based Organization: An Ideal Form Managing Complex Products and Systems?' *Research Policy*, 29, pp. 871–93.

Hofer, C. and Schendell, D. (1978). *Strategy Formulation: Analytical Concepts.* St Paul: West Publishing.

Hofstader, D. R. (1979). *Goedel, Escher, Bach: An Eternal Golden Braid.* New York: Basic Books.

Hofstede, G. (1991). *Cultures and Organizations: Software of the Mind.* London: HarperCollins.

Holland, J. H. (1995). *Hidden Order: How Adaptation Builds Complexity.* Cambridge: Perseus Books.

Holland, J. H. (1998). *Emergence from Chaos to Order.* Cambridge: Perseus Books.

Horgan, J. (1994). 'Profile: Philip W. Anderson'. *Scientific American*. November, pp. 19–22.

Huang, J. C. and Newell, S. (2003). 'Knowledge Integration Processes and Dynamics within the Context of Cross-Functional Projects'. *International Journal of Project Management*, 21, pp. 167–76.

Huber, G. P. (1991). 'Organizational Learning: The Contributing Process and the Literatures'. *Organization Science*, 2(1), pp. 88–116.

Huber, G. P. (1999). 'Facilitating Project Team Learning and Contributions to Organizational Knowledge'. *Creativity and Innovation Management*, 8(2), pp. 70–6.

Huemann, M. and Winkler, G. (1998). 'Project Management-Benchmarking: An Instrument of Learning'. In: R. A. Lundin and C. Midler (Eds), *Projects as Arenas for Renewal and Learning Processes* (pp. 71–8). Boston: Kluwer Academic Publishers.

Huemer, L., von Krogh, G., and Roos, J. (1998). 'Knowledge and the Concept of Trust'. In: G. von Krogh, J. Roos and D. Kleine (Eds), *Knowing in Firms: Understanding, Managing and Measuring Knowledge* (pp. 123–45). London: SAGE Publications.

Huff, A. S. (1990). *Mapping Strategic Thought.* New York: Wiley & Sons.

Husserl, E. (1948). *Erfahrung und Urteil: Untersuchungen zur Genealogie der Logik* (Experience and Opinion: Studies on Genealogy of Logic). Hamburg: Claassen & Goverts.

Husserl, E. (1950). 'Ideen zu einer Phänomenologie und phänomenologishen Philosophie' (Thoughts about a Phenomenology and Phenomenological Philosophy). *Husserliana*, 3. The Hague: Nijhoff.

Husted, K. and Michailova, S. (2002). 'Diagnosing and Fighting Knowledge-Sharing Hostility'. *Organizational Dynamics*, 31(1), pp. 60–73.

Janoff-Bulman, R. (1992). *Shattered Assumptions: Towards a New Psychology of Trauma.* New York: Free Press.

Jantsch, E. (1980). *The Self-Organizing Universe: Scientific and Human Implication of the Emerging Paradigm of Evolution.* Oxford: Pergamon Press.

Jashapara, A. (2004). *Knowledge Management: An Integrated Approach.* Harlow: Pearson Education Ltd.

Johnson-Laird, P. N. (1987). *Mental Models: Towards a Cognitive Science of Language, Inference, and Consciousness.* New York: Cambridge University Press.

Järvenpää, S. L., Knoll, K., and Leidner, D. (1998). 'Is Anybody Out There? The Antecedents of Trust in Global Virtual Teams'. *Journal of Management Information Systems*, 14(4), Spring, pp. 29–64.

Kadefors, A. (2004). 'Trust in Project Relationships – Inside the Black Box'. *International Journal of Project Management*, 22, pp. 175–82.

Kast, F. E. and Rosenzweig, J. E. (1981). *Organization and Management: A Systems and Contingency Approach.* London: McGraw-Hill.

Katz, D. and Kahn, R. L. (1966). *The Social Psychology of Organizations.* New York: John Wiley & Sons.

Katz, R. (1982). 'The Effects of Group Longevity on Project Communication and Performance'. *Administrative Science Quarterly*, 27, pp. 81–104.

Kauffman, S. A. (1993). *The Origins of Order: Self-Organization and Selection in Evolution.* University of Pennsylvania and Santa Fe Institute: Oxford University Press.

Keegan, A. and Turner, R. (2001). 'Quantity versus Quality in Project-Based Learning Practices'. *Management Learning*, 32(1), pp. 77–98.

Keller, W. (1996). 'Absorptive Capacity: On the Creation and Acquisition of Technology in Development'. *Journal of Development Economics*, 49, pp. 199–227.

Kemper, S. (1984). 'The Development of Narrative Skills: Explanations and Entertainment'. In: S. A. Kuczaj, II (Ed.), *Discourse Development: Progress in Cognitive Development Research* (pp. 99–124). New York: Springer-Verlag.

Kerfoot, D. and Knights, D. (1998). 'Managing Masculinity in Contemporary Organizational Life: A Managerial Project'. *Organization*, 5(1), pp. 7–26.

Kerzner, H. (1997). *In Search of Excellence in Project Management.* New York: John Wiley & Sons.

Kim, D. H. (1993). 'The Link between Individual and Organizational Learning'. *Sloan Management Review*, Fall, pp. 37–50.

Kim, D. H. (1994). 'From Individual to Shared Mental Models'. *The Systems Thinker*, 5(3), pp. 5–6.

Kim, D. H. (1998). 'The Link between Individual and Organizational Learning'. In: D. A. Klein (Ed.), *The Strategic Management of Intellectual Capital.* Boston: Butterworth-Heinemann.

Kim, D. H. (1999). *Introduction to Systems Thinking.* Waltham: Pegasus Communications Inc.

King, W. R. (2007). 'Keynote Paper: Knowledge Management: A Systems Perspective'. *International Journal of Business Systems and Research*, 1(1), pp. 5–28.

Klimoski, R. and Mohammed, S. (1994). 'Team Mental Model: Construct or Metaphor?' *Journal of Management*, 20(2), pp. 403–37.

Klir, G. J. (1985). *Architecture of Systems Problem Solving.* New York: Plenum Press.

Kogut, B. and Zander, U. (1992). 'Knowledge of the Firm, Combinative Capabilities, and the Replication of Technology'. *Organization Science*, 3(3), pp. 383–97.

204   *Bibliography*

Kogut, B. and Zander, U. (1996). 'What Firms Do? Coordination, Identity, and Learning'. *Organization Science*, 7(5), pp. 502–18.

Kolb, D. A. (1984). *Experimental Learning – Experience as the Source of Learning and Development*. Englewood Cliffs: Prentice-Hall.

Koskinen, K. U. (2000). 'Tacit Knowledge as a Promoter of Project Success'. *European Journal of Purchasing & Supply Management*, 6, pp. 41–7.

Koskinen, K. U. (2003). 'Evaluation of Tacit Knowledge Utilization in Work Units'. *Journal of Knowledge Management*, 7(5), pp. 67–81.

Koskinen, K. U. and Pihlanto, P. (2003). 'Trust in a Project Management Context'. In *Proceedings of the NORDNET 2003 Conference 'Project Management: Dreams, Nightmares, and Realities'*. Oslo.

Koskinen, K. U., Pihlanto, P. and Vanharanta, H. (2003). 'Tacit Knowledge Acquisition and Sharing in a Project Work Context'. *International Journal of Project Management*, 21(4), pp. 281–90.

Koskinen, K. U. (2004). 'Knowledge Management to Improve Project Communication and Implementation'. *Project Management Journal*, 35(2), pp. 13–19.

Koskinen, K. U. (2005a). 'Metaphoric Boundary Objects as Co-Ordinating Mechanisms in the Knowledge Sharing of Innovation Processes'. *European Journal of Innovation Management*, 8(3), pp. 323–35.

Koskinen, K. U. (2005b). 'Role of Metaphoric Boundary Objects in the Development of a Company's Strategic Vision'. *International Journal of Management Concepts and Philosophy*, 1(2), pp. 156–76.

Koskinen, K. U. (2005c). 'Learning That Took Place in Office Equipment Retailers during a Technological Discontinuity'. *International Journal of Learning and Intellectual Capital*, 2(4), pp. 408–21.

Koskinen, K. U. and Pihlanto, P. (2006). 'Competence Transfer from Old Timers to Newcomers Analyzed with the Help of the Holistic Concept of Man'. *Knowledge and Process Management*, 13(1), pp. 3–12.

Koskinen, K. U. and Pihlanto, P. (2008). *Knowledge Management in Project-Based Companies: An Organic Perspective*. London: Palgrave Macmillan.

Koskinen, K. U. (2009a). 'Project-Based Company's Vital Condition: Structural Coupling. An Autopoietic View'. *Knowledge and Process Management*, 16(1), pp. 13–22.

Koskinen, K. U. (2009b). 'Characterising Knowledge Transfer in Project-Based Companies'. *Innovative Management Journal*, 3, pp. 16–27.

Koskinen, K. U. and Mäkinen, S. (2009). 'Role of Boundary Objects in Negotiations of Project Contracts'. *International Journal of Project Management*, 27, pp. 31–8.

von Krogh, G. and Vicari, S. (1993). 'An Autopoiesis Approach to Experimental Strategic Learning'. In: P. Lorange, B. Chakravarthy, J. Roos, and A. van de Ven (Eds), *Implementing Strategic Processes: Change, Learning and Co-Operation* (pp. 394–410). London: Blackwell.

von Krogh, G. and Roos, J. (1995a). *Organizational Epistemology*. New York: St Martin's Press.

von Krogh, G. and Roos, J. (1995b). 'Conversation Management'. *European Management Journal*, 13(4), pp. 390–4.

von Krogh, G. and Roos, J. (1996a). 'Five Claims of Knowing'. *European Management Journal*, 14(4), pp. 423–6.

von Krogh, G. and Roos, J. (1996b). 'Arguments on Knowledge and Competence'. In: G. von Krogh and J. Roos (Eds), *Managing Knowledge: Perspectives on Cooperation and Competition* (pp. 100–15). London: SAGE Publications.

von Krogh, G., Roos, J., and Slocum, K (1996a). 'An Essay on Corporate Epistemology'. In: G. von Krogh and J. Roos (Eds), *Managing Knowledge: Perspectives on Cooperation and Competition* (pp. 157–83). London: SAGE Publications.

von Krogh, G., Roos, J., and Yip, G. (1996b). 'A Note on the Epistemology of Globalizing Firms'. In: G. von Krogh and J. Roos (Eds), *Managing Knowledge: Perspectives on Cooperation and Competition* (pp. 203–17). London: SAGE Publications.

von Krogh, G., Ichijo, K., and Nonaka, I. (2000). *Enabling Knowledge Creation: How to Unlock the Mystery of Tacit Knowledge and Release the Power of Innovation.* New York: Oxford University Press.

Lachman, R., Nedd, A., and Hining, B. (1994). 'Analyzing Cross-National Management and Organizations: A Theoretical Framework'. *Management Science*, 25(1), pp. 91–102.

LaFasto, F. and Larson, C. (2001). *When Teams Work Best.* Thousand Oaks: SAGE Publications.

Lam, A. (2000). 'Tacit Knowledge, Organizational Learning and Social Institutions: An Integrated Framework'. *Organization Studies*, 21(3), pp. 487–513.

Lampel, J. (2001). 'The Core Competencies of Effective Project Execution: The Challenge of Diversity'. *International Journal of Project Management*, 19, pp. 471–83.

Lane, P. J. and Lubatkin, M. (1998). 'Relative Absorptive Capacity and Interorganizational Learning'. *Strategic Management Journal*, 19, pp. 461–77.

Lant, T. K. and Mezias, S. J. (1990). 'Managing Discontinuous Change: A Simulation Study of Organizational Learning and Entrepreneurship'. *Strategic Management Journal*, 11, pp. 147–79.

Larson, C. and LaFasto, F. (1989). *Teamwork – What Must Go Right/What Can Go Wrong.* Newbury Park: SAGE Publications.

Laszlo, E. (1972). *The Systems View of the World.* New York: George Brazilier.

Latour, B. (1986). 'Visualization and Cognition: Thinking with Eyes and Hands'. *Knowledge and Society: Studies in the Sociology of Culture Past and Present.* 6, pp. 1–40.

Laudon, K. C. and Laudon, J. P. (2000). *Management Information Systems: Organization and Technology in the Network Enterprise.* Upper Saddle River: Prentice-Hall.

Laufer, A. and Hoffman, E. J. (2000). *Project Management Success Stories: Lessons of Project Leaders.* New York: John Wiley & Sons.

Lee, J. N. (2001). 'The Impact of Knowledge Sharing, Organizational Capability and Partnership Quality on IS Outsourcing Success'. *Information and Management*, 38(5), pp. 323–35.

Lee, G. G. and Bai, R. J. (2003). 'Organizational Mechanisms for Successful IS/IT Strategic Planning in the Digital Era'. *Management Decision*, 41(1), pp. 32–42.

Lencioni, P. M. (2002). 'Make Your Values Mean Something'. *Harvard Business Review*, July, pp. 113–17.

Leonard-Barton, D. (1995). *Wellsprings of Knowledge.* Boston: Harvard Business School Press.

Leonard-Barton, D. and Sensiper, S. (1998). 'The Role of Tacit Knowledge in Group Innovation'. *California Management Review*, 40(3), pp. 112–32.

Leroy, F. and Ramanantsoa, B. (1997). 'The Cognitive and Behavioral Dimensions of Organizational Learning in a Merger: An Empirical Study'. *Journal of Management Studies*, 34(6), pp. 871–94.

Leseure, M. J. and Brookes, N. J. (2004). 'Knowledge Management Benchmarks for Project Management. *Journal of Knowledge Management*, 8(1), pp. 103–16.

Leskinen, J. (1997). *Avoin, tasaveroinen keskustelu työpaikalla* (Open and Equal Discussion at the Work Place). Helsinki: Työturvallisuuskeskus.

Levitt, B. and March, J. G. (1988). 'Organizational Learning'. *Annual Review of Sociology*, 14, pp. 319–40.

Levy, D. (1994). 'Chaos Theory and Strategy: Theory, Application, and Managerial Implications'. *Strategic Management Journal*, 15, pp. 167–78.

Lewicki, R. J. and Bunker, B. B. (1996). 'Developing and Maintaining Trust in Work Relationships'. In: R. M. Kramer and T. R. Tyler (Eds), *Trust in Organizations: Frontiers of Theory and Research* (pp. 114–39). Thousand Oaks: SAGE Publications.

Lewis, J. D. and Weigert, A. (1985). 'Trust as Social Reality'. *Social Forces*, 63(4), pp. 967–85.

Liebeskind, J. B. (1996). 'Knowledge, Strategy, and the Theory of the Firm'. *Strategic Management Journal*, 17, pp. 93–107.

Lindkvist, L., Söderlund, J., and Tell, F. (1998). 'Managing Product Development Projects: On the Significance of Fountains and Deadlines'. *Organization Studies*, 17(6), pp. 931–51.

Lindkvist, L. (2004). 'Governing Project-Based Firms: Promoting Market-Like Processes within Hierarchies'. *Journal of Management and Governance*, 8, pp. 3–25.

Lindkvist, L. and Söderlund, J. (2002). 'What Goes on in Projects? On Goal-Directed Learning Processes'. In: K. Sahlin-Andersson and A. Söderholm (Eds), *Beyond Project Management* (pp. 278–91). Malmö: Liber.

Lindskold, S. (1978). 'Trust Development, the GRIT Proposal, and the Effects of Conciliatory Acts on Conflict and Cooperation'. *Psychological Bulletin*, 85, pp. 772–93.

Livingston, I. (2006). *Between Science and Literature: An Introduction to Autopoiesis*. Chicago: University of Illinois Press.

Locke, D. (1984). *Project Management*. New York: St Martin's Press.

Loew, R., Stengel, I., Bleimann, U., and McDonald, A. (1999). 'Security Aspects of an Enterprise-Wide Network Architecture'. *Internet Research: Electronic Networking Application and Policy*, 9(1), pp. 8–15.

Long, C. and Vickers-Koch, M. (1995). 'Using Core Capabilities to Create Competitive Advantage'. *Organizational Dynamics*, 24(1), pp. 7–22.

Lord, R. G. and Brown, D. J. (2001). 'Leadership, Values, and Subordinate Self-Concepts'. *The Leadership Quarterly*, 12, pp. 133–52.

Lorenz, E. N. (1993). *The Essence of Chaos*. Seattle: University of Washington Press.

Love, P. E. D., Fong, P. S. W., and Irani, Z. (2005). *Management of Knowledge in Project Environments*. Amsterdam: Elsevier.

Luhmann, N. (1979). *Trust and Power*. Chichester: John Wiley & Sons.

Luhmann, N. (1982). *The Differentiation of Society*. New York: Columbia University Press.

Luhmann, N. (1986). 'The Autopoiesis of Social Systems'. In: F. Geyer and J. van der Zouwen (Eds), *Sociocybernetic Paradoxes* (pp. 172–92). Beverly Hills: SAGE Publications.

Luhmann, N. (1987). 'The Representation of Society within Society'. *Current Sociological*, 35, pp. 101–8.

Luhmann, N. (1988). 'The Unity of the Legal System'. In: G. Teubner (Ed.), *Autopoietic Law: A New Approach to Law and Society* (pp. 12–35). Berlin: Walter de Gruyter.

Luhmann, N. (1990a). 'The Autopoiesis of Social Systems'. In: N. Luhmann (Ed.), *Essays of Self-Reference* (pp. 1–20), New York: Columbia University Press.

Luhmann, N. (1990b). *Essays of Self-Reference.* New York: Columbia University Press.

Luhmann, N. (1992). *Ecological Communication.* Cambridge: Polity Press.

Luhmann, N. (1995a). *Social Systems.* Stanford: Stanford University Press.

Luhmann, N. (1995b). *Gesellschaftsstruktur und Semantik 4: Studien zur Wissenssoziologie der modernen Gesellschaft* (Structure of Society and Semantic 4: Studies on Knowledge-Sociology of Modern Society). Frankfurt am Main: Suhrkamp.

Luhmann, N. (2000). *Organisation und Entsheidung* (Organization and Decision). Opladen: Westdeutscher Verlag.

Lundin, R. A. and Söderholm, A. (1995). 'A Theory of the Temporary Organization'. *Scandinavian Journal of Management*, 11(4), pp. 437–55.

Lundin, R. A. and Midler, C. (1998). 'Evolution of Project as Empirical Trend and Theoretical Focus'. In: R. A. Lundin and C. Midler (Eds), *Projects as Arenas for Renewal and Learning Processes* (pp. 1–9). Norwell: Kluwer Academic Publishers.

Lundin, R. A. (2000). 'Business in a World of Projects'. In: D. P. Slevin, D. I. Cleland and J. K. Pinto (Eds), *Management Research at the Turn of the Millenium – Proceedings of PMI Research Conference 2000, 21–24 June 2000 Paris* (pp. 73–8). Newton Square: Project Management Institute.

Lundin, R. A. and Hartman, F. (2000). 'Pervasiveness of Projects in Business'. In: R. A. Lundin and F. Hartman (Eds), *Projects as Business Constituents and Guiding Motives* (pp. 1–10). Dordrecht: Kluwer Academic Publishers.

Lyles, M. A. (1988). 'Learning among Joint Venture Sophisticated Firm'. *Management International Review*, 28, pp. 85–98.

Lyles, M. A. and Schwenk, C. R. (1992). 'Top Management, Strategy and Organizational Knowledge Structures'. *Journal of Management Studies*, 29, pp. 155–74.

Lyles, M., von Krogh, G., Roos, J., and Kleine, D. (1996). 'The Impact of Individual and Organizational Learning on Formation and Management of Organizational Cooperation'. In: G. von Krogh and J. Roos (Eds), *Managing Knowledge: Perspectives on Cooperation and Competition* (pp. 82–99). London: SAGE Publications.

Lyytinen, K. and Klein, H. (1985). 'The Critical Theory of Jürgen Habermas as a Basis for a Theory of Information Systems'. In: E. Mumford, R. Hirschheim, G. Fitzgerald, and A. T. Wood-Harper, (Eds), *Research Methods in Information System* (pp. 219–36). Amsterdam: North-Holland.

MacIntyre, A. (1981). *After Virtue.* London: Duckworth.

Mahoney, I. and Pandian, J. R. (1992). 'The Resource-Based View within the Conversation of Strategic Management'. *Strategic Management Journal*, 13, p. 363.

Mandelbrot, B. (1967). 'How Long is the Coast of Britain? Statistical Self-Similarity and Fractional Dimension'. *Science*, 156, pp. 636–9.

Mangham, I. L. and Overington, M. A. (1987). *Organizations as Theatre: A Social Psychology of Dramatic Appearances*. Chichester: John Wiley & Sons.

Mathieu, J. E., Heffner, T. S., Goodwin, G. F., Salas, E., and Cannon-Bowers, J. A. (2000). 'The Influence of Shared Mental Models on Team Process and Performance'. *Journal of Applied Psychology*, 85(2), pp. 273–83.

Maturana, H. R and Varela, F. J. (1973). 'Autopoiesis and Cognition: The Realization of the Living'. In: R. S. Cohen and M. W. Wartofsky (Eds), *Boston Studies in the Philosophy of Science*, Volume 42. Dordecht: D. Reidel Publishing Co.

Maturana, H. R. (1975). 'The Organization of the Living: A Theory of the Living Organization'. *International Journal of Man-Machine Studies*, 7, pp. 313–32.

Maturana, H. R. (1978). 'Biology of Language: The Epistemology of Reality'. In: G. A. Miller and E. Lenneberg (Eds), *Psychology and Biology of Language and Thought* (pp. 27–63). New York: Academic Press.

Maturana, H. R. and Varela, F. J. (1980a). *Autopoiesis and Cognition: The Realization of the Living*. London: D. Reidel Publishing Co.

Maturana, H. R. and Varela, F. J. (1980b). 'Autopoiesis: Reproduction, Heredity and Evolution'. In: M. Zeleny (Ed.), *Autopoiesis, Dissipative Structures and Spontaneous Orders* (pp. 45–79). Boulder: Westview Press.

Maturana, H. R. and Varela, F. J. (1987). *The Tree of Knowledge*. London: New Science Library, Shambhala.

Maturana, H. R. (1988). 'Reality: The Search for Objectivity or the Quest for a Compelling Argument'. *Irish Journal of Psychology*, 9(1), pp. 25–82.

Maturana H. R. (1991). 'Science and Daily Life: The Ontology of Scientific Explanations'. In: F. Steier (Ed.), *Research and Reflexivity* (pp. 30–52). Beverly Hills: SAGE Publications.

Maula, M. (2000). 'The Senses and Memory of a Firm – Implications of Autopoiesis Theory for Knowledge Management'. *Journal of Knowledge Management*, 4(2), pp. 157–61.

Maula, M. (2006). *Organizations as Learning Systems: 'Living Composition' as an Enabling Infrastucture*. London: Elsevier Science, Advanced Series in Management.

McDermott, R. (1999). 'Why Information Technology Inspired But Cannot Deliver Knowledge Management'. *California Management Review*, 41(4), pp. 103–17.

McDermott, R. and O'Dell, C. (2001). 'Overcoming Cultural Barriers to Sharing Knowledge'. *Journal of Knowledge Management*, 5(1), pp. 76–85.

Meacham, J. A. (1983). 'Wisdom and the Context of Knowledge: Knowing That One Doesn't Know'. *Contributions in Human Development*, 8, pp. 111–34.

Mead, G. H. (1962). *Mind, Self, and Society*. Chicago: University of Chicago Press.

Meehan, B. and Richardson, I. (2002). 'Identification of Software Process Knowledge Management'. *Software Process Improvement and Practice*, 7, pp. 47–55.

Merleau-Ponty, M. (1963). *The Structure of Behaviour*. Boston: Beacon Press.

Meyer, J. W. and Scott, R. (1983). *Organizational Environments: Ritual and Rationality*. Beverly Hills: SAGE Publications.

Meyerson, D., Weick, K. E., and Kramer, R. M. (1996). 'Swift Trust and Temporary Groups'. In: R. M. Kramer and T. R. Tyler (Eds), *Trust in Organizations: Frontiers of Theory and Research* (pp. 166–95). Thousand Oaks: SAGE Publications.

Mingers, J. (1995). *Self-Producing Systems*. New York: Plenum.

Mingers, J. (1997). 'Systems Typologies in the Light of Autopoiesis: A Reconceptualization of Boulding's Hierarchy, and a Typology of Self-Referential Systems. A Research Paper'. *Systems Research and Behavioral Science*, 14, pp. 303–13.

Mingers, J. and Stowell, F. (1997). *Information Systems: An Emerging Discipline*. London: McGraw-Hill.

Mingers, J. (2002). 'Can Social Systems Be Autopoietic? Assessing Luhmann's Social Theory'. *The Sociological Review*, 50(2), pp. 278–99.

Mingers, J. (2006). *Realising Systems Thinking: Knowledge and Action in Management Science*. New York: Springer Science + Business Media Inc.

Mitleton-Kelly, E. (2003). 'Ten Principles of Complexity and Enabling Infrastructures'. In: E. Mitleton-Kelly (Ed.), *Complex Systems and Evolutionary Perspectives on Organizations: The Application of Complexity Theory on Organizations* (pp. 23–50). London: Elsevier Science, Advanced Series in Management.

Mollona, E. (2008). 'A Competence View of Firms as Resource Accumulation Systems: A Synthesis of Resource-Based and Evolutionary Models of Strategy-Making'. In: J. Morecroft, R. Sanchez, and A. Heene (Eds), *Systems Perspectives on Resources, Capabilities, and Management Processes* (pp. 93–125). Bingley: Emerald Group Publishing House.

Mooradian, N. (2005). 'Tacit Knowledge: Philosophic Roots and Role in KM'. *Journal of Knowledge Management*, 9(6), pp. 104–13.

Moorman, C., Deshpandé, R., and Zaltman, G. (1993). 'Factors Affecting Trust in Market Research Relationships'. *Journal of Marketing*, 57, pp. 81–101.

Morecroft, J. (1988). 'System Dynamics and Microworlds for Policymakers'. *European Journal of Operational Research*, 35(3), pp. 301–21.

Morecroft, J. (2007). 'Resource Management under Dynamic Complexity'. In: J. Morecroft, R. Sanchez, and A. Heene (Eds), *Systems Perspectives on Resources, Capabilities, and Management Processes* (pp. 19–39). Bingley: Emerald Group Publishing House.

Morecroft, J. Sanchez, R., and Heene, A. (2007). 'Integrating Systems Thinking and Competence Concepts in a New View of Resources, Capabilities, and Management Processes'. In: J. Morecroft, R. Sanchez, and A. Heene (Eds), *Systems Perspectives on Resources, Capabilities, and Management Processes* (pp. 3–16). Bingley: Emerald Group Publishing House.

Morgan, G. (1996). *Images of Organization*. Thousand Oaks: SAGE Publications.

Morin, E. (1982). 'Can We Conceive of a Science of Autonomy?' *Human Systems Management*, 3, pp. 201–306.

Morris, P. W. G. (1988). 'Managing Project Interfaces – Key Points for Project Success'. In: D. I. Cleland and W. R. King (Eds), *Project Management Handbook* (pp. 3–36). New York: Van Nostrand Reinhold Company.

Mullins, L. J. (2007). *Management and Organizational Behaviour*. Harlow: Prentice-Hall.

Myers, C. and Davids, K. (1992). 'Knowing and Doing: Tacit Skill at Work'. *Personnel Management*, February, pp. 45–7.

Mäkilouko, M. (2001). *Leading Multinational Project Teams: Formal, Country Specific Perspective*. Tampere: Tampere University of Technology.

Nass, C. (1994). 'Knowledge or Skills: Which Do Administrators Learn from Experience?' *Organization Science*, 5(1), pp. 38–50.

Nelson, R. R. and Winter, S. G. (1982). *An Evolutionary Theory of Economic Change*. Cambridge: The Belknap Press of Harvard University Press.

Nelson, R. R. (1994). 'Why Do Firms Differ, and How Does It Matter?' In: R. P. Rumelt, D. E. Schendel, and D. J. Teece (Eds), *Fundamental Issues in Strategy* (pp. 247–69). Boston: Harvard Business School Press.

Nelson, R. R. (1995). 'Recent Evolutionary Theorizing about Economic Change'. *Journal of Economic Literature*, XXXIII, March, pp. 48–90.

Newell, S., Robertson, M., Scarbrough, H., and Swan, J. (2002). *Managing Knowledge Work*. Basingstoke: Palgrave Macmillan.

Newell, S., Bresnen, M., Edelman, L., Scarbrough, H., and Swan, J. (2006). 'Sharing Knowledge across Projects: Limits to ICT-Led Project Review Practices'. *Management Learning*, 37, p. 167.

Nonaka, I. (1988). 'Creating Organizational Order Out of Chaos'. *California Management Review*, Spring, pp. 57–73.

Nonaka, I. (1991). 'The Knowledge-Creating Company'. *Harvard Business Review*, 69 (November–December), pp. 96–104.

Nonaka, I. (1994). 'A Dynamic Theory of Organizational Knowledge Creation'. *Organization Science*, 5(1), pp. 14–37.

Nonaka, I. and Takeuchi, H. (1995). *The Knowledge-Creating Company*. New York: Oxford University Press.

Nooteboom, B. (1996). 'Globalisation, Learning & Strategy'. *EMOT Workshop*. Durham: Durham University of Durham.

O'Connor, J. and McDermott, I. (1997). *The Art of Systems Thinking: Essential Skills for Creativity and Problem Solving*. London: Thorsons.

Olson, D. R. (1977). 'From Utterance to Text: The Bias of Language in Speech and Writing'. *Harvard Educational Review*, 47, pp. 257–81.

O'Reilly, C. A. (1989). 'Corporations, Culture and Commitment: Motivation and Social Control in Organizations'. *California Management Review*, Summer, pp. 9–25.

Orlikowski, W. J. (2002). 'Knowing in Practice: Enacting a Collective Capability in Distributed Organizing'. *Organization Science*, 13(3), pp. 249–73.

Orr, J. (1990). 'Sharing Knowledge, Celebrating Identity: War Stories and Community Memory in a Service Culture'. In: D. S. Middleton and D. Edwards (Eds), *Collective Remembering: Memory in Society* (pp. 169–89). Beverly Hills: SAGE Publications.

Orr, J. (1996). *Talking about Machines: An Ethnography of a Modern Job*. Ithaca: Cornel University Press.

Orton, D. J. and Weick, K. E. (1990). 'Loosely Coupled Systems: A Reconceptualization'. *Academy of Management Review*, 15, pp. 203–23.

Osterloh, M. and Frey, B. (2000). 'Motivation, Knowledge Transfer, and Organizational Forms'. *Organization Science*, 11(5), pp. 538–50.

Østerberg, T. (1988). *Metasociology*. Oslo: Norwegian University Press.

Otala, M. (1995), 'The Learning Organization: Theory into Practice'. *Industry and Higher Education*, 8(3), pp. 157–64.

Packendorff, J. (2002). 'The Temporary Society and Its Enemies: Projects From an Individual Perspective'. In: K. Sahlin-Andersson and A. Söderholm (Eds), *Beyond Project Management. New Perspectives on the Temporary – Permanent Dilemma* (pp. 39–58). Malmö: Liber.

Pamkowska, M. (2008). 'Autopoiesis in Virtual Organizations'. *Informatica Economică*, 1(45), pp. 33–9.

Paoli, M. and Prencipe, A. (2003). 'Memory of the Organisation and Memories within the Organisation'. *Journal of Management and Governance*, 7, pp. 145–62.

Parboteeah, P. and Jackson, T. W. (2007). 'An Autopoietic Framework for Organisational Learning'. *Knowledge and Process Management*, 14(4), pp. 248–59.

Penrose, E. (1959). *The Theory of the Growth of the Firm*. New York: John Wiley & Sons.

Peteraf, M. A. (1993). 'The Cornerstones of Competitive Advantage: A Resource-Based View'. *Strategic Management Journal*, 14, pp. 179–91.

Peters, T. J. and Waterman Jr, R. H. (1982). *In Search of Excellence*. New York: Harper & Row Publishers.

Pfeffer, J. (1981). *Power in Organizations*. Marshfield: Pitman.

Piaget, J. (1936). *The Origins of Intelligence in Children*. New York: W. W. Norton & Company Inc.

Pihlanto, P. (2000). 'An Actor in an Individual Situation: The Holistic Individual Image and Perspectives on Accounting Research'. *Series Discussion and Working Papers 4: 2000*. Turku: Publications of the Turku School of Economics and Business Administration.

Pihlanto, P. (2002). 'Understanding Behaviour of the Decision-Maker in an Accounting Context'. *The Theater Metaphor for Conscious Experience and the Holistic Individual Image*. Turku: Publications of the Turku School of Economics and Business Administration. Series A-1: 2002.

Pihlanto, P. (2005). 'From Economic Man to the Holistic Individual. A Quest for a Realistic Notion of the Human Actor'. In: S. Tengblad, R. Solli, and B. Czarniawska (Eds), *The Art of Science* (pp. 87–110). Copenhagen: Liber & Copenhagen Business School Press.

Pihlanto, P. (2009). *Decision-Maker in Focus: Holistic Individual in the Theater of Consciousness*. Köln: LAP LAMBERT Academic Publishing AG & Co.

Pinto, J. K. and Kharbanda, O. P. (1995). *Successful Project Managers: Leading Your Team to Success*. New York: Van Nostrand Reinhold.

Pinto, J. K. and Onsrud, H. J. (1995). 'Sharing Geographic Information Across Organizational Boundaries: A Research Framework'. In: H. J. Onsrud and G. Rushton (Eds), *Sharing Geographic Information* (pp. 44–64). New Brunswick: Center for Urban Policy Research.

Polanyi, M. (1966). *The Tacit Dimension*. New York: Anchor Books.

Polkinghorne, D. E. (1988). *Narrative Knowing and the Human Sciences*. Albany: State University of New York Press.

Pondy, L. R. and Mitroff, I. (1979). 'Beyond Open Systems Models of Organization'. In: B. M. Straw (Ed.), *Research in Organizational Behavior*, 1, pp. 3–39. Greenwich: JAI Press.

Popper, K. (1977). 'The Worlds 1, 2 and 3'. In: K. Popper and J. Eccles (Eds), *The Self and Its Brain* (pp. 36–50). Berlin: Springer International.

Postman, L. (1976). 'Methodology of Human Learning'. In: W. K. Estes (Ed.), *Handbook of Learning and Cognitive Processes, Vo. 4. Attention and Memory* (pp. 11–69). Hillsdale: Lea Lawrence Erlbaum Associates, Publishers.

Postrel, S. (1999). 'Islands of Shared Knowledge: Specialization and Mutual Understanding in Problem-Solving Teams'. *Organization Science*, 13(3), pp. 303–20.

Powell, W. W. (1996). 'Trust-Based Forms of Governance'. In: R. M. Kramer and T. R. Tyler (Eds), *Trust in Organizations: Frontiers of Theory and Research* (pp. 51–67). Thousand Oaks: SAGE Publications.

Prahalad, C. K. and Hamel, G. (1990). 'The Core Competence of the Corporation'. *Harvard Business Review*, 68(3), pp. 79–91.

Prahalad, C. K. and Hamel, G. (1994). 'Strategy as a Field of Study: Why Search for a New Paradigm?' *Strategic Management Journal*, 15, pp. 5–16.

Prencipe, A. and Tell, F. (2001). 'Inter-Project Learning: Processes and Outcomes of Knowledge Codification in Project-Based Firm'. *Research Policy*, 30, pp. 1371–94.

Priem, R. L. and Butler, J. E. (2001). 'Is the Resource-Based "View" a Useful Perspective for Strategic Management Research?' *Academy of Management Review*, 26(1), pp. 22–40.

Propp, V. (1968). *Morphology of the Folktale*. Austin: University of Texas Press.

Quinn, J. B. (1996). 'Strategies for Change'. In H. Mintzberg and J. B. Quinn (Eds) *The Strategy Process: Concepts, Contexts, Cases* (pp. 3–10). New Jersey: Prentice-Hall.

Quinn, J. B., Anderson, P., and Finkelstein, S. (1996). 'Managing Professional Intellect: Making the Most of the Best'. *Harvard Business Review*, 74(2), pp. 71–80.

Raelin, J. A. (2001). 'Public Reflection as the Basis of Learning'. *Management Learning*, 32(1), pp. 11–30.

Raivola, R. and Ropo, E. (1991). *Jatkuva koulutus ja elinikäinen oppiminen* (Continuous Training and Life Long Learning). Tampere: TAY Julkaisusarja A: Tutkimusraportti, 9.

Reason, P. and Hawkins, P. (1988). 'Storytelling as Inquiry'. In: P. Reason (Ed.), *Human Inquiry in Action: Developments in New Paradigm Research* (pp. 79–101). London: SAGE Publications.

Reber, A. S. (1989). 'Implicit Learning and Tacit Knowledge'. *Journal of Experimental Psychology: General*, 118(3), pp. 219–35.

Reed, R. and DeFilippi, R. J. (1990). 'Causal Ambiguity, Barriers to Imitation, and Sustainable Competitive Advantage'. *Academy of Management Review*, 15(1), pp. 88–102.

Reich, B. H. and Wee, S. Y. (2006). 'Searching for Knowledge in the PMBOK® Guide'. *Project Management Journal*, 37(2), pp. 11–25.

Reich, H. R. (2007). 'Managing Knowledge and Learning in IT projects: A Conceptual Framework and Guidelines for Practice'. *Project Management Journal*, 38(2), pp. 5–17.

Repenning, N. P. (1999). *Resource Dependence in Product Development Improvement Efforts*. Massachusetts Institute of Technology Sloan School of Management Department of Operations Management/System Dynamics Group.

Repenning, N. P. (2001). 'Understanding Fire Fighting in New Product Development'. *The Journal of Product Innovation Management*, 18, pp. 285–300.

Revans, R. W. (1982). *The Origins and Growth of Action Learning*. Lund: Studentlitteratur.

Ring, P. S. and van de Ven, A. (1994). 'Developmental Processes of Cooperative Interorganizational Relationships'. *Academy of Management Review*, 19(1), pp. 90–118.

Robbins, S. P. (2003). *Organizational Behavior*. Upper Saddle River: Prentice-Hall.

Robbins, S. P. and Judge, T. A. (2009). *Organizational Behavior*. Upper Saddle River: Pearson Education Inc.

Robertson, M. and Hammersley, G. (2000). 'Knowledge Management Practices within a Knowledge-Intensive Firm: The Significance of the People Management Dimension'. *Journal of European Industrial Training*, 24(2/3/4), pp. 241–53.

Robertson, M., Sørensen, C. and Swan, J. (2001). 'Survival of the Leanest: Intensive Knowledge Work and Groupware Adaption'. *Information Technology & People*, 14(4), pp. 334–52.

Rogers, E. (1995). *Diffusion of Innovations*. New York: Free Press.

Rokeaach, M. (1973). *The Nature of Human Values*. New York: Free Press.

Ronen, S. (1986). *Comparative and Multinational Management*. New York: John Wiley & Sons.

Rosenberg, N. (1982). *Inside the Black Box: Technology and Economics*. Cambridge: Cambridge University Press.

Rousseau, D. M., Sitkin, S. B., Burt, R. S., and Camerer, C. (1998). 'Not So Different After All: A Cross-Discipline View of Trust'. *Academy of Management Review*, 23(3), pp. 383–404.

Rubenstein-Montano, B., Liebowitz, J., Buchwalter, J., McCaw, D., Newman, B., and Rebeck, K. (2001). 'A Systems Thinking Framework for Knowledge Management'. *Decision Support Systems*, 31, pp. 5–16.

Rumelt, R. P. (1995). 'Inertia and Transformation'. In: C. A. Montgomery (Ed.), *Resource-Based and Evolutionary Theories of the Firm: Towards a Synthesis* (pp. 101–32). London: Kluwer Academic Publishers.

Ruuska, K. (1999). *Projekti hallintaan* (Project under Control). Helsinki: Suomen Atk-kustannus Oy.

Ruuska, I. and Vartiainen, M. (2005). 'Characteristics of Knowledge Sharing Communities in Project Organizations'. *International Journal of Project Management*, 23(5), pp. 374–9.

Ryle, G. (1949). *The Concept of Mind*. London: Hutchinson.

Sachs, P. (1995). 'Transforming Work: Collaboration, Learning and Design'. *Communications of the ACM*, 38(9), pp. 36–44.

Sanchez, R., Heene, A., and Thomas, H. (1996). *Dynamics of Competence-Based Competition: Theory and Practice in the New Strategic Management*. Oxford: Elsevier.

Sanchez, R. (1997). 'Strategic Management at the Point of Inflection: Systems, Complexity and Competence Theory'. *Long Range Planning*, 30(6), pp. 939–46.

Sanchez, R. and Heene, A. (1997). 'A Competence Perspective on Strategic Learning and Knowledge Management'. In: R. Sanchez and A. Heene (Eds), *Strategic Learning and Knowledge Management* (pp. 3–15). Chichester: Wiley.

Sanchez, R. (2001). *Knowledge Management and Organizational Competence*. Oxford: Oxford University Press.

Sanchez, R. and Heene, A. (2008). 'Managing Strategic Change: A Systems View of Strategic Organizational Change and Strategic Flexibility'. In: J. Morecroft,

R. Sanchez, and A. Heene (Eds), *Systems Perspectives on Resources, Capabilities, and Management Processes* (pp. 71–91). Bingley: Emerald Group Publishing House.

Sarala, U. (1993). *Madaltuvat organisaatiot ja irseohjautuvat pienryhmät: kahvikerhosta oppivaan organisaatioon* (Lowering Organizations and Self-controlled Small Groups). Espoo: Nurmiprint.

Scarbrough, H., Swan, J., Laurent, S., Bresnen, M., Edelman, L., and Newell, S. (2004). 'Project-Based Learning and the Role of Learning Boundaries'. *Organization Studies*, 25(9), pp. 1579–600.

Schatz, B. R. (1991). 'Building an Electronic Community System'. *Journal of Management Information Systems*, 8(3), pp. 87–107.

Schein, E. H. (1980). *Organizational Psychology*. New Jersey: Prentice-Hall.

Schein, E. H. (1985). *Organizational Culture and Leadership: A Dynamic View*. San Francisco: Jossey-Bass Publishers.

Schein, E. H. (1987). *Process Consultation: Lessons for Managers and Consultants*. Reading: Addison-Wesley.

Schilling, M. (1988). 'Technological Lockout: An Integrative Model of Economic and Strategic Driving Technology Success and Failure'. *Academy of Management Review*, 23(2), pp. 267–84.

Schutz, A. (1970). *On Phenomenology and Social Relations*. Chicago: University of Chicago Press.

Scott, W. R. (1987). *Organizations: Rationale, Natural, and Open Systems*. Englewood Cliffs: Prentice-Hall.

Seidl, D. (2005). *Organizational Identity and Self-Transformation: An Autopoietic Perspective*. Hants: Ashgate Publishing Limited.

Senge, P. M. (1990). *Fifth Discipline: The Art and Practice of the Learning Organization*. New York: Doubleday Currency.

Sense, A. J. (2008). 'Conceptions of Learning and Managing the Flow of Knowledge in the Project-Based Environment'. *International Journal of Managing Projects in Business*, 1(1), pp. 33–48.

Shannon, C. E. and Weaver, W. (1949). *The Mathematical Theory of Communication*. Chicago: University of Illinois Press.

Shapiro, D., Sheppard, B. H., and Cheraskin, L. (1992). 'Business on a Handshake'. *The Negotiation Journal*, 8, pp. 365–78.

Sheppard, B. H. and Tuchinsky, M. (1996). 'Micro-OB and the Network Organization'. In: R. M. Kramer and T. R. Tyler (Eds), *Trust in Organizations: Frontiers of Theory and Research* (pp. 140–65). Thousand Oaks: SAGE Publications.

Simmons, A. (2002). *The Story Factor: Secrets of Influence from the Art of Storytelling*. New York: Basic Books.

Simon, H. A. (1981). *The Sciences of the Artificial*. Cambridge: MIT Press.

Simon, H. A. (1991). 'Bounded Rationality and Organizational Learning'. *Organization Science*, 2, pp. 125–34.

Simon, H. A. (1993). 'Strategy and Organizational Evolution'. *Strategic Management Journal*, 14, pp. 131–42.

Sivula, P., van den Bosh, F. A. J., and Elfring, T. (1997). 'Competence Building by Incorporating Clients into the Development of a Business Service Firm's Knowledge Base'. In: R. Sanchez and A. Heene (Eds), *Strategic Learning and Knowledge Management* (pp. 121–37). Chichester: Wiley.

Skyttner, L. (1996). *General Systems Theory: An Introduction*. Houndsmill: Macmillan.

Slocum, J. W. (1995). 'Group Culture'. In: N. Nicholson (Ed.). *Blackwell Encyclopedic Dictionary of Organizational Behavior* (pp. 124–5). Oxford: Blackwell.

Smircich, L. (1983). 'Concepts of Culture and Organizational Analysis'. *Administrative Science Quarterly*, 28, pp. 339–58.

Smith, K. (1982). 'Philosophical Problems in Thinking about Organizational Change'. In: P. S. Goodman (Ed.), *Change in Organizations* (pp. 316–73). San Francisco: Jossey-Bass.

Smith, M. J. (1984). 'Contingency Rules Theory, Context, and Compliance Behaviors'. *Human Communication Research*, 10, pp. 489–512.

Smith, K. and Berg, D. N. (1987). *Paradoxes of Group Life*. San Francisco: Jossey-Bass.

Snowden, D. (2002). 'Complex Acts of Knowing: Paradox and Descriptive Self-Awareness'. *Journal of Knowledge Management*, 6(2), pp. 100–11.

Sorri, M. and, Gill, J. H. (1989). *A Post-Modern Epistemology: Language, Truth and Body*. Lewiston: E. Mellan Press.

Sowa, J. F. (2006). 'Processes and Causality'. http://www.jfsowa.com/ontology/causal.htm, retrieved 5 December 2006.

Spencer Brown, G. (1979). *The Laws of Form*. New York: E. P. Dutton.

Spencer, Jr, L. M. and Spencer, S. (1993). *Competence at Work: Models for Superior Performance*. New York: John Wiley & Sons.

Spender, J-C. (1996a). 'Making Knowledge the Basis of a Dynamic Theory of a Firm'. *Strategic Management Journal*, 17 December, pp. 45–62.

Spender, J-C. (1996b). 'Organizational Knowledge, Learning and Memory: Three Concepts in Search of a Theory'. *Organizational Knowledge*, 9(1), pp. 63–78.

Spender, J-C. and Grant, R. M. (1996). 'Knowledge and the Firm: Overview'. *Strategic Management Journal*, 17 December, pp. 5–10.

Stacy, R. (2001). *Complex Responsive Processes in Organizations: Learning and Knowledge Creation*. London: Routledge.

Star, S. L. (1989). 'The Structure of Ill-Structured Solutions: Boundary Objects and Heterogeneous Problem Solving'. In: L. Gasser and M. N. Huhns (Eds), *Distributed Artificial Intelligence, Volume II* (pp. 37–54). Pitman, London: Morgan Kaufman Publishers Inc.

Star, S. L. and Griesemer, J. R. (1989). 'Institutional Ecology, "translations" and Boundary Objects: Amateurs and Professionals in Berkeley's Museum of Vertebrate Zoology, 1907–39'. *Social Studies of Science*, 19, pp. 387–420.

Starbuck, W. H. (1992). 'Learning by Knowledge-Intensive Firms'. *Journal of Management Studies*, 29, pp. 713–40.

Steele, L. W. (1989). *Managing Technology*. New York: McGraw-Hill Book Company.

Stein, E. W. (1995). 'Organizational Memory: Review of Concepts and Recommendations for Management'. *International Journal of Information Management*, 15(2), pp. 17–32.

Steiner, G. A. (1969). *Top Management Planning*. New York: Macmillan.

Sterman J. D. (2000). *Business Dynamics: Systems Thinking and Modeling for a Complex World*. Boston: Irwin McGraw-Hill.

Sternberg, R., Wagner, R., Williams, W., and Horvath, J. (1995). 'Testing Common Sense'. *American Psychologist*, 50(11), pp. 912–27.

Ståhle, P. and Grönroos, M. (1999). *Knowledge Management – tietopääoma yrityksen kilpailutekijänä* (Knowledge Management – Knowledge Capital as a Competitive Advantage of a Firm). Helsinki: WSOY.

Suda, L. V. (2006). 'The Meaning and Importance of Culture for Project Success'. *Project Perspectives*, 1, pp. 48–52.

Sveiby, K. E. (1997). *The New Organizational Wealth: Managing and Measuring Knowledge Based Assets*. San Francisco: Berret Koehler publishers.

Swan, J. A., Newell, S., Scarbrough, H., and Hislop, D. (1999). 'Knowledge Management and Innovation: Networks and Networking'. *Journal of Knowledge Management*, 3, pp. 262–75.

Swieringa, J. and Wierdsma, A. (1992). *Becoming a Learning Organization*. Wokingham: Addison-Wesley.

Szulanski, G. (1996). 'Exploring Internal Stickiness: Impediments to the Transfer of Best Practices within the Firm'. *Strategic Management Journal*, 17, pp. 27–43.

Tannen, D. (1995). 'The Power of Talk: Who Gets Heard and Why'. *Harvard Business Review*, September–October, pp. 138–48.

Teale, M., Dispenza, V., Flynn, J., and Currie, D. (2003). *Management Decision-Making: Towards an Integrated Approach*. Harlow: Pearson Education Limited.

Teece, D. J., Pisano, G., and Shuen, A. (1997). 'Dynamic Capabilities and Strategic Management'. *Strategic Management Journal*, 18(7), pp. 509–33.

Teece, D. J. (1998). 'Capturing Value from Knowledge Assets: The New Economy, Markets for Know-How, and Intangible Assets'. *California Management Review*, 40(3), pp. 55–76.

Teubner, G. (1991). 'Autopoiesis and Steering: How Politics Profit from the Normative Surplus of Capital'. In: R. J. in 't Veld, L. Schaap, C. J. A. M. Termeer, and M. J. W. van Twist (Eds), *Autopoiesis and Configuration Theory: New Approaches to Social Steering* (pp. 127–43). Dordrecht: Kluwer Academic Publishers.

Thamhain, H. J. and College, B. (1993). 'Effective Leadership for Building Project Teams, Motivating People, and Creating Optimal Organizational Structures'. In: P. C. Dinsmore (Ed.), *The AMA Handbook of Project Management* (pp. 248–58). New York: American Management Association.

Thiry, M. and Deguire, M. (2007). 'Recent Developments in Project-Based Organisations'. *International Journal of Project Management*, 25, pp. 649–58.

Trevino, L. K., Lengel, R. H., and Daft, R. L. (1987). 'Media Symbolism, Media Richness, and Media Choice in Organizations – A Symbolic Interactionist Perspective'. *Communication Research*, 14(5), pp. 553–74.

Tsai, W. (2001). 'Knowledge Transfer in Intraorganizational Networks: Effects of Network Position and Absorptive Capacity on Business Unit Innovation and Performance', *Academy of Management Journal*, 44(5), pp. 996–1004.

Tsoukas, H. (1991). 'The Missing Link: A Transformational View of Metaphors in Organizational Science'. *Academy of Management Review*, 16(3), pp. 566–85.

Tsoukas, H. (1993). 'Analogical Reasoning and Knowledge Generation in Organization Theory'. *Organization Studies*, 14(3), pp. 323–46.

Tsoukas, H. (1996). 'The Firm as a Distributed Knowledge System: A Constructionist Approach'. *Strategic Management Journal*, 17, Special Issue, pp. 11–25.

Tsoukas, H. and Vladimirou, E. (2001). 'What Is Organizational Knowledge?' *Journal of Management Studies*, 38(7), pp. 973–93.

Tuckman, B. and Jensen, N. (1977). 'Stages of Small Group Development Revisited'. *Group and Organizational Studies*, 2, pp. 419–27.

Tuomi, I. (1996). 'The Firm as a Distributed Knowledge System: A Constructionist Approach'. *Strategic Management Journal*, 17 December, pp. 11–26.

Turner, J. R. and Keegan, A. (1999). 'The Management of Operations in the Project-Based Organization'. In: K. Artto, K. Kähkönen, and K. Koskinen (Eds), *Managing Business by Projects* (pp. 57–85). Helsinki: Project Management Association Finland.

van Twist, M. J. W. and Schaap, L. (1991). 'Introduction to Autopoiesis Theory and Autopoietic Steering'. In: R. J. in't Veld, L. Schaap, C. J. A. M. Termeer, and M. J. W. van Twist, *Autopoiesis and Configuration Theory: New Approaches to Social Steering* (pp. 31–44). Dordrecht: Kluwer Academic Publishers.

Underwood, B. J. (1982). *Studies in Learning and Memory: Selected Papers*. New York: Praeger.

Usher, R. S. (1989). 'Locating Experience in Language: Towards a Poststructuralist Theory of Experience'. *Adult Education Quarterly*, 40(1), pp. 23–32.

van de Ven, A. H. (1992). 'Suggestions for Studying Strategy Process: A Research Note'. *Strategic Management Journal*, 13, Special Issue, pp. 169–88.

Varela, F. J., Maturana, H. R., and Uribe, R. (1974). 'Autopoiesis: The Organization of Living Systems, Its Characterization and a Model'. *Biosystems*, 5(4), pp. 187–96.

Varela, F. J. (1979). *Principles of Biological Autonomy*. Amsterdam: North-Holland.

Varela, F. J. (1981). 'Describing the Logic of the Living: The Adequacy and Limitations of the Idea of Autopoiesis'. In: M. Zeleny (Ed.), *Autopoiesis: A Theory of Living Organization* (pp. 36–48). New York: North Holland.

Varela, F. J., Thompson, E., and Rosch, E. (1991). *Embodied Mind: Cognitive Science and Human Experience*. Cambridge: MIT Press.

Varela, F. J. (1996). 'The Early Days of Autopoiesis: Heinz and Chile'. *Systems Research*, 13, pp. 407–16.

Venzin, M., von Krogh, G., and Roos, J. (1998). 'Future Research into Knowledge Management'. In: G. von Krogh, J. Roos, and D. Kleine (Eds), *Knowing in Firms: Understanding, Managing and Measuring Knowledge* (pp. 26–66). London: SAGE Publications.

Vicari, S., von Krogh, G., Roos, J., and Mahnke, V. (1996). 'Knowledge Creation through Cooperative Experimentation'. In: G. von Krogh and J. Roos (Eds), *Managing Knowledge: Perspectives on Cooperation and Competition* (pp. 184–202). London: SAGE Publications.

Vicari, S. and Troilo, G. (1999). 'Organizational Creativity: A New Perspective from Cognitive Systems Theory'. In: G. von Krogh, I. Nonaka,. and T. Nishiguchi (Eds), *Knowledge Creation: A Source of Value* (pp. 63–88). London: Macmillan.

Vygotsky, L. (1986). *Thought and Language*. Boston: Massachusetts Institute of Technology.

Wagner, R. and Sternberg, R. (1985). 'Practical Intelligence in Real-World Pursuits: The Role of Tacit Knowledge'. *Journal of Personality and Social Psychology*, 49, pp. 436–58.

Walker, D. H. T., Maqsood, T. and Finegan, A. (2005). 'The Culture of The Knowledge Advantage (K-Adv)-An Holistic Strategic Approach to the Management of Knowledge'. In: A. S. Kazi (Ed.), *Knowledge Management in the Construction Industry: A Socio-Technical Perspective* (pp. 223–48). Helsinki: Idea Group Publishing.

Walsh, J. (2003). *The Art of Storytelling: Easy Steps to Presenting an Unforgettable Story*. Chicago: Moody.

Walsh, J. P. and Ungson, G. R. (1991). 'Organizational Memory'. *Academy of Management Review*, 16(1), pp. 57–91.

Warren, K. (2007). 'Operationalizing the Impact of Competence-Building on the Performance of Firms' Resource Systems'. In: J. Morecroft, R. Sanchez, and A. Heene (Eds), *Systems Perspectives on Resources, Capabilities, and Management Processes* (pp. 41–55). Bingley: Emerald Group Publishing House.

Weathly, M. J. (1992). *Leadership and the New Science*. San Francisco: Berrett-Koehler Publishers.

Webber, A. M. (1993). 'What's So New About the New Economy'. *Harvard Business Review*, January–February.

Weick, K. E. (1979). *The Social Psychology of Organizing*. Reading: Addison-Wesley.

Weick, K. E. and Roberts, K. H. (1993). 'Collective Mind in Organizations: Heedful Interrelating on Flight Decks'. *Administrative Science Quarterly*, 38, pp. 357–81.

Weinberg, G. M. (2001). *An Introduction to General Systems Thinking. Silver Anniversary Edition*. New York: Dorset House Publishing.

Wenger, E. (1998). *Communities of Practice: Learning, Meaning and Identity*. Cambridge: Cambridge University Press.

Wernerfelt, B. (1984). 'A Resource-Based View of the Firm'. *Strategic Management Journal*, 5, pp. 171–80.

West, M. A. (1997). *Developing Creativity in Organizations*. Leicester: The British Psychological Society.

Whitehill, M. (1997). 'The Knowledge-Base View of the Firm: Implications for Management Practice'. *Long Range Planning*, 30(3), pp. 450–4.

Wiig, K. M. (1997). 'Integrating Intellectual Capital and Knowledge Management'. *Long Range Planning*, 30(3), pp. 399–405.

Williams, A. (1996). 'Groupware: The Text Ware of Office Automation'. *Industrial Management & Data Systems*, 96(6), pp. 11–13.

Winograd, T. and Flores, F. (1987). *Understanding Computers and Cognition*. Norwood: Ablex Publishing.

Winter, S. (1987). 'Knowledge and Competence as Strategic Assets'. In: D. Teece (Ed.), *The Competitive Challenge – Strategies for Industrial Innovation and Renewal* (pp. 159–84). Cambridge: Ballinger Publishing.

Zahra, S. A. and George, G. (2002). 'Absorptive Capacity: A Review, Reconceptualization, and Extension'. *Academy of Management Review*, 27(2), pp. 185–203.

Zander, U. and Kogut, B. (1995). 'Knowledge and the Speed of the Transfer and Imitation of Organizational Capabilities: An Empirical Test'. *Organization Science*, 6, pp. 76–92.

Zeleny, M. (1980). *Autopoiesis, Dissipative Structures, and Spontaneous Social Orders*. Boulder: Westview Press.

Zeleny, M. (1981). *Autopoiesis: A Theory of Living Organization*. New York: North Holland.

Zimmerman, B. and Hurst, D. K. (1993). 'Breaking the Boundaries: The Fractal Organization'. *Journal of Management Inquiry*, 2(4), December, pp. 334–55.

Zollo, M. and Winter, S. G. (2002). 'Deliberate Learning and the Evolution of Dynamic Capabilities'. *Organization Science*, 13(3), pp. 339–51.

Index

Page numbers in **bold** refer to figures, page numbers in *italic* refer to tables